ECOLOGY:
SELECTED CONCEPTS

ECOLOGY: SELECTED CONCEPTS

David B. Sutton
University of California, Santa Barbara

N. Paul Harmon
Harmon Associates

John Wiley & Sons, Inc.

New York · London · Sydney · Toronto

Editors: Judy Wilson and Irene Brownstone
Production Manager: Ken Burke
Editorial Supervisor: Lorna Cunkle
Artists: Heather Kortebein, Carl Brown, and Lorna Cunkle
Composition and Make-up: Winn Kalmon

Library of Congress Cataloging in Publication Data

Sutton, David B.
    Ecology: selected concepts.

    (Self-teaching guides)
    Bibliography: p. 273
    1. Ecology--Programmed instruction. I. Harmon,
N. Paul, joint author. II. Title.
(QH541.2.S93)   574.5'07'7   73-8715
ISBN 0-471-83830-6

Printed in the United States of America

73   74   10 9 8 7 6 5 4 3 2 1

to

Lawrence W. Swan

Foreword

In <u>A</u> <u>Child's</u> <u>Christmas</u> <u>in</u> <u>Wales</u> Dylan Thomas, that too short-lived golden-voiced troubadour of our times, told of his disappointment as a child at being given "a book that told me everything about the wasp except <u>Why</u>." Thus, in one pithy phrase, the poet crystallized the most widespread complaint of the common man against contemporary science, that it has produced too many details of the <u>How</u> of things for even a Leonardo to master, without answering the simple, nagging question <u>Why</u>.

I think it must have been someone in the nineteenth century who first explicitly called attention to these two questions and insisted that science is concerned only with <u>How</u>. This abandonment of a portion of the field of inquiry on the part of science had something in it of the religious spirit of renunciation, but the scientific renunciation was made precisely to exclude religious approaches to the world. To the question "Why do honey bees make honey?" religiously trained biologists like John Ray in the eighteenth century had given replies in this form: "It is one of the inspiring examples of the Providence that oversees the affairs of Man that bees should make honey for his delectation." The Providence postulated was equally capable of explaining the very undelectable sting of the bee by asserting that the pains produced in Man are a testing of his faith in Providence; more, "they develop his character."

The trouble with such a postulation is, of course, that the Providence postulated is a "waterproof hypothesis." Both good and evil are equally well "explained"; in fact, one cannot conceive of an observation that would falsify the hypothesis of an all-wise Providence. Since the hypothesis "explains" everything it <u>explains</u> nothing. It was postulations like this that led most scientists, a hundred years ago, to give up asking <u>Why</u>. The science that developed from this renunciation was more rigorous than its predecessor, and it possessed a certain Spartan beauty; but it was a bare beauty. It was not enough for the ordinary man. Nor should it have been.

The same century that saw the institutionalization of this renunciation in science also laid the foundations of a scientific edifice in which the question <u>Why</u> could be asked and answered without recourse to waterproof hypotheses. The two main planks in the new edifice of science are called "evolution" and "ecology," and Charles Darwin was as much responsible for them as anyone. But there is a momentum in intellectual progress as in all other human affairs, and most of the thrust of science in the century following the publication of the <u>Origin</u> <u>of</u> <u>Species</u> was in the <u>How</u> direction. It was only in the 1960's that the direction of science shifted and <u>Why</u> again became a respectable question to ask. Environmental problems and a deepening concern with the goals of human endeavors made it necessary to take up once more this almost tabooed question.

But history never really repeats, never really reverts to an earlier position. The Why of our time is not the same Why that John Ray asked. The ecological Why is not only rigorously answerable; it is also much richer in meaning than its theological progenitor. This richness must be appreciated if we are to avoid repeating old errors.

It is one of the many merits of this book by David Sutton and Paul Harmon that it makes the intellectual dimensions of the new Why clear in the first two dozen pages. Clarity is, in fact, a central virtue of the entire text. Now that ecology is fashionable the inquiring mind is in danger of being smothered in a plethora of facts. "Information overload" is one of the most serious dangers facing the conscientious citizen who wants to understand what environmental problems are all about. To protect himself, the reader must refuse to read most of the material thrust at him. This means that the small proportion that he does read must give him a clear and deep understanding of the most fundamental principles of ecology, together with their application to the environmental problems we cannot escape.

The needed understanding of the essentials of ecology should, in my opinion, come easily to any careful reader of Sutton and Harmon's text. None other that I know of packs so many important ideas in so small a space, following such a careful step-by-step development. I found the text a joy to work through. I trust that a multitude of others will share this joy.

Garrett Hardin
Professor of Human Ecology
University of California, Santa Barbara

To the Reader

Ecology: Selected Concepts can be used as a self-teaching guide or as a supplementary course text. It is intended primarily to provide the reader with a clear understanding of the basic concepts of ecology and the major human implications of these concepts. As an introductory book, only a casual understanding of high school biology or chemistry is required. Terms such as evolution or population are defined as they are used.

This book is programmed, which means that you will be asked to respond to questions at certain points. It is neither a formal text nor a workbook. Unlike a workbook, this book is self-contained and provides answers for all the questions it asks. Unlike a text, this program helps you to learn by asking you questions and providing you with self-tests. This assures you that you have understood what has been presented. Because the questions add to the length of the book, the amount of information covered is not as much as in the average beginning ecology textbook. But our book is designed so that you actually master everything that is presented.

To ensure its design for efficient self-study, the book has been tested on students similar to yourself, then revised until we feel confident that our explanations and questions will be effective in conveying the basic concepts of ecology and the human environmental implications.

To make the best use of this book, you should know how it is organized and what the different elements can do for you. Read the following description carefully. Each of the twelve chapters contains the following:

- A Title Page: The learning objectives of the chapter are stated on the title page. By examining these objectives you can determine what general information the chapter contains. If you feel you already know the material included, take the Self-Test. If you pass it, you can safely skip the chapter.

- The Self-Study Frames: The body of each chapter is divided into numbered frames, each presenting a block of information, a general discussion, and one or more questions. You will learn the most if you read the frame summary (the indented material at the beginning of each frame) and the discussion, then write out your responses to the questions without looking back at the discussion or looking at the answers provided below the short dashed line. After you have given your answer, compare it with the one below the dashed line. If your answer is very different, reread the frame until you are sure you understand why the authors thought the printed answer was best. The frames are arranged so that they build on one another. To understand frames at the end of a chapter, you must first have completed the earlier ones. Thus, skipping any frames or reading them out of sequence will usually slow you down.

- A Self-Test: This can be used as a pre-test to see if you know the subject matter well enough to safely skip the chapter. Or, after you have read the chapter, it can be a quiz to gauge your mastery of the material. After you have completed the test, compare your responses with those provided at the end of the Self-Test. If you miss any questions on the Self-Test, review the frames indicated in parentheses following the answers. The chapters build on one another just as the frames do, so you should not go from one chapter to the next until your Self-Test results indicate that you have mastered the earlier chapter.

We have used many graphs, charts, and illustrations. Study them carefully; often they integrate information and concepts far better than words can.

Many of the questions, both in the frames and in the Self-Tests, call for you to write a short paragraph or explanation. In the future when you talk or think about ecology or environmental problems, you generally will not be trying to answer a multiple-choice question! You will be trying to explain a concept to someone or apply that concept to solving some problem. Here you have a chance to practice. Obviously your answer will not be exactly the same as ours. Don't worry about the exact words. You should, however, compose an answer with the same overall idea and the same general points as ours.

Whenever you need to review a chapter, either before taking the chapter Self-Test or perhaps after finishing the book, just read the indented summaries at the beginning of each frame. The important points are highlighted there. To further assist you in rapid study and review, we have included a combined index-glossary, which includes most of the technical terms in the book. A comprehensive exam, which can be used either as a final test or as additional chapter tests, is available upon request from the publisher. If you are using this book in conjunction with an ecology textbook, the cross-reference chart should help you correlate the two. If you wish to delve deeper into any particular topic, you can find additional sources of information in the bibliography.

Many people have given us help during the preparation of this book—family, friends, students who read and tested the materials, and various members of the John Wiley editorial and production staffs. We want to thank each of these people. We especially want to thank Irene Brownstone of Wiley who has been invaluable in helping us through several edits.

Although we have tried to make this book as useful as possible, only you can tell us if we have succeeded in communicating the material to you. Therefore, we would appreciate your suggestions on how we might improve

the book. Please address any comments about <u>Ecology</u>: <u>Selected Concepts</u>
to:

Editor, Self-Teaching Guides
John Wiley & Sons, Inc.
605 Third Avenue
New York, New York   10016

September 1973   D. B. S.
Santa Barbara, California   N. P. H.

CROSS-REFERENCE CHART

The cross-reference chart on the following page indicates the pages in some of the popular ecology and environmental studies texts corresponding to each chapter in Ecology: Selected Concepts. Below is a bibliography of the texts in the chart.

Boughey, Arthur S., Man and the Environment (New York: Macmillan, 1971).

Clapham, W. B., Jr., Natural Ecosystems (New York: Macmillan, 1973).

Colinvaux, P. A., Introduction to Ecology (New York: John Wiley & Sons, 1972).

Ehrlich, Paul R., and Ehrlich, Anne H., Population/Resources/Environment, 2nd ed. (San Francisco: W. H. Freeman, 1972).

Kormondy, Edward J., Concepts of Ecology (Englewood Cliffs, N. J.: Prentice-Hall, 1969).

Murdoch, William W., ed., Environment (Stamford, Conn.: Sinauer Assoc., 1971).

Odum, Eugene P., Fundamentals of Ecology, 3rd ed. (Philadelphia: W. B. Saunders, 1971).

Smith, Robert Leo, Ecology and Field Biology (New York: Harper & Row, 1966).

Southwick, Charles H., Ecology and the Quality of Our Environment (New York: Van Nostrand Reinhold, 1972).

Wagner, Richard H., Environment and Man (New York: W. W. Norton, 1971).

Chapters in Ecology: Selected Concepts	Boughey	Clapham	Colinvaux	Ehrlich	Kormondy	Murdoch	Odum	Smith	Southwick	Wagner
1 Ecological and Systems Concepts	1-17	---	115-126 229-245	---	1-6	1-27	3-8 276-292	---	103-114	---
2 Concepts of Energy	---	17-25	145-152 285-294	62-63	7-14	326-335	37-43	27-28	115-123	---
3 Feeding Relationships & Productivity	---	25-37	129-143 152-166 167-180	101-104	21-33	---	63-85	29-48	135-145	---
4 Human Energy Consumption	---	---	---	61-69 104-138 193-197	14-21	53-69 89-115	43-63	---	278-281	443-449
5 Astronomical & Geosystem Cycles	313-339	1-16 53-54	262-265	145-156	---	189-210	---	---	13-23	170-195
6 The Water Cycle	343-367	49-53	256-260 265-267	75-77 156-159	35-40 178-189	135-154 213-254	97-99 432-444	52-54	6-13 276-278	93-132
7 Biogeochemical Cycles and Nutrient Budgets	---	37-49	197-218	197-201 229-234	40-60	---	86-105	48-59	124-134	---
8 Population Characteristics & Dynamics	---	79-99	309-328 369-379	---	62-86	---	162-195	341-363	163-208	---
9 Factors Affecting Population Size	---	57-79	273-307 328-355 381-505	---	86-111	---	195-233	363-425	209-239	---
10 Human Populations	236-311	---	---	5-55	166-178	31-51 416-434	510-516	---	37-61	426-461
11 The Structure and Function of Ecosystems	---	102-134	71-90 550-572	---	113-163	---	140-159 251-273	11-26 98-155	243-270	---
12 Human Ecosystems	---	229-237	571-572 579-581	193-245	---	53-69 117-133 339-357	267-270	---	---	60-74 360-382

Contents

Introduction

"Not only will men of science have to grapple with the sciences
that deal with man, but—and this is a far more difficult matter
—they will have to persuade the world to listen to what they
have discovered. If they cannot succeed in this difficult enter-
prise, man will destroy himself by his halfway cleverness."

Bertrand Russell

A bacteriologist takes from his cabinet a freshly prepared glass container
half-filled with a food material. He carefully opens it and touches a glass
rod with a few bacteria to the surface of the nutrient. The container is then
sealed and placed in a warm spot. For the bacteria in that dish, the glass
container is the entire universe. The environment is well-suited for the bacteria's growth and reproduction. In 4 days a healthy bacterial colony the
size of a dime is established. In 6 days the colony has become as large as a
fifty-cent piece. Rapid growth and reproduction continue for these 6 days,
then suddenly disaster strikes. The end comes quickly for two reasons.
First, as the bacteria have consumed the food and multiplied, they have
given off waste products. These are toxic, and at a certain point the amount
of waste products in the glass container becomes too great and the bacteria
begin to die of self-poisoning. Second, the food runs out, and after a few
hours any bacteria that have not died of poisoning starve to death.

This particular study is worth further consideration for its broader implications to human life. Scientists commonly use mathematical models to explain the data they gather. In the case of population growth, like that of
bacteria, graphs are often drawn, on which the number of organisms are
plotted against time. Examine figure I.1.

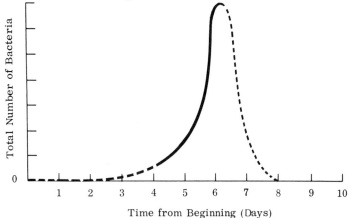

Figure I.1   Bacteria population growth curve

The curve in figure I.1 shows, in an abstract way, the history of the bacterial colony. The first part, the bold part of the line, is called an <u>exponential</u> <u>curve</u>. Mathematically, it tells us that an event is occurring at a rapidly accelerating rate, similar to the progression 2, 4, 8, 16, 32, 64, 128, for example. In other words, growth is proceeding as a series of doublings. The startling point is that the last term in this series of doublings is greater than the sum of all the previous terms. Indeed, it is hard to grasp the speed of such a rate of change, and soon the growth seems out of control. Consider this simple example: If you tore a page out of this book and held it edgewise, it would appear very thin, approximately 1/10 millimeter or about 1/254 of an inch. Assume you folded it in half or doubled it. It would then be 0.2 mm thick. If you folded it again, it would be 0.4 mm thick. The third doubling would result in a folded piece of paper about 0.8 mm thick. This is still not very impressive, but continue and see what happens. After 8 doublings, the paper is about 1 inch thick. At 12, one foot. After 20 doublings, if that were physically possible, it would be 256 feet thick! Now let's jump ahead a few steps to where the curve begins its dramatic upward climb. At 37 doublings, the paper would be 3000 miles thick, equal to the distance from New York to Los Angeles! After 43 doublings it would be 240,000 miles thick, the distance from the earth to the moon! And after 52 doublings, the wad of paper would be 93 million miles thick, and would reach from the earth to the sun. This growth in the thickness of a page resulting from repeated doubling is graphed in figure I.2.

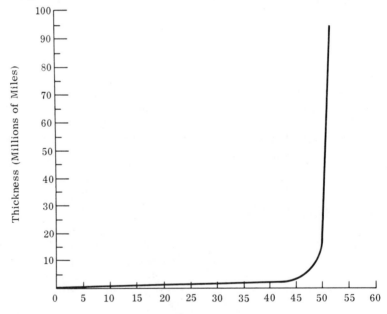

Figure I.2   The exponential growth in thickness
—as a page in this book is doubled successively,
the thickness grows at an exponential rate.
(After Miller, 1972)

Understanding how abstractions like exponential growth relate to real human problems is a matter of perspective. Individual human beings vary in their perceptions of the future. Most of us are only concerned with the immediate present and rarely look beyond next week, month, or year. The same limited perspective applies to when we examine problems in geographical space. Most of us only consider the area immediately around ourselves. We may consider the entire neighborhood, but we rarely think in terms of how something will affect people in other countries or nations. Unfortunately, as the world becomes increasingly complex, such limited perspective becomes more and more dangerous. Indeed, ignorance of events puts a person at the mercy of change, rather than in control of the future. For example, a country which ignores population growth today might well find itself unable to provide adequate schools, homes, food, jobs, and recreational space for its new inhabitants in the future. The world is becoming more and more interrelated and only a person with a perspective broadly extended in both time and space can understand what is happening or will soon occur. The survival of mankind in the immediate future depends on the ability of scientists and political leaders to anticipate developing events, and not just to react to crises. On the personal level, if in the next decade you are to be prepared for change, you will have to expand your own time and space perspective.

Because the world is changing in many ways at an exponential rate, you need to prepare for the future by learning how to cope with change—how to handle new and constantly changing information. It is no longer enough to know how to deal with present day information and problems. "The future," says Alvin Toffler in Future Shock, "is coming faster all the time." In order to adapt, you must understand the nature of exponential growth and what the future holds whenever you find that something is increasing at an exponential rate.

For example, today's world population is growing at an unprecedented exponential rate. Every time your pulse beats, the population of the world will have increased by more than one human being. There are almost 140 more people added a minute, 8,000 an hour, 190,000 a day, and 70,000,000 a year. The world population reached 3.9 billion in mid-1972 and is growing at the rate of almost 2 percent annually, which means that it will double in about 35 years. The human population, the consumption of natural resources, and the adverse effect of both on the environment are all growing at an exponential rate. Can we expect such growth to continue indefinitely?

One of the most important and comprehensive recent studies in human ecology, made by an international research team at the Massachusetts Institute of Technology (MIT), indicated we cannot. This study, recently published as a book—The Limits to Growth—undertook to determine the limits to population and technological growth. System Dynamics analysis and computer simulation techniques were employed to build a world model to determine how various factors would interact in the near future. The project team isolated five major factors that they felt ultimately affected future growth. These include:

• Human population (total number of persons)

- Industrial output per capita (dollar equivalent of goods and services produced per person per year)

- Agricultural production (food measured in kilograms per person per year)

- Nonrenewable natural resources (fraction of nonrenewable natural resources left)

- Pollution (wastes of all kinds that must necessarily be "produced" as "by-products" of producing the other four factors)

There was no single variable called "technology" since different technologies affect different variables (e.g., birth control pills affect population while new drilling techniques affect available resources). Assumptions about technological "breakthroughs" were considered in projecting each of the five major factors given above. Based on a very complex world model that hypothesized how the five major variables interact, the MIT team projected the future to the year A.D. 2100. They assumed there would be no major change in the physical, economic, or social patterns that are currently governing the development of the earth. Their projection is shown in figure I.3.

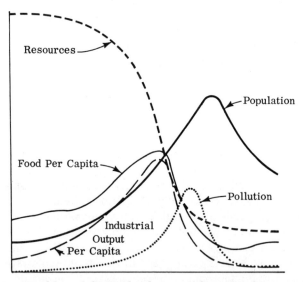

Figure I.3 World model standard run (After Meadows et al., 1972)

Notice that food production, industrial output, and human population are currently growing at an exponential rate. By about 2000 A.D., however, rapidly declining natural resources are expected to cause a sharp drop in food and industrial output. Pollution, the unwanted but ever present by-product of food production and industrial output, will also decline. Human population will continue to rise but then drop sharply as the fall in industrial output and food production have their effect. Significantly, the drop in human population results from a sharply increased death rate. Births continue to rise sharply until well beyond A.D. 2100.

Some people have suggested that the basic MIT model is wrong. They feel, for example, that it doesn't give enough weight to technological break-throughs that will allow man to create new resources or use old resources in new ways. Yet the MIT scientists did attempt to take all of these things into account. They even included a model that assumed that all known re-sources were doubled, fully exploited, and seventy-five percent recycled. They projected that pollution controls could reduce current pollution by 75 percent and anticipated that available high yield agricultural lands might be doubled. Finally, they assumed that a perfect birth control device could be developed, made available to everyone, and willingly used by everyone as soon as received. The results of these assumptions are plotted in figure I.4.

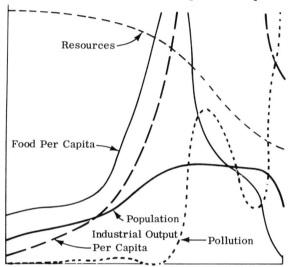

Figure I.4 World model with "unlimited" resources, pol-lution controls, increased agricultural productivity, and "perfect" birth control. (After Meadows et. al., 1972)

Notice that in figure I.4 food output and industrial output are programmed to grow exponentially, and both go off the top of the chart. Human population levels off and for a time pollution is controlled by new technologies. The en-tire human population of the earth begins to approach the U.S. standard of living by 2000. Then everything seems to go wrong. The soil is destroyed, and food output turns sharply down. Increased industrial output continues to diminish even the vastly increased resources. Pollution, after being checked by technological devices, again begins its steep exponential rise. A little after A.D. 2000 the human population starts to decline sharply as the death toll rises rapidly. Still not a very pleasant picture! Of greatest significance, all of the assumptions tried did not change one basic fact—that if any part of a system (e.g., food, total resources) is limited, exponential growth will sooner or later use up that limited resource and the system will fail. The fate of the bacteria in their glass-contained world pretty much tells the story.

The average person with the typical space-time perspective may not realize it, but in the very near future mankind is going to face a very serious crisis. Most people fail to understand this because they perceive future events in terms of the past. But a long history of growth does not imply a long future of progress. Few realize that mankind's history over the past two or three generations has been characterized by several exponential growth trends. This very rapid growth is unique in human history, and the sharp shot upward that occurs in the later stages of exponential growth is going to be a great shock to most of mankind. Of course, the signs are already present. About 34,000 individual human beings—mostly young children —died of starvation during the last 24 hours! Most of the signs are showing up in the underdeveloped areas of the world at this point, so we do not notice them, unless we make a real effort to expand our space perspective. Pollution and gas, oil, and electrical shortages are closer to home, however, and they will grow rapidly. No one will be able to ignore the near future too much longer.

Even though we who live in the United States do not encounter the pressing population problems that several other areas of the world must deal with, we do face severe moral problems. It is our country that is currently and rapidly using up a large part of the entire world's supply of protein and nonrenewable mineral resources, and at the same time is producing much of the pollution that is spreading from the U.S. to the farthest reaches of our planet. Leadership in solving the world environmental crisis must come from those who have a perspective that is liberally extended in time and space—and that must include all of you who are reading this book.

We began this introduction by talking about exponential growth because we wanted to emphasize that, like other natural laws, it cannot be ignored. Nor can it be patched over by new technological breakthroughs for more than a limited period of time. Nature's laws always exact their price whether we want to pay it or not. We can ignore an exponential growth pattern for awhile, but sooner or later we realize that it will not wither away from our inattention. To expect this would be equivalent to picking up a rock, dropping it, and hoping that for some reason that particular rock would suddenly become an exception to the law of gravity. That is an exception no reasonable person should expect to occur. It is far more reasonable to try to learn to live in accordance with the law of gravity than to hope it will not apply in your particular case. Most of us respect the law of gravity—but we are just beginning to learn the natural laws of ecological energy flow, population growth, biogeochemical cycles, and various balances in nature. Once exponential growth begins its vertical ascent, there will not be time left in which to apply what you have learned.

This book is designed to give you a general introduction to the basic principles of ecology and some of the human environmental implications. It will help you understand the nature and complexity of some of the problems mankind will have to face in the next few decades. It will not give you many answers, but hopefully it will give you a perspective that will help you to intelligently evaluate the answers proposed by others, or to begin to seek some of your own.

PART ONE
The Nature of Ecosystems

In Part One we define ecology and put it into perspective as a science, and we introduce the four major viewpoints used throughout this book—energy, cycles, populations, and ecosystems. These viewpoints are the specific subjects of Parts Two through Five. In this part we present basic concepts, and our definitions and explanations are broad and general.

This part also introduces some general systems concepts. The systems approach is a way of explaining things, similar to language or mathematics. For a complex problem, we need a way of thinking that can grasp its reality all at once—as a whole thing—not as a series of simple problems to be solved one at a time. The systems approach tries to do this, and thus it is a valuable tool in understanding ecology. We will use systems explanations throughout the rest of the book to explain various ecological concepts, and you will probably also encounter systems explanations in areas outside of ecology.

CHAPTER ONE
Ecological and Systems Concepts

When you complete this chapter, you will be able to

- match these terms with their definitions: ecology, human ecology, energy, cycle, population, community, ecosystem, and biosphere;

- identify the goal of science;

- explain the role of models in science;

- explain the use of different viewpoints or perspectives in science;

- define system, open system, and cybernetic system;

- explain set point, negative feedback, homeostatic plateau, and positive feedback;

- explain the relationship between supersystems, systems, and subsystems;

- explain in what respects all biological systems are both open and cybernetic systems;

- describe an ecosystem in informal systems terms.

If you think that you have already mastered these objectives and might skip all or part of this chapter, turn to page 26 at the end of this chapter and take the Self-Test. The results will allow you to evaluate your current knowledge of this chapter's contents. If you answer all of the questions correctly, you are ready to begin the next chapter. If you miss any questions, you should study the frames indicated after the answers to the Self-Test.

If this material is new to you, or if you choose not to take the Self-Test now, proceed to frame 1.

1. <u>Ecology</u> is the science that studies the interactions between living organisms and their environment.

No living organism exists in isolation. Organisms interact with one another and with the chemical and physical components of the nonliving environment. The basic unit of organism-environment interaction resulting from the complex interplay of living and nonliving elements in a given area is called an ecosystem. The ecosystem concept is central to the science of ecology—in fact, ecology has been defined as the study of ecosystems.

Despite the ecological insights contained in the writings of ancient Greek philosophers, ecology has only been considered a science in its own right since the beginning of this century. Because it developed from natural history, ecology is normally considered a branch of the biological sciences and is often called environmental biology.

<u>Human ecology</u> is the study of ecosystems as they affect and are affected by human beings. Human ecology draws together knowledge and experience from many branches of learning and considers chemical, economic, political, social, and ethical questions, as well as strictly biological ones.

As man's interactions with the environment have become more drastic, more people have become concerned with human ecology (environmental studies). Today a committee assigned to work on a particular human ecological problem is likely to include physicists, systems analysts, city planners, biologists, chemists, economists, historians, politicians, corporate executives, union leaders, and behavioral scientists. Each must contribute his special knowledge if the problem is to be solved.

(a) Define ecology. _____

_____

_____

(b) Define human ecology. _____

_____

_____

– – – – – – – – – – – – – – – – – – –

(a) the science that studies the interactions between living organisms and their environment (or the science that studies ecosystems); (b) the study of ecosystems as they specifically affect and are affected by human beings

2. Science is an activity that is basically concerned with making predictions about the future. Scientists develop models in order to make predictions. They develop elaborate techniques for collecting and organizing information. At some point, enough information is accumulated so that relationships can be discovered among the various pieces of information.

Models are developed to explain the relationships that might exist between the various pieces of information. A good theory or model integrates many separate pieces of information (facts) in a consistent and orderly manner. An idealized model is shown in figure 1.1.

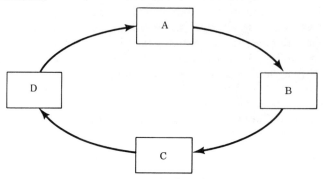

Figure 1.1   Idealized model

How would a scientist use this model? Let's say he has a well established bacterial colony that is rapidly increasing in numbers. He would first determine the present state of affairs; suppose the colony is in state B. Using the model, he can predict that at some point in the future, state C will exist. (He could also "predict" that state B had been preceded by state A.)

Although models mimic the real world, they never match reality on a one to one basis. Some elements are always missing. Otherwise, the models wouldn't be models—they'd be reality! Models always simplify reality—a good model pinpoints the key elements that vary in a particular situation (variables), those needed to make accurate predictions. In their simplest forms models are usually verbal or graphic. More sophisticated models are based on mathematical or statistical formulations.

Some situations seem very complex. Yet, if only a few important variables are involved, a very simple model can give great insight into the complexity. For example, before Darwin, the origin of the multitudes of animals and plants seemed extremely complex. But Darwin's natural selection model makes the origin of all the animals and plants seem comparatively simple, natural, and logical.

The closer a scientist's model matches reality, the more accurate the predictions he is able to make. Scientists constantly revise and refine models seeking a closer and closer match between the model (theory) and the reality (as judged by the accuracy of the predictions generated by the model). If a model can generate predictions about things we want to know about, and if it makes those predictions more accurately and simply than any competing model (and more accurately than chance), then the model is used and represents the current state of knowledge in that particular area of science.

Ecologists work to organize man's knowledge about the interactions that occur in nature. They build models of these interactions, so they can predict what will happen in the future. Living things interact with their environment in many very complex ways. Ecology is a relatively young science, and not surprisingly there are many matters about which ecologists cannot make very accurate predictions. However, in the past 50 years, ecologists have developed a number of useful conceptual models.

Why are scientists concerned with constructing models? _____

_____

_____

– – – – – – – – – – – – – – – – – – –

Models simplify reality by pinpointing what seem to be the key variables in a given situation, and thus they allow scientists to make predictions about the future, and making predictions is the goal of science.

3.   When <u>biotic</u> <u>components</u> (living organisms) and <u>abiotic</u> <u>components</u> (nonliving things) interact in a regular and consistent way they can be viewed as <u>systems</u>. Ecologists are especially concerned with population systems, communities, and ecosystems.

Dr. Eugene P. Odum has suggested that we view the areas of biological study as a spectrum composed of many levels of organization, each level representing a type of biological system. He uses the diagram in figure 1.2.

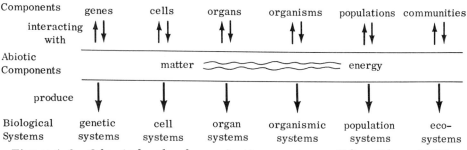

Figure 1.2 Odum's levels of organization spectrum (After Odum, 1971)

Notice that each level of organization (running from left to right) involves a biotic component interacting with an abiotic component through the exchange of matter and energy. Each interacting level produces a functional biological system. For example, you are a biological organism, so you use energy and various material substances from your external environment to maintain a system at the organismic level of organization. You exchange the food you eat and the air you breathe for the wastes eliminated and the air exhaled. In addition, your bodily system includes many smaller <u>subsystems</u>. You are composed of organs; they in turn are composed of cells and genetic material. In each case the system persists because of interactions with the abiotic components of the physical environment (exchanges of matter and energy).

At first glance it might seem that small, simple things occur to the left and large, complex things occur to the right. This view would be too simplistic. Each of the biotic components represents a level of organization with its own complexities and its own "laws." The problems of cell structure and function are just as complex as the problems of communities, and a knowledge of one level will not necessarily help a scientist solve the major problems of another level—either to the right or to the left of it on the spectrum. Knowing about one level may help you think about another level, but each level is a new system with complexities and interactions that cannot be predicted from a knowledge of another level.

Consider H_2O—water. It has unique properties that are not found in either H—hydrogen, or O—oxygen. Even if you knew all about hydrogen and oxygen in their free states, you would not be able to predict that combining them would produce something with the properties of water. And the same thing is true in reverse: You would not intuitively think that water, a liquid, would break up into two highly flammable gases.

Ecologists are mainly concerned with the right side of this organizational spectrum—especially populations, communities, and ecosystems. Before proceeding, let's explicitly define each of these important terms:

- Population: a group of organisms, all of one kind (species), living within a specific area. We can speak of a population of catfish in a pond, the population of starlings in Central Park, or the population of mice in your granddad's barn.

- Community: all of the populations of organisms that exist and interact in a given area. The community includes the entire living (biotic) component of an area. For instance, a desert community refers to all the plants, animals, and microbes living in a specific desert area.

- Ecosystem: a community and the related nonliving environment interacting together as a whole. To the biotic component we now add the abiotic component of the external environment, thus making a relatively self-sustaining system. When we consider a desert community plus its soil, climate, temperature, water, mineral cycles, and sunlight, we are studying a desert ecosystem.

When we consider all living organisms on or around the earth, we are looking at the biosphere.

(a) Ecologists are mainly concerned with what levels of Odum's "levels of

organization spectrum"? _____

_____

(b) An ecosystem is a community interacting with _____

_____.

- - - - - - - - - - - - - - - - - -

(a) populations, communities, and ecosystems; (b) abiotic components
(the nonliving environment)

4.   In addition to looking at the organizational levels with which
      ecologists concern themselves, several viewpoints or perspec-
      tives are also possible within each of these levels. We use the
      term viewpoint to stress that the system itself—the interacting
      reality of biotic and abiotic components—remains the same.
      For purposes of model building, however, it is useful at times
      to look at a particular system from different vantage points.
      Each viewpoint allows us to build a different model and make
      different predictions, but we should remember that no one
      viewpoint is more valid than any other. They are each more
      or less useful, depending upon the sort of prediction we want
      to make.

Probably one of the best examples of different viewpoints comes from
modern physics in the study of light. In certain situations, physicists approach light as if it were a wave phenomenon, transmitted through space like
waves on the surface of a pond. In other situations, physicists hold that light
is composed of tiny particles which are given off by a light-emitting object.
Both views are quite successful in building models that explain certain characteristics of light and predict its future behavior. Each viewpoint is useful
in illustrating certain properties of light which the other does not explain.
Because of the different and important predictions obtained from each of the
models, both viewpoints are regarded as valid. In this book we will study
ecology successively from four major viewpoints:

- The Energy Viewpoint: When we organize information about the interrelationships of biotic and abiotic factors on the basis of energy flow,
  we are viewing ecosystems from an energy perspective. Energy is
  defined as the ability to do work. Energy is the cause of all activity;
  energy transforms matter; and life itself exists only because it contains
  and expends energy. Energy passes through an ecosystem and in the
  process gives the ecosystem a special sort of order. The greater the
  organizational complexity of an organism, a population, or an ecosystem, the greater the amount of energy needed to maintain the system.

- The Cycles Viewpoint: Another way of looking at ecosystem interactions
  is from the perspective of cycles. Using the term cycle in its most
  general sense, we can view a whole class of phenomena simply as a
  sequence of events that recur regularly. Some cycles, such as the
  astronomical, atmospheric, and geologic cycles, do not necessarily
  involve living organisms. Most cycles, however, involve not only
  abiotic but also biotic components. These cycles are called biogeochemical cycles. Biogeochemical cycles include the oxygen cycle, the
  carbon cycle, the nitrogen cycle, the phosphorus cycle, and the cycles
  of various other minerals.

- The Populations Viewpoint: Population is one of the most fundamental
  groupings in ecology. As previously noted, populations are composed
  of all the members of one kind (species) of organism living within a
  given area. In addition to the characteristics of individual organisms,

populations have characteristics of their own. An individual organism may be born and die, but only populations have birth rates and death rates. A population extends through time and has its own birth, its times of expansion and contraction, and it may perhaps die (extinction).

- The <u>C</u>ommunities <u>or</u> <u>E</u>cosystems <u>V</u>iewpoint: When we study the interactions of all populations (hence all organisms) in a given area, we are looking at the community level of organization. Just as populations have characteristics separate from the individual organisms that make up the population, communities have properties separate from any one of the populations in the community. In a process called succession, communities evolve from simple to more complex (mature) interactions. In mature communities, even though some populations may be increasing and others decreasing, a general balance of energy flow and productivity is maintained. A community along with its abiotic interactions is called an ecosystem.

These four major viewpoints are discussed in detail in the remaining four parts of the book. First, however, we will consider some basic systems concepts that will be used throughout the book to describe and explain the viewpoints.

(a) Energy is the most valid of the four viewpoints. _____
                                                                    (true/false)

(b) Explain your answer. _____

_____

_____

(c) In what sense can we say that the population viewpoint is different from

the individual viewpoint and from the community viewpoint? _____

_____

_____

_____

– – – – – – – – – – – – – – – – – – –

(a) false

(b) The validity of a viewpoint is relative. For some purposes the energy viewpoint is valid. For other purposes it isn't especially useful. Each viewpoint is more or less valid depending upon the sort of predictions we want to make.

(c) Populations have characteristics that are different from those possessed by individual organisms or by a community. For example, populations have birth rates but individuals do not. And no individual population can display succession because it is a unique property of several populations acting together as a community.

5. A _system_ is a collection of parts or events that can be seen
    as a single whole thing because of the interdependence and
    interaction of those parts or events. The _systems_ _approach_
    is a way of thinking about the world, an approach to problem
    solving and model development which involves thinking about
    a complex series of events or things as a single whole.

An airplane is composed of many parts. These parts include mechanical
engine parts, controls, seats, and the components of the superstructure of
the plane. A plane in flight also includes fuel, a pilot, and passengers. Yet,
when we see a plane fly overhead, we can think of it as a single, whole thing
—a transportation system. Likewise, an ecological area may contain many
species of plants and animals all interacting with each other and with such
abiotic factors as climate and geography. We can think of all these organisms, abiotic factors, and interactions as one single thing—an ecosystem.

We will consider two basic types of systems:

- Open Systems: systems that depend upon the outside environment to
  provide inputs and accept outputs.

- Cybernetic Systems: systems that use some sort of feedback mechanism to regulate themselves.

6. Open systems process inputs and produce outputs. They do
    this in a more or less set way, and the amount of output pro-
    duced is directly related to the amount of input received.
    To continue functioning, open systems constantly require
    new inputs. The easiest way to diagram such a system is
    the box model (see figure 1.3).

Input(s) → | System | → Output(s)

Figure 1.3   General model of open system

A "black box" is a simple model of an open system. A black box takes
one thing and, by some unknown manipulation, changes it to something else.
For many of us, TV is a black box that takes inputs of electricity and electromagnetic waves and changes them into picture and sound (see figure 1.4).
TV is also an open system in that if its inputs are cut off, then it ceases to
function (make outputs).

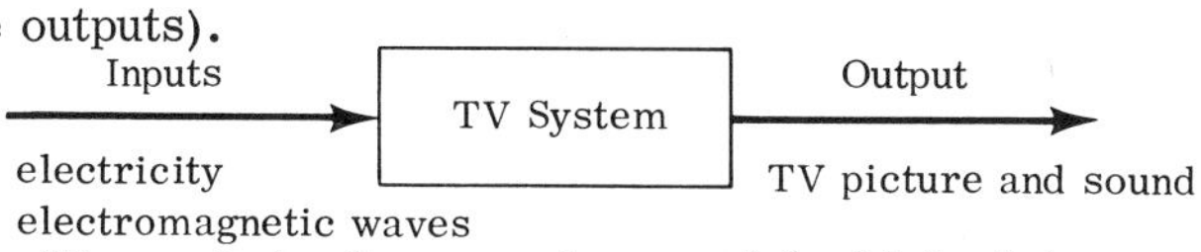

Inputs → | TV System | → Output

electricity   TV picture and sound
electromagnetic waves

Figure 1.4   Open system model of television

The parts or pieces of a system or of a black box are called _system_ components or _elements_. As a scientist discovers relationships among system
components, he groups and relates them. These related groups are called
subsystems. A system that is slightly understood might be diagrammed as
in figure 1.5. System XYZ is composed of three subsystems, and subsystem
Y is broken down into its two components.

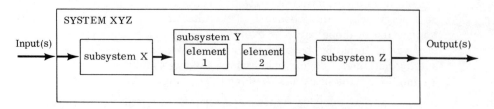

Figure 1.5   Open system with components

In this text we will often use open system diagrams to illustrate how various components are interrelated by common output-input paths. For example, figure 1.6 shows a series of interrelated system components.

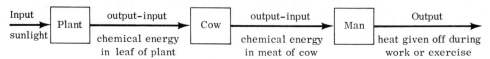

Figure 1.6   Series of open system components
connected by output-input

An example of a mechanical open system is a switch-controlled heater (figure 1.7). When you turn the switch on, electricity enters the heater system and produces a heat output. It continues to accept electrical inputs and produce heat outputs at a relatively constant rate as long as its input is continued (as long as the switch is left on).

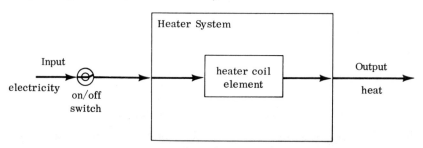

Figure 1.7   A heater system as an example of an open system

Define an open system. _____

_____

_____

– – – – – – – – – – – – – – – – – – – –

An open system is a collection of parts or events that act as a single thing and take inputs from the outside environment, change them, and produce outputs. To continue functioning, open systems always need new inputs.

7.   Cybernetic systems use feedback to exercise some degree of self-control. The basic idea behind feedback is that some of the output of the system is used to control some future input to the system. Cybernetic systems usually have an <u>ideal</u> <u>state</u> or <u>set</u> <u>point</u>, the state or point at which the system maintains itself.

A concrete example of a cybernetic system is a heater-thermostat system whose set point is the point (temperature) at which the householder sets the dial. When the set point is exceeded, an internal mechanism is activated and input to the system is reduced, curbing the tendency to exceed the set point. The same thing happens in reverse when the set point is not being reached. The internal mechanism increases the system's input until the set point is reached. In the case of most thermostats this mechanism is a heat-sensitive metal spring that expands or contracts as the temperature rises or falls and thus makes or breaks contact. In either case, the feedback that causes the readjustment to the set point is called <u>negative</u> <u>feedback</u>. The feedback is referred to as negative because it halts or reverses a tendency or movement away from the set point. In this book we will normally use a <u>figure-eight</u> <u>diagram</u> (figure 1.8) to represent any simple cybernetic negative feedback system.

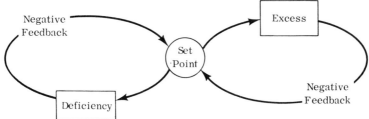

Figure 1.8   A figure-eight diagram

Let's consider one specific mechanical example in detail. See figure 1.9. The thermostat regulates the input of electricity to the heater. (Some person made an input to the thermostat—gave it a set point—but thereafter the thermostat simply works to maintain that set point.) When the temperature rises, a metal spring expands, and cuts off the electricity by breaking the electrical connection to the heater coil. When the temperature falls, the metal contracts and the electrical connection is reestablished, thus turning on the heating coil again. Figure 1.10 is a figure-eight diagram of the thermostat-heater system. Both figures, 1.9 and 1.10, are on the following page.

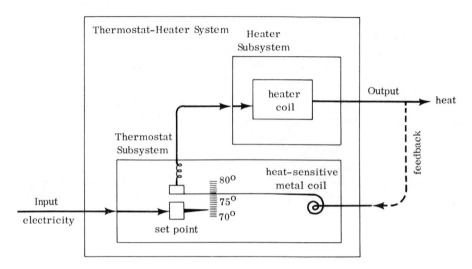

Figure 1.9   A thermostat-heater system
as an example of a cybernetic system

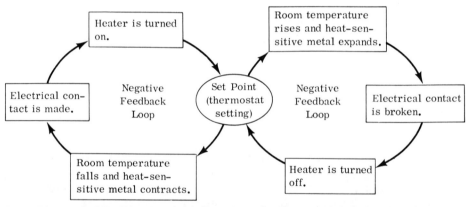

Figure 1.10   Figure-eight diagram of a thermostat-heater system

(a) Define a cybernetic system. _____

_____

(b) Draw the simplest possible general diagram of a cybernetic system.

(c) Feedback that slows down and eventually halts or reverses a tendency

away from a set point is called _____.

– – – – – – – – – – – – – – – – – – –

_____

(a) A cybernetic system is a collection of parts or events that act as a single thing and regulates its activities about an ideal state or set point. Cybernetic systems use feedback to maintain this ideal state.

(b)

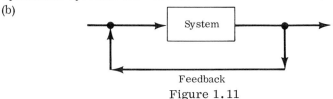

Feedback

Figure 1.11

A figure-eight diagram would also be acceptable.

(c) negative feedback

8.   Cybernetic systems can also display <u>positive feedback</u>. Positive feedback is a continually increasing tendency away from the system's set point.

For an example of positive feedback, let us look at the temperature of the human body. It is maintained by a most remarkable thermostat. For external temperatures between 62° and 90°F an elaborate series of negative feedback mechanisms maintains the body's temperature around its set point of 98.6°F. As body temperature rises, these mechanisms lower heat production and increase heat loss (through sweating and radiation). As body temperature decreases, the body responds by increasing heat production and diminishing heat loss (through decreased sweating and surface circulation, as well as increased shivering). At extreme temperatures, however, these elements of the body's cybernetic heat regulation system may break down. In higher temperatures the body is unable to lose heat fast enough and positive feedback takes over. The body's metabolic processes proceed faster, which serve to elevate body temperature even more. This in turn hastens the metabolic rate which again increases body temperature. This vicious cycle ultimately results in death. The normal negative feedback mechanisms can also fail at extremely low temperatures, initiating positive feedback: lower body temperatures, reduction in rate of metabolism, and death. It is easy to see why positive feedback is sometimes referred to as runaway feedback.

Figure 1.12 is a diagram of the human body's cybernetic heat regulation system. Both negative and positive feedback processes are illustrated.

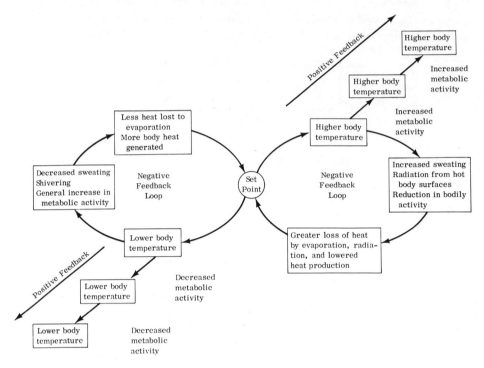

Figure 1.12   Diagram of human body's
cybernetic heat regulation system

Why does negative feedback occur in some cases and positive feedback occur in others? One answer is that a cybernetic system has a homeostatic plateau—that is, the system has certain limits within which negative feedback will occur. Beyond that plateau (outside those limits)—when the variation from the set point becomes too great—positive feedback takes over. Figure 1.13 illustrates these limits and the homeostatic plateau for temperature regulation in mammals. The figure is on the next page.

Two common examples of positive feedback are reproduction and bank interest rates. In both cases, products (children or money) produce more products, ad infinitum. In both cases, pursued far enough, some sort of disaster would occur (total space or money available in the world would run out).

(a) Define positive feedback. _____

_____

(b) Explain the concept of a homeostatic plateau. _____

_____

_____

– – – – – – – – – – – – – – –

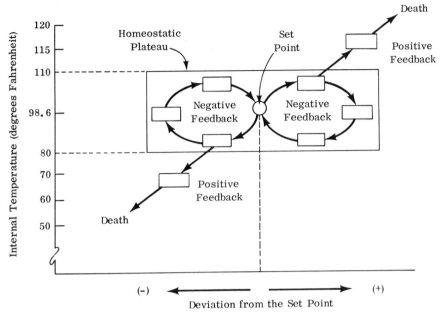

Figure 1.13   Temperature regulation in mammals
and the homeostatic plateau

(a) Positive feedback is a continually increasing tendency away from
the system's set point.

(b) The homeostatic plateau defines an area (set of limits) within which
the system can use negative feedback to regulate itself about a set point.
If some tendency away from the set point exceeds the limits of the homeostatic plateau, positive feedback occurs, which pushes the system even
further away from its set point and eventually results in the "death" of
the system.

9.   As a general rule, we can say that any system is composed
        of smaller systems—subsystems—and is itself a part of some
        larger system—a supersystem. If we choose to study a par-
        ticular subsystem Q of system X, we refer to Q as a system
        in its own right and apply systems concepts in analyzing it.
        For example, we see if it has a set point, we study its inputs
        and outputs, and we examine its negative and positive feed-
        back tendencies.

     Generally, when we ask how something works we are asking for a descrip-
tion of the system's subsystems. Thus, we describe how a man gets energy,
in part, by describing his circulatory system. We explain how circulation
occurs by examining the heart, blood vessels, etc. We explain how the heart
works by describing its parts and their interactions.

When we ask <u>why</u> something works we are asking about the supersystem to which a particular system belongs. Thus, we explain <u>why</u> a boiler was built a certain way by saying that it was designed to fulfill a particular role in a steam engine. We explain <u>why</u> steam engines are built by referring to the railroad train for which the steam engine is a part. And, we explain <u>why</u> a railroad train follows the course it does by talking about a particular railroad system of tracks, cities, and schedules.

This can all be summarized by saying that a system never stands alone. A system is a level of explanation. When the object of our study changes, our system may become a subsystem within a new larger study area. Or, we may go from our first system to one of its components and study its parts and interactions. The complexity of ecology and systems thinking lies in the interrelatedness of all the various components and concepts.

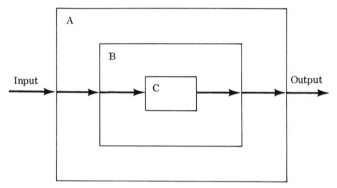

Figure 1.14

Examine figure 1.14.

(a) If A is a system, B and C are _____.

(b) If B is a system, then C (but not A) is a _____.

(c) If B is a system, then A is a _____.

(d) If you were asked <u>how</u> B works, you would probably explain it in terms of

_____.

(e) If you were asked <u>why</u> B exists, you would probably explain it in terms of

_____.

(f) Does a system ever stand alone, outside the context of any other system?

_____

- - - - - - - - - - - - - - - - - -

(a) subsystems (or components or elements); (b) subsystem (or component or element); (c) supersystem; (d) C and the other subsystems that comprise it; (e) A—the supersystem that it is contained within; (f) no

10. All biological systems are necessarily open systems. To stay alive, not to mention grow, the system must take in food and nutrients from outside itself. The system must also give off heat as it carries on chemical processes (respiration, for example). However, each level of an open biological system contains cybernetic systems. The cybernetic systems operating at a particular level (within a particular open system) give that level its unique characteristics.

Briefly review Odum's levels of organization spectrum, figure 1.2 on page 11. Each of the biological systems identified is an open system. They all take in energy and give off energy. Odum isolated genes, cells, organs, organisms, populations, and communities as six separate levels or systems. Each of these open systems or levels contains important cybernetic systems. When we say that population systems have characteristics different from those found in organismic systems, we are saying that there are cybernetic systems operating at the level of populations that are not apparent when we examine organisms by themselves.

Thus, a cell (system) is an open system because it constantly acquires food from outside itself and eliminates wastes. It also contains cybernetic systems, for example, membranes which control the entry and exit of cellular materials. If limits are exceeded, negative feedback mechanisms correct the situation. The cell can <u>live</u> because it is an open system. It exists <u>as a cell</u> because of the cybernetic systems that hold its "cell" characteristics intact.

We will usually examine an ecological viewpoint—energy, for example—as an open system first, finding the general system inputs and outputs. Then we will ask how the system handles these inputs and still preserves its own identity, which will bring us to the cybernetic systems within the open system.

(a) All living systems are _____.

(b) We classify living systems into levels because each level contains
_____ that give that level a special identity.

(c) A cell is a(n) _____.

(d) A cell contains several _____ that maintain its characteristic cellular traits.

- - - - - - - - - - - - - - - - - -

(a) open systems; (b) cybernetic systems; (c) open system; (d) cybernetic systems

11. In this text we are concerned with systems or models that can be described in verbal or graphic terms. These are sometimes called <u>informal</u> <u>systems</u> or <u>models</u>. With more knowledge, scientists refine their models from verbal to graphic and finally to mathematical terms. Mathematical systems models can

make predictions of specific future outputs (specified quantities and qualities). Mathematical models of systems are
sometimes called <u>formal</u> <u>models</u>.

To make formal models, ecologists must first translate complex ecological data into mathematical symbols in order to make formal statements and
establish formulas. This is a difficult theoretical and practical problem, for
ecological systems are often very complex. Once physical or biological concepts are stated in mathematical terms, however, various manipulations are
possible and increased predictive power usually results. Computers are
immensely useful in this effort.

We shall use very little mathematics in this book, but as ecology becomes
more sophisticated and makes more accurate predictions, you may reasonably
expect that many of the explanations and laws described here will assume
mathematical form.

12.   Ecologists commonly use the term <u>ecosystem</u> to describe a
       system that contains both living and nonliving components
       (a community interacting with its abiotic surroundings). An
       ecosystem is composed of subsystems with their own char-
       acteristics and interactions, but the ecosystem is more use-
       fully viewed as a single whole thing.

We could regard the entire planet earth as a single open ecosystem, as
in figure 1.15. The earth ecosystem is obviously an open system: It constantly needs inputs of energy and it constantly gives off used energy in the
form of heat. But, like other ecosystems, it also has cybernetic subsystems
with their set points and feedback cycles.

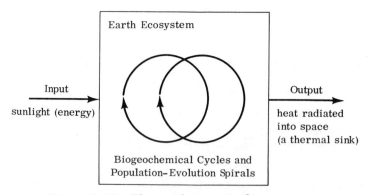

Figure 1.15   The earth as a single ecosystem

Actually, the earth as a whole is too large and complex to be usefully
viewed as an ecosystem. There is nothing technically wrong with viewing
it as such, but as a matter of practicality, we tend to limit the use of the
word <u>ecosystem</u> to a set of interacting organisms that we can fruitfully study
with our present instruments and concepts. A forest, a pond, a city, or a
certain altitude on a mountain—all constitute typical, workable ecosystems.

In studying a particular ecosystem, we must always determine the role of time. We can view an ecosystem as a static thing and study the interactions of the system's components as if they were constant and unchanging. Or, we can view an ecosystem as a dynamic entity whose components are constantly evolving and thereby modifying the system itself. Applying this latter view is often difficult, but when successful, we have a very realistic view of a portion of our world.

However, even when we take the evolution of ecosystem components into account, we exclude really dramatic changes from the ecosystem concept. For example, consider a swamp. The swamp's history may go back to the retreat of the last glacier at the end of the last Ice Age. If, however, men drained the swamp and built a factory on that ground, we would say that the swamp ecosystem had ceased to exist, and some new ecosystem had begun. A particular ecosystem can extend in time, but only as long as the majority of its components or interactions remain substantially unchanged.

Finally, we would like to reemphasize that no system stands alone. Every ecosystem is part of a larger ecosystem—extending to at least the whole earth. Likewise, ecosystems contain ecosystems which contain ecosystems, down to the most basic environmental relationships. And ecosystems are related horizontally as well, since some of the inputs of any one ecosystem are sure to be former outputs of some other ecosystem.

SELF-TEST

This Self-Test is designed to show you whether or not you have mastered this chapter's objectives. Answer each question to the best of your ability. In most cases, to define or explain you should write one to three brief sentences. Correct answers and review instructions are given at the end of the test.

1. Match the following terms:

_____(a) ecology

_____(b) human ecology

_____(c) energy

_____(d) cycle

_____(e) population

_____(f) community

_____(g) ecosystem

_____(h) biosphere

(1) a sequence of events that occur regularly.
(2) the science that studies the interactions between living organisms and their environment.
(3) all living organisms on or around the planet earth.
(4) a group of organisms, all of one kind, living in a given area.
(5) the ability to do work.
(6) the study of ecosystems as they affect and are affected by human beings.
(7) all of the populations or organisms that exist and interact in a given area.
(8) a community and the related non-living environment interacting as a whole.

2. The goal of science is to _____.

3. In physics, light can be viewed as either a wave or a particle. What does this illustrate? _____

_____

4. Which ecological perspective or viewpoint is ultimately most important? Explain your answer. _____

_____

5. Define system. _____

_____

_____

_____

6. What is an open system? _____

_____

_____

7. What is a cybernetic system? _____

_____

_____

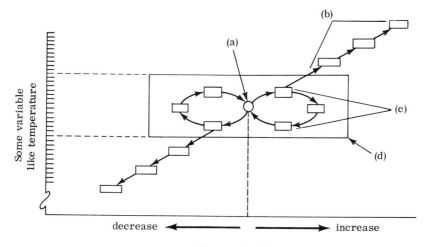

Figure 1.16

8. Label figure 1.16.

(a) _____   (b) _____

(c) _____   (d) _____

9. Examine figure 1.17. Then answer the questions on the following page.

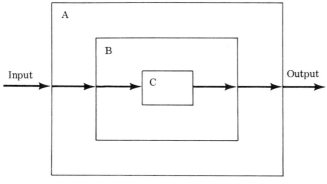

Figure 1.17

(a) Relative to system B, A is a _____

(b) Relative to system B, C is a _____

(c) Relative to system A, B is a _____

(d) Relative to system C, B is a _____

(e) Relative to system B, the question "<u>how</u> does B work?" can be explained in terms of _____.

(f) Relative to system B, the question "<u>why</u> does B exist?" can be explained in terms of _____.

10. Organisms are one level on Odum's levels of organization spectrum.

(a) Are organisms open systems? Explain. _____

_____

_____

(b) What systems give organisms their unique level characteristics?
Explain. _____

_____

_____

11. Ecosystems are living systems. Based on that information, give several
general properties of ecosystems. _____

_____

_____

_____

ANSWERS TO SELF-TEST

Compare your answers to the questions on the Self-Test with the answers given below. If all of your answers are correct, you are ready to go on to the next chapter. If you missed any questions, review the frames indicated in parentheses following the answer. If you miss several questions, you should probably reread the entire chapter carefully.

1. (a) 2 (frame 1)　　　　(b) 6 (frame 1)
   (c) 5 (frame 4)　　　　(d) 1 (frame 4)
   (e) 4 (frames 3 and 4)　(f) 7 (frames 3 and 4)
   (g) 8 (frames 1, 3, and 4) (h) 3 (frame 3)

2. to make accurate predictions of future events (frame 2)

3. the importance of looking at the same system from different viewpoints or perspectives; or the use of different models for different purposes (frame 4)

4. No one perspective is more important than any other. The validity or importance of a viewpoint depends on your purpose. Particular viewpoints are more or less valid depending upon the sort of predictions we want to make. (frame 4)

5. A system is a collection of parts or events that can be seen as a single whole thing because of the consistent interdependence and interaction of those parts or events. (frame 5)

6. Open systems depend upon the outside environment to provide inputs and accept outputs. (frames 5 and 6)

7. Cybernetic systems are systems that use some sort of feedback mechanism to regulate themselves. (frames 5 and 7)

8. (a) set point; (b) positive feedback; (c) negative feedback; (d) homeostatic plateau (frames 5-8)

9. (a) supersystem; (b) subsystem; (c) subsystem; (d) supersystem; (e) subsystem C; (f) supersystem A (frame 9)

10. (a) Yes, they require inputs from their environment to continue to exist and they must make outputs.
    (b) Cybernetic systems give each level its unique characteristics. The cybernetic systems with their negative feedback mechanisms keep a system at a particular level in a state of balance, maintain its essential character (set point), and prevent it from changing into something different. (frame 10)

11. You should have mentioned at least the following: They receive inputs and produce outputs. Some of their unique characteristics are maintained by cybernetic systems—they have feedback mechanisms and a homeostatic plateau. They are subsystems of larger systems and they themselves contain subsystems. (frame 12)

PART TWO

Energy in Ecosystems

Energy is a very mysterious concept. It is involved in every single event in the universe from frogs to photons. Energy is everywhere, in everything. It is one of the most fundamental concepts of physics, yet physicists say that they really do not understand it very well. One thing they do believe, however, is that energy never appears from or disappears into nothing. Energy can always be accounted for, just as your bank can account for your money. If we cannot account for some energy, we must have made a mistake, because nature's "energy accounts" are always balanced. In analyzing complex systems, energy accounting can furnish us with important insights. Environmentalists are beginning to realize that the energy viewpoint can be an extremely useful analytical tool.

Part Two is composed of three chapters. Chapter 2 identifies the fundamental principles that underlie any understanding of energy. The earth is treated as an open system receiving continuous energy inputs from the sun and returning energy to space as heat. The distribution of solar radiation is discussed, and the First and Second Laws of Thermodynamics are introduced.

Chapter 3 describes how energy acts to organize an ecosystem. The path that energy takes through food chains and food webs is traced as each living organism is considered an individual open system converting its energy input into new tissue, waste, and heat.

The concept of community productivity and some of its human implications are introduced in Chapter 4. Man depends on energy derived from the sun to keep his biological and technological machinery running. This chapter also discusses the changing patterns of human energy consumption as well as some problems arising from man's failure to properly balance his energy-account books.

CHAPTER TWO

Concepts of Energy

When you complete this chapter, you will be able to

- identify the sun as the source of all energy on earth;

- explain the importance of wavelength to both incoming sunlight and reflected heat;

- describe how plants capture solar energy by means of photosynthesis;

- describe how plants and animals acquire energy from food by means of respiration;

- state the First Law of Thermodynamics and explain its basic ecological implications;

- state the Second Law of Thermodynamics and explain its basic ecological implications.

If you think that you have already mastered these objectives and might skip all or part of this chapter, turn to page 43 at the end of this chapter and take the Self-Test. The results will allow you to evaluate your current knowledge of this chapter's contents. If you answer all of the questions correctly, you are ready to begin the next chapter. If you miss any questions, you should study the frames indicated after the answers to the Self-Test.

If this material is new to you, or if you choose not to take the Self-Test now, proceed to frame 1.

1.   From the energy viewpoint, the earth is an open system. For life to exist, the earth must constantly receive inputs of energy from the sun and make outputs of heat energy which are passed to outer space. Energy from the sun maintains all of the life processes in the earth ecosystem. Life on earth is possible only because a continuous flow of solar energy (solar radiation)

arrives from the sun daily. At the same time, large amounts of heat energy leave the earth and pass into the vast heat "sink" of space.[1] A stable earth ecosystem is maintained because of the continuous input of solar radiation and the constant outflow of heat. The relatively constant temperature of the earth's surface is one result of the constant input-output energy balance maintained by the earth ecosystem.

The sun is a sort of hydrogen bomb, a huge mass of hydrogen that is constantly changing some of itself into helium, with the incidental emission of a huge amount of energy in the form of electromagnetic waves (radiation). These waves flow outward from the sun in all directions. The earth, which would be just a dot in the sky if it were viewed from the sun, is touched by only about 1/50,000,000 of the sun's electromagnetic waves.

2.   Solar energy is radiated toward the earth, but the atmosphere keeps some solar radiation from reaching the earth. Only about 50 percent of the sunlight reaching the earth's upper atmosphere actually continues to the earth's surface. Heat from the earth is constantly rising and passing to outer space.

As shown in figure 2.1 on the next page, over one-third of the solar energy reaching the earth's atmosphere is reflected back into space by clouds, atmospheric dust, and reflecting surfaces on earth (snow, oceans, sand). Another 14 percent or so of the solar energy never reaches the surface. It is absorbed by gases as it penetrates into the earth's atmosphere. Of the remaining 50 percent, about 25 percent comes directly to the earth's surface. The other 25 percent is first scattered by clouds, dust, and so forth, but eventually it is radiated to the earth by clouds and particles in the atmosphere.

Most of the sun's energy is radiated in electromagnetic waves with lengths from 0.2 to 4.0 microns.[2] This spectrum ranges roughly from the ultraviolet through the infrared (see figure 2.2 on the next page). About half of the sun's energy is radiated in wavelengths that fall in the visible spectrum and can be seen by the human eye (0.39 to 0.76 microns). Most of these "short" wavelengths pass directly through the earth's upper atmosphere because the clouds, dust, and other atmospheric components are effectively "transparent" to short wavelengths.

A very special exception bears mentioning. A layer of ozone in the earth's upper atmosphere actively absorbs ultraviolet radiation. Ultraviolet radiation, with a very short wavelength, has a high energy content that is capable of breaking the bonds of large organic molecules which compose living organisms. The early atmosphere of the earth was probably transparent to ultraviolet radiation since it most likely lacked oxygen. But with the emergence

---

1. The term "sink" refers to a place that absorbs huge energy outputs. Relative to earth, outer space is a heat or thermal sink.

2. One micron is equal to 1/10,000 of a centimeter (or about 1/25,000 of an inch), and the abbreviation for micron is μ, the Greek letter mu.

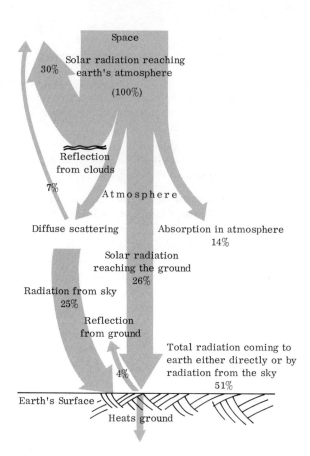

Figure 2.1   Energy input to earth's surface at midday

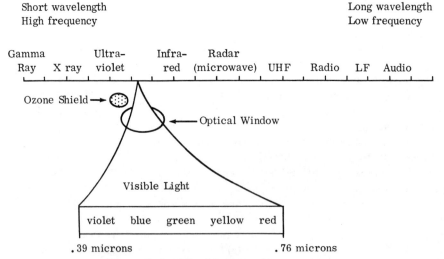

Figure 2.2   Electromagnetic spectrum

of photosynthetic activity, oxygen (O_2) was introduced into the atmosphere. Ozone (O_3) was soon formed and provided the shield needed in order for life to evolve onto land. This filter of ozone allows light of short wavelengths (the visible spectrum) through, while it absorbs the very short wavelengths of ultraviolet radiation that would otherwise kill earth's present life forms.

The solar radiation that passes through the atmosphere and is absorbed at the earth's surface is expended in a variety of processes. It drives the major atmospheric cycles (as we will see in Part Three), melts ice, evaporates water, and generates winds, waves, and currents, as well as powering all of the organisms existing on earth.

Most of the energy that reaches the earth is reflected by the surface of the earth itself. But, significantly, the earth generally reflects radiations in very long wavelengths (about 12 microns). This means that most energy comes to the earth as visible sunlight and is radiated back into space in the form of heat. This is significant because the earth's atmosphere is <u>not</u> transparent to heat radiation and thus temporarily holds a large portion of the energy radiated from the earth's surface. The same carbon dioxide (CO_2) and water vapor in the atmosphere that permitted the incoming short wavelength radiation to reach the surface of the earth now absorb the infrared (longer wavelength) radiation and temporarily prevent the heat from leaving, much like the glass roof of a greenhouse, which gives the phenomenon its name—the <u>greenhouse</u> <u>effect</u>. Figure 2.3 is a visual summary of the primary energy inputs and outputs of the earth ecosystem. You may view that figure on the following page. Remember that these events are going on continually.

As you can see, life depends on both the clarity and the opaqueness of the atmosphere: It requires an atmospheric window that will admit visible light and absorb ultraviolet. It requires an atmosphere somewhat opaque to heat, so that the energy that is reflected from the earth's surface can be retained and distributed for a time before escaping into space.

There has been much speculation lately that man's activities might affect the earth's overall heat balance. As a result of burning fossil fuels, the CO_2 content of the atmosphere has increased by 12 percent since 1890. One would expect that an increase in atmospheric CO_2 would increase the greenhouse effect and thus the surface temperature of the earth. By 1940 it was estimated that the mean world temperature had increased by 0.35°C (0.63°F) due to man's recent fuel burning activities. After 1940 the temperatures began to decline, even though the CO_2 content continued to rise at an ever-increasing rate. The most common speculation is that the increased reflectivity of the earth's atmosphere has more than compensated for the increased greenhouse effect. More particles in the atmosphere as well as clouds resulting from high-flying jet aircraft tend to reduce the amount of incoming sunlight by increasing the amount reflected. It seems that we are carrying on a global experiment with our climate and weather without anyone really knowing what's going on. Indeed, it seems to be fortunate, thus far, that the two opposing forces—the greenhouse effect that raises the earth's surface temperature and the reflectivity that tends to lower it—seem to counterbalance each other. Thus, even before we discuss how solar radiation is used by living organisms, we can see that it interacts with abiotic factors to create the type of abiotic environment in which living things can survive.

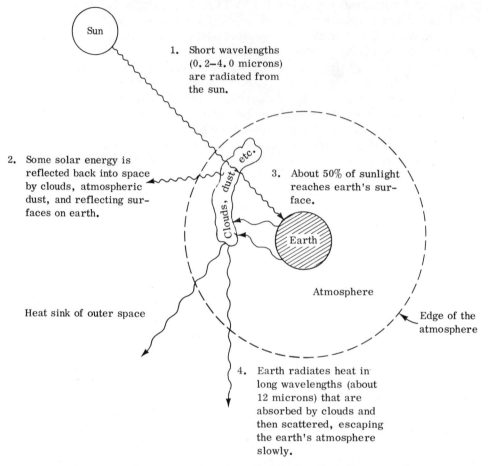

1. Short wavelengths (0.2–4.0 microns) are radiated from the sun.

2. Some solar energy is reflected back into space by clouds, atmospheric dust, and reflecting surfaces on earth.

3. About 50% of sunlight reaches earth's surface.

Heat sink of outer space

Atmosphere

Edge of the atmosphere

4. Earth radiates heat in long wavelengths (about 12 microns) that are absorbed by clouds and then scattered, escaping the earth's atmosphere slowly.

Figure 2.3   Energy inputs and outputs of earth ecosystem

What might happen if the sun radiated energy at wavelengths of 12 microns?

_____

_____

_____

- - - - - - - - - - - - - - - -

The energy would be absorbed and reflected by the clouds above the earth, and the energy reaching earth would probably be insufficient to allow life. Or, the energy would not be in a form that living plants could use in photosynthesis, so that life would not be as we know it.

3.   In plants sunlight is transformed by means of <u>photosynthesis</u> into complex chemical molecules. Later, when either plants or animals (who eat plants or other animals to obtain these

complex, energy-rich molecules) need energy, they break down these molecules, releasing the energy stored in them.

About one-half of the sunlight that reaches the earth's surface is of a wavelength that can be used in the photosynthetic process. The sunlight that strikes plants is converted from radiant energy into chemical energy in the presence of a complex substance called <u>chlorophyll</u>. Ecologists sometimes refer to this process as <u>fixing solar energy</u>. Without photosynthesis, which provides living organisms with the energy to build complex molecules, life could not exist.

Biological systems store the energy that they obtain from sunlight in large food molecules. The chemical bonds of force that hold these complex molecules together represent stored chemical energy that can be released when the organism needs energy. All biological systems can break down molecular bonds (in a process called respiration) and thereby release the energy contained in these bonds to do the work of living. But only photosynthetic plants possess the ability to build the initial food molecules, and for this reason they are called <u>autotrophs</u> or self-feeders. All other living organisms depend upon autotrophs for the food molecules (in the form of autotroph tissue) that they must have to live.

The photosynthetic formula (in its simplest form) is represented in figure 2.4. Six carbon dioxide and twelve water molecules are changed, by means of sunlight and chlorophyll, into one sugar molecule (glucose), six oxygen molecules, and six water molecules. The carbon (C) formerly present in the carbon dioxide is now part of the sugar-glucose. Compounds containing carbon are called organic compounds and include all foods (proteins, fats, carbohydrates) and living tissue. In this case, the glucose is the organic molecule that is "storing" energy.

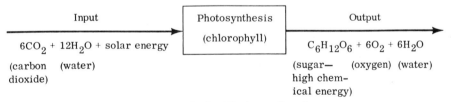

Figure 2.4   Photosynthesis

Actually, the process of photosynthesis is far more complex than this equation suggests. There are more than a hundred steps to this production of glucose from carbon dioxide and water.

Describe photosynthesis. How is it important? _____

_____

_____

_____

_____

– – – – – – – – – – – – – – – – – – –

_____

Photosynthesis is the process whereby plants capture sunlight and use it to produce chemical compounds.

Formula: $6CO_2 + 12H_2O \xrightarrow{\text{sunlight + chlorophyll}} C_6H_{12}O_6 + 6O_2 + 6H_2O$

Photosynthesis is important because it is the only significant way that living things can capture solar energy.

4. Plants store solar energy in complex energy-rich chemical molecules by means of photosynthesis. Heterotrophs ("other-feeding" organisms) are consumers of green plants. They have no way of fixing solar energy and must obtain the energy-rich chemicals from plant tissue. Both plants and animals then release the energy from these chemicals in a process called respiration.

Let us look at these events in detail. As photosynthesis occurs, energy is bonded into each sugar molecule ($C_6H_{12}O_6$). Other energy-rich substances such as fats and proteins are subsequently produced from chemical interactions between the glucose and other substances. Within both plants and animals these complex food molecules undergo a series of changes which channel the available energy into various life processes. These changes are collectively known as respiration. As the foodstuff molecules are combined with oxygen, the energy is transferred to smaller "packages" of high energy chemical bonds. These high energy bonds are found in a compound known to biologists as ATP (adenosine triphosphate). ATP is found in the cells of each living organism and is the common energy currency used in the organism's biochemical reactions. It can be "saved" for future use or "spent" for building and repairing cellular structures and for performing various cellular functions. Respiration involves more than seventy sequential chemical reactions, but the net reaction is summarized in figure 2.5.

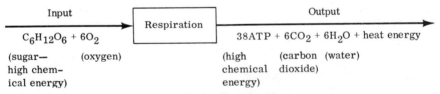

Figure 2.5 Respiration

As you read this, your body's cells are maintaining your life by combining the energy-rich molecules originally formed in photosynthesis with appropriate proteins called enzymes and giving you energy to contract your muscles, force blood through your heart, and keep your body temperature at about 98.6°F. In the process the cells are also releasing carbon dioxide (CO_2), which you expel from your lungs with every breath, and water (H_2O), which you exhale or perspire. As you live and work the energy you use is converted to heat, which constantly radiates from your body and into the atmosphere. In this you are similar to all living systems, and like all living systems your existence is totally dependent upon the energy of the sun.

(a)   Describe how solar energy is made available to animals.   _____

_____

_____

_____

_____

(b)   Examine figure 2.6 and fill in the blanks below.

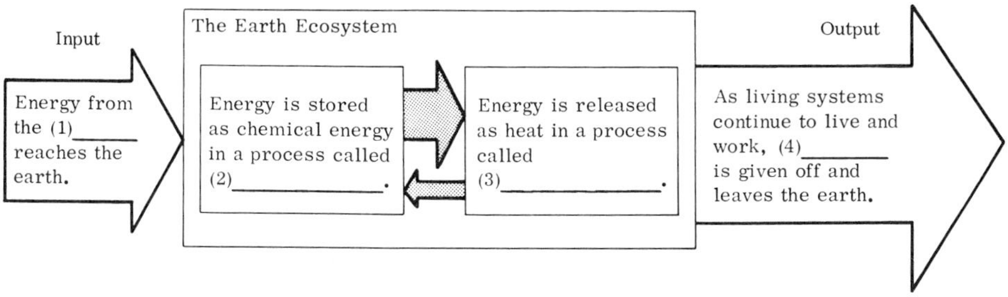

Figure 2.6

(1) _____   (2) _____

(3) _____   (4) _____

- - - - - - - - - - - - - - - - - - -

(a) By means of photosynthesis, plants store energy in energy-rich
chemical molecules. Animals eat the tissue of plants and thus obtain
these chemicals. Then they release the energy from these chemicals
in the process of respiration.
(b) (1) sun;   (2) photosynthesis;   (3) respiration;   (4) heat

5.   All energy processes are controlled by two very general laws
        —the laws of thermodynamics, which give the relationships be-
        tween the different forms of energy. The First Law of Ther-
        modynamics states that energy can be transformed from one
        form to another but can never be created or destroyed.

     Energy is defined as the ability to do work. It can take many forms,
such as nuclear energy, radiant energy (visible light, ultraviolet light,
x-rays, etc.), chemical energy, heat energy, or the energy associated with
mass itself ($E = mc^2$).[3] The First Law of Thermodynamics (often called
conservation of energy)' requires that the total amount of energy in all its
forms remain constant. The First Law tells us that we can't get something
for nothing. Although the amount of energy in various forms may change, the
sum in all forms must remain constant.

_____

3. $E = mc^2$ stands for Einstein's celebrated formula for the conversion of
mass to energy (energy = mass × velocity of light squared).

(a) Define energy. _____

_____

(b) What is the First Law of Thermodynamics? _____

_____

_____

– – – – – – – – – – – – – – – – – –

    (a) the ability to do work; (b) The First Law of Thermodynamics
states that energy can neither be created nor destroyed, only transformed
from one form to another.

6.   The Second Law of Thermodynamics states that each time
energy is transformed it tends to go from a more organized
and concentrated form to a less organized and more dispersed form. The ecological implication of the Second Law
of Thermodynamics is that the transfer of energy from one
user to another is never very efficient. In every transfer
some energy becomes so disorganized or dispersed that it
is no longer useful.

    The two laws of thermodynamics imply that it should be possible to ac-
count for all energy that occurs in ecological systems (that is, where it
comes from, where it goes) and that as energy flows through ecological
systems, less and less of it will be available to do work at each successive
step.

What is the Second Law of Thermodynamics? What is its major implication

for ecosystems? _____

_____

_____

– – – – – – – – – – – – – – – – – –

    The Second Law of Thermodynamics states that energy tends to go from
a more organized and concentrated state to a less organized state. This
implies that as energy is processed through an ecosystem, less and less
of it is available in a usable (organized and concentrated) form.

7.   Violations or apparent contradictions of the First and Second
Laws of Thermodynamics invariably stem from an incomplete
accounting of the whole system. Both biological organisms
and man-made machines are capable of organizing diffuse substances from their environment (transforming disorder into
order). These processes appear to negate the tendency toward
disorder imposed by the Second Law of Thermodynamics. But

a <u>complete</u> accounting of all the consequences soon reveals
that the disorder in the system as a whole (the process and
the surroundings) invariably increases.

For example, the fuel and other energy expended by man and machine in
the generation of electricity are only partly converted into concentrated electrical energy. A large portion of the total energy is degraded into relatively
useless heat. In addition to this waste heat, the electrical energy output from
the plant is also ultimately degraded to heat as it is transmitted and used in
everything from light bulbs to electric motors.

All human activity—from the breaking down and using of food by our cells
to the running of machines—requires energy. As this energy is used, heat
is given off. No technological innovation can free us from this consequence
of the Second Law of Thermodynamics. In future chapters we will consider
some of the implications of releasing excessive heat into the environment.

Both the First and Second Laws of Thermodynamics are demonstrated in
the one-way flow of energy through the biosphere shown in figure 2.7. The
energy from the sun is not destroyed as it flows through the earth's ecosystem, but is rather <u>degraded</u> from a more concentrated form of energy capable
of driving reactions and performing work into the most diffuse kind of energy
—heat. In other words, the First Law insists that the total amount of energy
in the universe remain constant while the Second Law insists that concentrated,
usable energy must continually diminish.

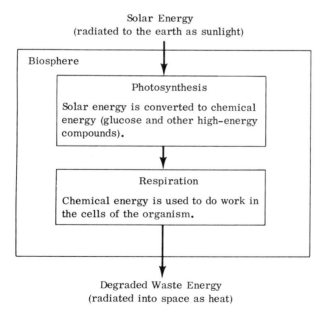

Figure 2.7   Energy flow and transformation in the biosphere

What is indicated if an ecologist thinks he can account for all energy coming into and leaving a particular ecosystem, but finds that considerably more energy leaves than enters the ecosystem?

_____

_____

_____

_____

– – – – – – – – – – – – – – – – – –

Since the ecosystem cannot create energy, it indicates that the ecologist is not adequately accounting for all entering energy. He should search for additional sources of energy entering the particular ecosystem.

SELF-TEST

This Self-Test is designed to show you whether or not you have mastered this chapter's objectives. Answer each question to the best of your ability. Correct answers and review instructions are given at the end of the test.

1. Solar radiation (sunlight) is important to living things on earth because it supplies them with _____.

2. What happens to incoming solar radiation with a wavelength between 0.2 and 4.0 microns when it reaches earth's atmosphere? What happens to radiation with a wavelength of 12 microns when it is reflected by the earth? _____

   _____

   _____

   _____

3. Describe how plants capture solar energy. _____

   _____

   _____

   _____

   _____

4. Describe how plants and animals obtain energy for their daily activities.

   _____

   _____

   _____

   _____

5. State the First Law of Thermodynamics (in your own words).

   _____

   _____

6. State the Second Law of Thermodynamics (in your own words).

   _____

   _____

7. From what law is the following statement derived: In any ecosystem, we ought to be able to account for all the incoming and outgoing energy.

8. What law implies the following statement: As energy passes through an ecosystem, it becomes less and less available to do work.

ANSWERS TO SELF-TEST

Compare your answers to the questions on the Self-Test with the answers given below. If all of your answers are correct, you are ready to go on to the next chapter. If you missed any questions, review the frames indicated in parentheses following the answer. If you miss several questions, you should probably reread the entire chapter carefully.

1. energy (frame 1)

2. Earth's atmosphere is relatively transparent to wavelengths of 0.2-4.0 microns (it lets sunlight in freely). Earth's atmosphere is relatively reflective of wavelengths of 12 microns (it keeps the heat on earth longer, instead of letting it escape back into space right away). (frames 1 and 2)

3. Sunlight strikes plants and, by means of a process called photosynthesis, is combined in the presence of chlorophyll with CO_2 (carbon dioxide) and H_2O (water) to produce complex, energy-rich molecules (sugar—$C_6H_{12}O_6$) as well as oxygen and water. The energy from the sunlight is stored in the "bonds" of the sugar molecules. (frame 3)

4. The solar energy stored in energy-rich chemical molecules by photosynthesis is released by plants and animals by a process called respiration. In this process the molecular bonds are broken, thereby releasing the energy stored in them. (frame 4)

5. Energy can neither be created nor destroyed, only transformed from one form to another. (frame 5)

6. Each time energy is transformed, it tends to go from a more organized and concentrated form to a less organized and more dispersed form. (frame 6)

7. First Law of Thermodynamics (frame 5)

8. Second Law of Thermodynamics (frame 6)

CHAPTER THREE

Feeding Relationships and Productivity

OBJECTIVES

When you complete this chapter, you will be able to

- define food chain and food web;
- define, discriminate between, and relate producers, consumers, decomposers, autotrophs, heterotrophs, herbivores, carnivores, and top carnivores;
- trace the flow of energy through a food chain;
- recognize a parasite and a detritus food chain;
- define trophic level and determine the trophic level of various organisms within food webs;
- state the Ten Percent Law and use it to determine the energy available to organisms at different trophic levels of an ecosystem;
- identify and describe pyramids of numbers, pyramids of biomass, and pyramids of energy;
- describe how food chains can concentrate certain chemicals as they pass from one organism to the next.

If you think that you have already mastered these objectives and might skip all or part of this chapter, turn to page 67 at the end of the chapter and take the Self-Test. The results will allow you to evaluate your current knowledge of this chapter's contents. If you answer all of the questions correctly, you are ready to begin the next chapter. If you miss any questions, you should study the frames indicated after the answers to the Self-Test.

If this material is new to you, or if you choose not to take the Self-Test now, proceed to frame 1.

1.   Energy moves about the biosphere in the form of energy-rich molecules that are first assembled and stored by <u>producers</u>. Producers are eaten by a series of <u>consumers</u>. Both producers and consumers obtain energy from these energy-rich molecules. Ultimately any energy fixed by producers or accumulated by consumers and not used by them is released by <u>decomposers</u>. These feeding relationships can be diagrammed as either <u>food</u> <u>chains</u> or <u>food</u> <u>webs</u>.

Energy flows through the biosphere in a sequence of steps from one organism to another. A <u>food</u> <u>chain</u> is a series of feeding relationships between organisms that shows who eats whom. The energy first trapped by photosynthesis is transferred from one organism to another with a rearrangement of chemical compounds at each step. At each step some of the energy becomes heat and escapes the system. An abstract food chain is diagrammed in figure 3.1.

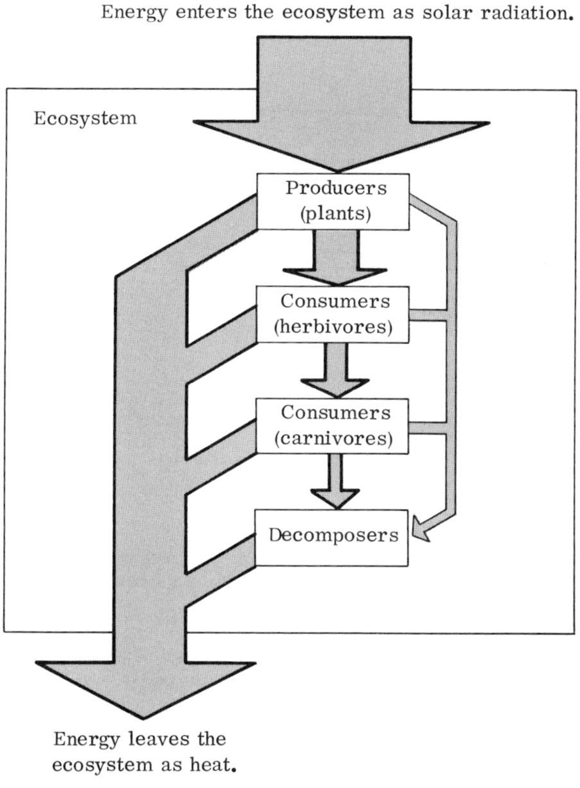

Energy enters the ecosystem as solar radiation.

Ecosystem

Producers
(plants)

Consumers
(herbivores)

Consumers
(carnivores)

Decomposers

Energy leaves the
ecosystem as heat.

Figure 3.1   Energy flow through an ecosystem—a food chain

Food chains are rarely isolated sequences. Several usually interweave to form a <u>food</u> <u>web</u>, a relatively complex series of feeding relationships.

Indicate the steps in figure 3.2 of an "ideal" food chain.

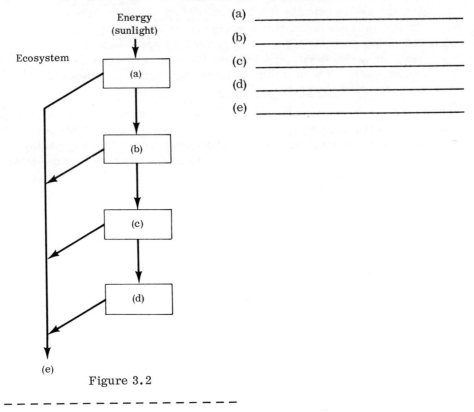

Figure 3.2

(a) _____

(b) _____

(c) _____

(d) _____

(e) _____

_ _ _ _ _ _ _ _ _ _ _ _ _ _ _ _ _ _ _

See page 47 for review.

2.   A <u>producer</u> (plant) uses sunlight and, by means of photosyn-
      thesis, produces energy-rich molecules. Most of the mole-
      cules produced simply increase the plant's tissue. Some of
      these molecules are broken down soon after they are made
      to fuel the plant's day-to-day life processes (including making
      additional tissue). In the course of its life, a plant uses most
      of the energy it fixes simply to stay alive or to produce off-
      spring. When it dies, the "dead" tissue still contains some
      energy, which is available to decomposing organisms—the
      decomposers. Or this dead tissue may yield its remaining
      energy to man; for instance, when we burn wood. Figure 3.3
      on the next page indicates the energy inputs and outputs of a
      typical producer.

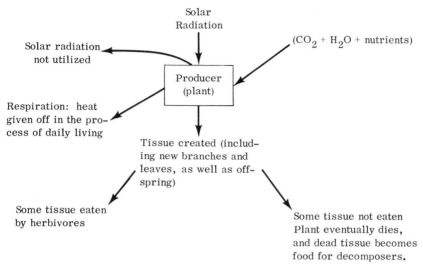

Figure 3.3   Energy inputs and outputs of a producer

3.   <u>Herbivores</u> are organisms that consume plant tissue.   Thus
     they obtain the energy-rich molecules that they can break
     down to release the energy they need to live.   Herbivores
     are heterotrophs ("other-feeding" organisms).   Like plants,
     herbivores expend most of the energy they obtain in living,
     growing, and reproducing.   This is diagrammed in figure 3.4.

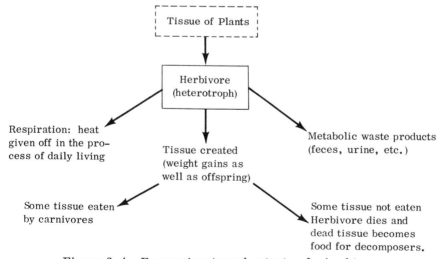

Figure 3.4   Energy inputs and outputs of a herbivore

To get some idea of the way one herbivore uses energy, look at figure
3.5 on the next page.   Notice that when the deer first eats food, some of it

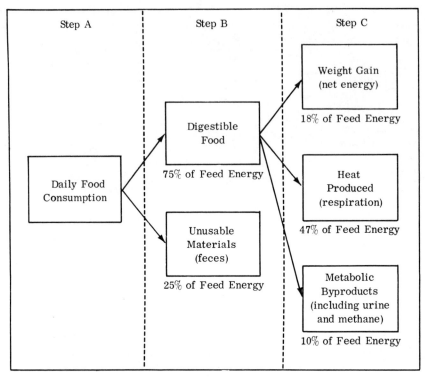

Figure 3.5 Relative values of the end products of energy
metabolism in the white-tailed deer. (After Cowan, 1962.)

is not digestible and is excreted as feces (Step B). In the process of using
the digestible food, some is released as gas and some as urine. Of that
energy used to live (Step C), most simply escapes as the heat produced in
respiration. Only a small proportion (about 18 percent) becomes a gain in
body weight. Of the deer's total intake of plant material, only the small portion that becomes tissue would be available to a carnivore who happened to
eat this deer.

Using thick and thin arrows to represent energy flow (that is, a very thick
arrow would represent a lot of energy), connect the boxes in figure 3.6.

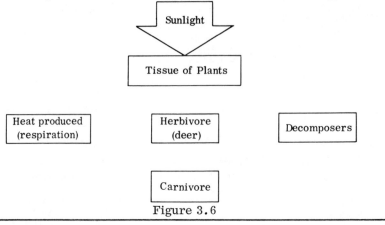

Figure 3.6

Figure 3.7 shows roughly how your arrows should look. (You might also have shown that some very small amount of plant tissue was directly consumed by decomposers.)

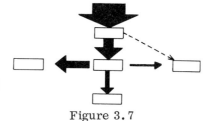

Figure 3.7

4. <u>Carnivores</u> are organisms that eat herbivores. Like herbivores, carnivores cannot obtain energy directly from sunlight. But instead of eating plant tissue to acquire energy-rich organic molecules, they eat herbivores. Also like herbivores, they expend their energy both in staying alive (respiration) and in tissue growth (growth and reproduction). See figure 3.8.

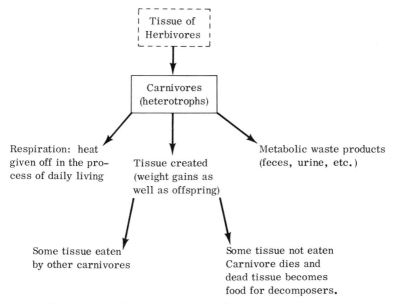

Figure 3.8 Energy inputs and outputs of a carnivore

Carnivores may also eat other carnivores. The last carnivore in a given food chain is called the <u>top carnivore</u>. Man is often a top carnivore. See figure 3.9 on the next page.

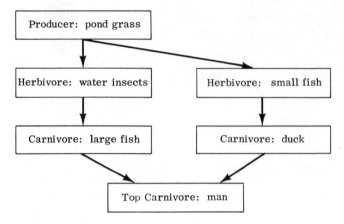

Figure 3.9   Simple food web with man as the top carnivore

5.   <u>Decomposers</u> live by obtaining energy-rich molecules from
        the tissue of dead organisms. Decomposers use much of
        their food intake in respiration but they also multiply, creat-
        ing new tissue. See figure 3.10.

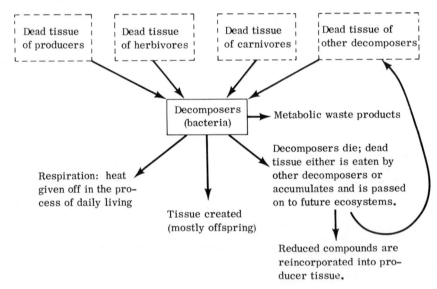

Figure 3.10   Energy inputs and outputs of a decomposer

Label the food chain in figure 3.11 on the opposite page.

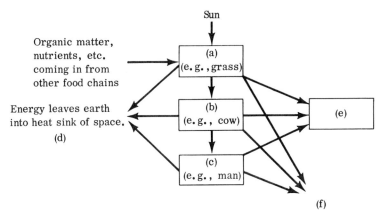

Figure 3.11

(a) _____   (b) _____

(c) _____   (d) _____

(e) _____   (f) _____

- - - - - - - - - - - - - - - - - -

(a) producer—plant;   (b) consumer—herbivore;   (c) consumer—carnivore;   (d) heat given off to stay alive—respiration;   (e) decomposers —bacteria;   (f) offspring and tissue not eaten

6.   We have been considering a generalized food chain where the energy goes from producer to primary consumer (herbivore) to secondary consumer (carnivore) to decomposers. There are no truly "general" food chains in nature. We have already mentioned, for example, that decomposers take their food from producers, herbivores, and even other decomposers, as well as carnivores. Special, but common, variations of the basic food chain pattern include parasite food chains and detritus food chains:

- Parasite Food Chains: food chains in which either the producer or the consumer is parasitized and therefore the food passes to a smaller organism rather than a larger one. See figure 3.12, on the next page.

- Detritus Food Chains: food chains in which the herbivores subsist on dead organic material (usually coming from outside the particular ecosystem), instead of eating producers.

An example of a detritus food chain is the aeolian zone in the Himalayas that was investigated by Dr. Lawrence Swan. Chlorophyll-bearing plants cannot live on these high mountains. In this zone the detritus input consists of wind-blown organic particles, especially pollen grains. Springtails and

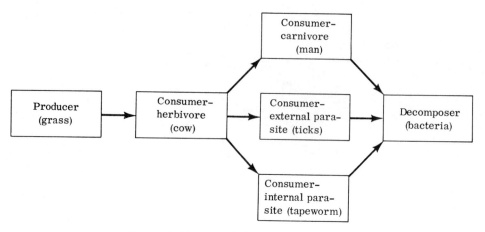

Figure 3.12   Food chain with parasites

mites live on these wind-blown particles and are eaten in turn by spiders.
The decomposers in this system are bacteria. This detritus food chain is
diagrammed in figure 3.13.

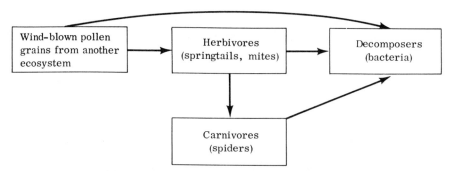

Figure 3.13   Aeolian detritus food chain

Obviously, a detritus ecosystem's borders could be expanded to include
producers, since no consumers can live without them. An ecosystem's
limits, however, are set for the purposes of a particular investigation.
Thus, although the basic pattern always works if one looks far enough, in
many studies it is useful to consider abbreviated or specialized versions of
food chains. From these examples you can also begin to see how simple
food chains can become expanded into food webs. No matter how the food
chain may vary from the basic pattern, however, the laws of thermodynamics
impose their invariable controls and limitations.

Draw a diagram of a parasitic food chain whose members consist of oak trees
that are parasitized by Spanish moss, squirrels that eat acorns but not the
Spanish moss, and bacteria that decompose everything else when the time
comes. Space is allowed for your drawing at the top of the next page.

- - - - - - - - - - - - - - - - - - -

Figure 3.14 illustrates how your diagram should appear.

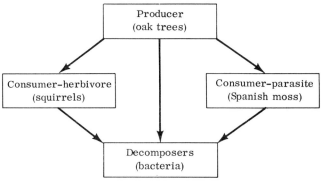

Figure 3.14

7.   The <u>trophic</u> <u>level</u> of an organism refers to the number of steps
     the organism is away from primary production. Primary pro-
     duction is trophic level one. One way of looking at food webs
     is to analyze different organisms according to the trophic lev-
     els they occupy.

More than one herbivore will probably feed on a given plant species.
Likewise, these primary consumers will often be preyed upon by more than
one carnivore and will most likely feed on several different types of plants.
So our generalized food chains become woven into an elaborate network of
interrelated food chains which we call a food web. If two organisms are the
same number of steps away from producers, we say that they occupy the
same trophic level. When we analyze food webs we can see that many different organisms, even though they do not prey on the same species, are on
the same trophic level. Examine figure 3.15 on the following page.

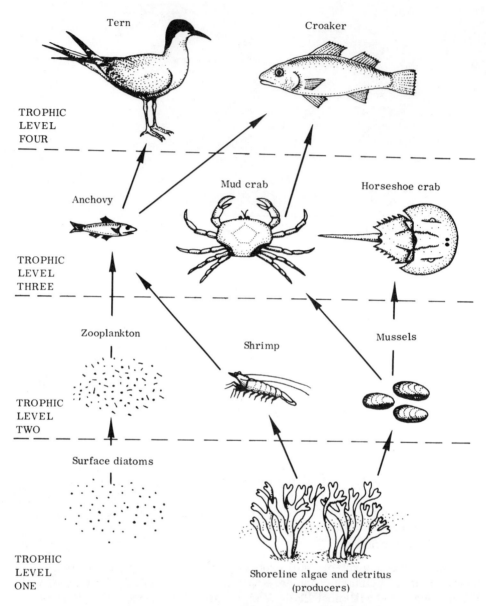

Figure 3.15   A shallow water ecosystem
with trophic levels illustrated

(a) Define trophic level. _____

_____

_____

(b)   A hypothetical food web is given in figure 3.16.   The organisms' names
have been replaced with letters.   Group the letters by trophic level.
A and B are producers.

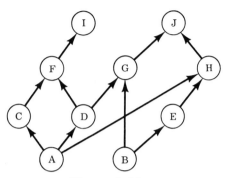

Figure 3.16

Organisms occupying <u>only</u> the first trophic level (1) _____
Organisms occupying only the second trophic level (2) _____
Organisms occupying only the third trophic level (3) _____
Organisms occupying only the fourth trophic level (4) _____
Organisms occupying <u>more</u> <u>than</u> <u>one</u> trophic level (5) _____

- - - - - - - - - - - - - - - - - - - -

(a) Trophic level is a term used to designate the number of steps away
from producers an organism is in a food web.   Producers are considered
trophic level one.
(b) 1 - A, B; 2 - C, D, E; 3 - F; 4 - I; 5 - H, G, J

8.   Putting all of our previous diagrams together and considering
all the organisms, we can get some idea of the energy flow
through an ecosystem.   To illustrate this we have used the
data from a study by Raymond L. Lindeman (1942) in which
he measured the fate of gram calories[1] per square centimeter
per year in Cedar Bog Lake in Minnesota (see figure 3.17
on the next page).

Figure 3.18 (on page 59) represents a much more detailed study by
H. T. Odum (1957) made at Silver Springs, Florida.   Dr. Odum's figures
represent kilocalories per square meter per year ($C/m^2/yr$).

---

1. A <u>gram</u> <u>calorie</u> is sometimes called a "small calorie" and is equivalent
to the amount of heat energy needed to raise the temperature of one gram of
water 1 degree centigrade (from 14.5 to $15.5^{o}C$).   In biology (and in diets)
we usually speak in terms of "large calories" or kilocalories which are 1000
small or gram calories.   Large calories are abbreviated C (or Kcal).

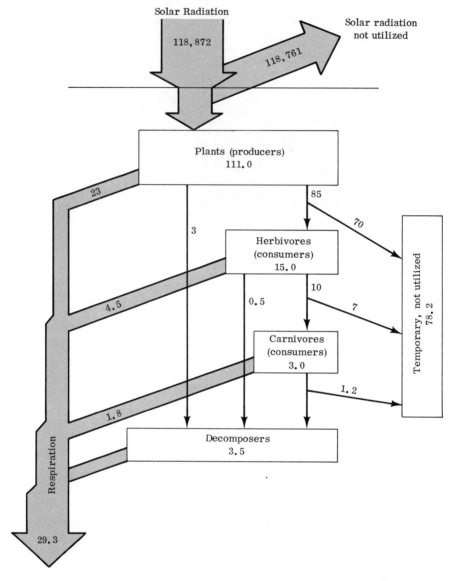

Figure 3.17   Fate of energy (gram calories per square centimeter
per year) in Cedar Bog Lake, Minnesota (After Lindeman, 1942)[2]

---

2. Since this study was limited to one year and since carnivores commonly
live longer than one year, no significant decomposition occurred. This study
did not keep track of decomposer respiration or the production of new decomposer tissue.

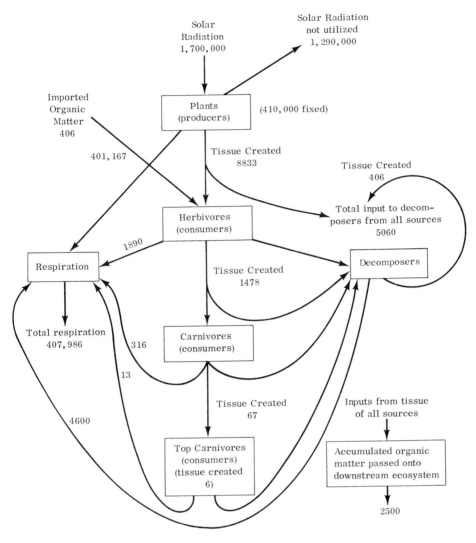

Figure 3.18 Energy flow in the Silver Springs
ecosystem (C/m^2/yr)^3 (Odum, 1957)

3. All imported organic matter is shown going into herbivores—actually some
of it went into plant tissue production, some went to carnivores, and some
went directly to decomposers.

Examine Figure 3.18:

(a) Approximately what percentage of initially fixed solar radiation ($410,000$ $C/m^2/yr$) was eventually dissipated in plant respiration?

_____

(b) Approximately what percentage of the initial plant tissue (8833 $C/m^2/yr$) did the top carnivore manage to obtain?

_____

(c) Approximately what percentage of the initial plant tissue did the decomposers receive from all sources?

_____

- - - - - - - - - - - - - - - - - - -

(a) over 95 percent ($401,000$ out of $410,000$);   (b) roughly 1 percent (67 out of 8833);   (c) about 50 percent (5060 out of 8833)

9.   As energy moves within a food web, most of it is lost in respiration. The Ten Percent Law states that only about 10 percent of the energy from one level can be captured by organisms on the next higher trophic level.

A major implication of the Second Law of Thermodynamics is that at each energy transfer considerable energy is lost. Because the energy loss is so excessive and because the First Law tells us that no new energy can be formed, the higher an organism's trophic level, the less energy is available to it. In biological transfers we can readily see how this is true. A plant must expend energy during photosynthesis. It uses energy to bring water and nutrients up from the ground and carbon dioxide in from the air, and it is constantly growing and reproducing. Animals expend considerable energy just locating the plants or animals they intend to eat and more energy in actually eating them, not to mention their constant cellular respiration. Thus it is not surprising that 80 to 90 percent of the energy received by organisms at one trophic level is used up before being transferred to the next level. Stated in another way, the total energy content of a trophic level in an ecosystem is only about one-tenth that of the preceding level. This is called the Rule of Ecological Tithe or the Ten Percent Law. As the total amount of energy available to an ecosystem is determined by the photosynthetic activity of the producers at the first trophic level, it is obvious that more usable energy is available to those organisms occupying lower levels. The Ten Percent Law places a practical upper limit on the number of trophic levels food webs can have. This limit is reached when organisms can no longer obtain enough energy to keep alive and reproduce. Most food webs have only about 4 or 5 trophic levels.

(a) Based on the Ten Percent Law, estimate the kilocalories (C) each of the members in the following food chain might add to its energy content, assuming each member of the chain ate the tissue of an organism in the preceding level. Write the figures in the blanks.

> Producer
> > produces 1000 C of tissue.
>
> Herbivore
> > adds _____ C of energy in the form of herbivore tissue.
>
> Carnivore
> > adds _____ C of energy in the form of carnivore tissue.
>
> Top Carnivore
> > adds _____ C of energy in the form of top carnivore tissue.

(b) What is the practical upper limit on the number of steps a food chain can have? Why? _____

_____

_____

_____

_____

– – – – – – – – – – – – – – – – – –

(a) Herbivore adds <u>100</u> C of energy; Carnivore adds <u>10</u> C of energy; Top Carnivore adds <u>1</u> C of energy.
(b) The practical upper limit is about 4 or 5 trophic levels, because a large amount of energy is lost at each level (at each energy transfer) so that ultimately there is insufficient energy (tissue) to sustain another organism.

10.   As you may imagine, the technical problems in determining energy flow in an ecosystem are quite complex, thus we are not able to fill in our models with all of the numbers we might theoretically desire. Nonetheless, the overall picture that you have gained from looking at both diagrams should be this:

- Only a very small part of the sunlight striking the producers is actually transformed into organic matter (energy-rich chemicals).

- Of the energy that the producer succeeds in capturing, a large part of it is used in respiration and eliminated from the system.

- The total amount of energy at each trophic level is much less than at the preceding level (80-90 percent less).

- Decomposers derive their energy from the dead tissue of organisms occupying all of the preceding steps (occupy all but the first trophic level). This is sometimes considered a separate detritus food chain.

11. Trophic structures for communities of organisms are often graphically represented by ecological pyramids.

We have seen how successive links in the food chain are represented by fewer numbers of individuals. The first links in the chain must produce enough to maintain themselves as well as nourish the next link. Each successive link from plant to herbivore to carnivore represents progressively less of the system's original energy. In addition, a smaller weight of living material (biomass) usually occurs along the food chain. In all these aspects —numbers, energy, and biomass—there is a pyramid effect in the community's trophic structure. Three types of ecological pyramids are shown in figure 3.19. In these examples, a hypothetical chain between alfalfa, a calf, and a boy is computed, based on the assumption that ten acres of alfalfa grow for one year.

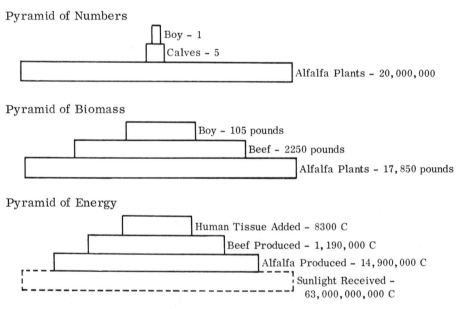

Pyramid of Numbers

Boy - 1
Calves - 5
Alfalfa Plants - 20,000,000

Pyramid of Biomass

Boy - 105 pounds
Beef - 2250 pounds
Alfalfa Plants - 17,850 pounds

Pyramid of Energy

Human Tissue Added - 8300 C
Beef Produced - 1,190,000 C
Alfalfa Produced - 14,900,000 C
Sunlight Received - 63,000,000,000 C

Figure 3.19 Types of ecological pyramids (Modified after Odum, 1971). (The drawings are based on a log scale.)

Notice that decomposer organisms are not represented on these ecological pyramids. The number of organisms is so large and their weight so small that they cannot be conveniently measured or graphed. Even though a considerable amount of energy flows through decomposers, its measurement poses many problems and is rarely undertaken. The omission of decomposers on ecological pyramids definitely limits their usefulness. They should, therefore, be viewed with caution so as not to ignore the vital role played by decomposers in ecosystems.

In figure 3.20, identify each of the trophic pyramids as to type.

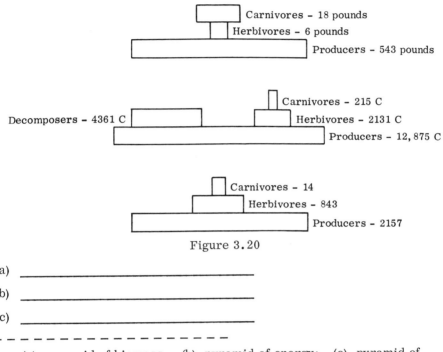

Figure 3.20

(a) _____

(b) _____

(c) _____

– – – – – – – – – – – – – – – – – –

(a) pyramid of biomass; (b) pyramid of energy; (c) pyramid of numbers

12. A fundamental characteristic of the food chain concept is the concentration of certain substances as they pass along the chain.

The energy received as food by an organism is only partially used to construct new tissue; about 50 percent is spent in respiration. Any substance that is neither involved in respiration nor easily excreted will tend to become concentrated in the organism's tissue. (See figure 3.21 on the following page.) This phenomenon is called <u>food</u> <u>chain</u> <u>concentration</u> or <u>biological</u> <u>magnification</u>, and it accounts for high concentrations of persistent pesticides and radioactive materials now found in many higher organisms. These concentrations may be several thousands of times higher than those found in the surrounding environment.

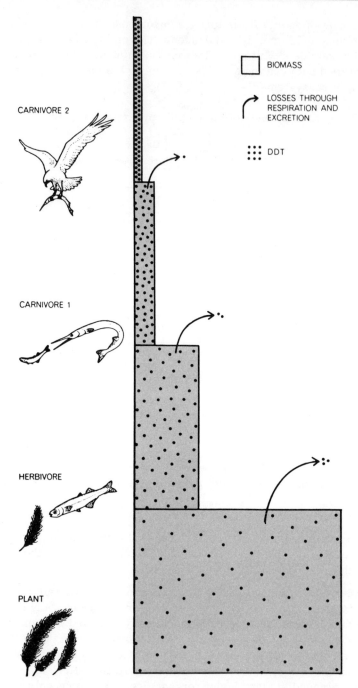

Figure 3.21. Concentration of DDT residues being passed along a simple food chain (From "Toxic Substances and Ecological Cycles" by George M. Woodwell, <u>Scientific</u> <u>American</u>, March 1967. Copyright © 1967 by Scientific American, Inc. All rights reserved.)

The levels of DDT found in some samples taken from a marsh along Long Island shore are pictured in figure 3.22. The numbers indicate residues of DDT and its derivatives in parts of DDT per million parts of wet body tissue. Notice that the level has been concentrated from 0.04 ppm in the plankton to 75 ppm in a gull. Accumulations in dead western grebes at Clear Lake, California, have been reported to be 80,000 times greater than the background level.

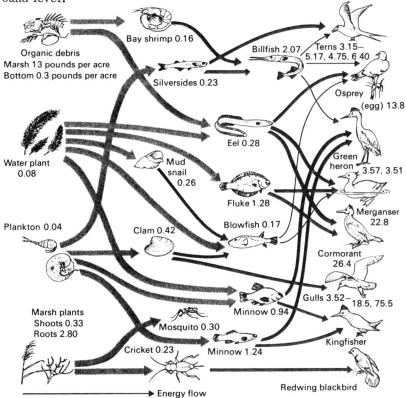

Figure 3.22 Levels of DDT in a Long Island shore food web (Adapted from "Toxic Substances and Ecological Cycles" by George M. Woodwell, Scientific American, March 1967. Copyright © 1967 by Scientific American, Inc. All rights reserved.)

Some biological concentration is called idiosyncratic concentration. This usually occurs due to selective absorption of a chemical by various tissues in an organism. For instance, the thyroid gland in vertebrates selectively removes iodine from the blood stream. Thus, radioactive iodine 131 is selectively absorbed into the thyroid gland when present in an organism's blood. Radioactive substances like strontium 90, which is similar in biological activity to calcium, and cesium 137, which behaves like potassium, can similarly concentrate in the bones. Figure 3.23 on the following page shows a simplified food web in which radioactive strontium is concentrated in the organisms of a freshwater community. This is based on the work of I. L. Ophel.

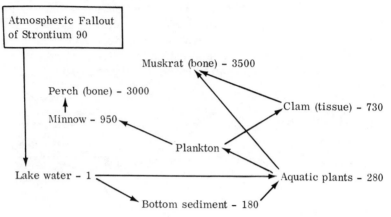

Figure 3.23   Accumulation of radioactive strontium
in a freshwater community expressed in parts per
million. (After Ophel, 1963)

(a) If figure 3.23 were tracing energy, we would expect the perch and musk-

rat to have _____ than the basic producers (the aquatic

                     much more/much less

plants).

(b) What mechanism is working in figure 3.23? _____

_____

(c) Briefly describe what is happening in the food web in figure 3.23.

_____

_____

_____

_____

(d) Does this have a relevance to man? Why or why not? _____

_____

_____

_____

- - - - - - - - - - - - - - - - - - -

(a) much less;   (b) food chain concentration;   (c) A substance not involved in respiration (strontium 90) is being concentrated in the tissue of
the organisms in this food chain. The higher the trophic level, the more
stored substance the animal has.   (d) Yes, it is relevant to man because
he sometimes functions as a top carnivore and could therefore accumulate
and store large amounts of chemicals subject to food chain concentration.

SELF-TEST

This Self-Test is designed to show you whether or not you have mastered this chapter's objectives. Answer each question to the best of your ability. Correct answers and review instructions are given at the end of the test.

1. Eating relationships between plants and animals can be diagrammed as either food _____ or food _____.

2. Identify each of the food relationship networks in figure 3.24.

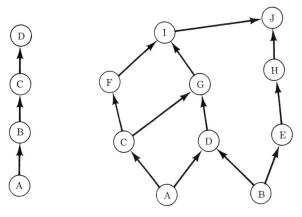

Figure 3.24

(a) _____   (b) _____

3. Match the following (there can be more than one match, so be complete).

_____ (a) grass   (1) producers
_____ (b) deer   (2) consumers
_____ (c) wolf   (3) decomposers
_____ (d) bacteria   (4) autotrophs
                                     (5) heterotrophs
                                     (6) herbivore
                                     (7) carnivore

4. Fill in the blanks below figure 3.25 on the next page.

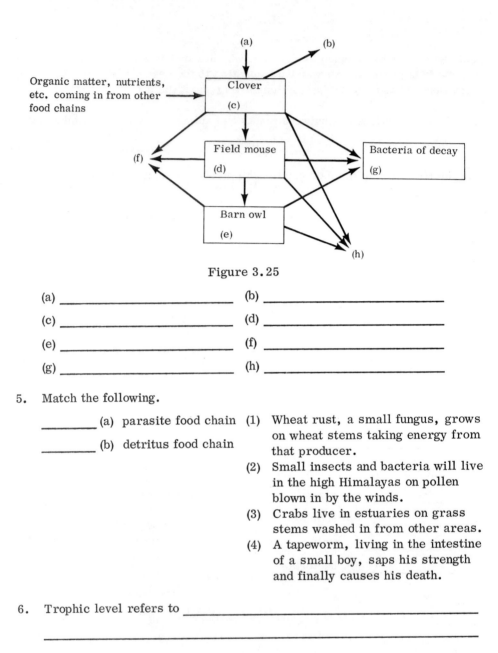

Figure 3.25

(a) _____   (b) _____

(c) _____   (d) _____

(e) _____   (f) _____

(g) _____   (h) _____

5. Match the following.

    _____ (a) parasite food chain   (1) Wheat rust, a small fungus, grows
                                             on wheat stems taking energy from
    _____ (b) detritus food chain   that producer.
                                         (2) Small insects and bacteria will live
                                             in the high Himalayas on pollen
                                             blown in by the winds.
                                         (3) Crabs live in estuaries on grass
                                             stems washed in from other areas.
                                         (4) A tapeworm, living in the intestine
                                             of a small boy, saps his strength
                                             and finally causes his death.

6. Trophic level refers to _____

    _____

7. Examine the food web in figure 3.26 on the facing page: 1 and 2 are pro-
    ducers. Fill in the blanks below the figure with the appropriate numbers.
    Numbers can be used more than once.

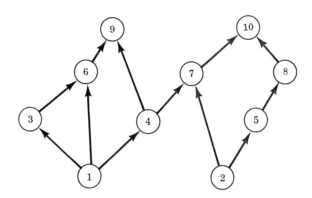

Figure 3.26

(a) _____ Organisms occupying <u>only</u> the first trophic level

(b) _____ Organisms occupying <u>only</u> the second trophic level

(c) _____ Organisms occupying <u>only</u> the third trophic level

(d) _____ Organisms occupying <u>only</u> the fourth trophic level

(e) _____ Organisms occupying more than one trophic level

8. State the Ten Percent Law. _____

_____

9. Fill in the following blanks.

Producer V captures 12,400 C of energy from sunlight.

(a) Herbivore W acquires _____ C by eating all of the Producer V crop.

(b) Carnivore X acquires _____ C by eating Herbivore W.

(c) Top Carnivore Y acquires _____ C by eating Carnivore X.

(d) Decomposer Z acquires _____ C by eating Top Carnivore Y.

10. Identify the figures below and on the following page.

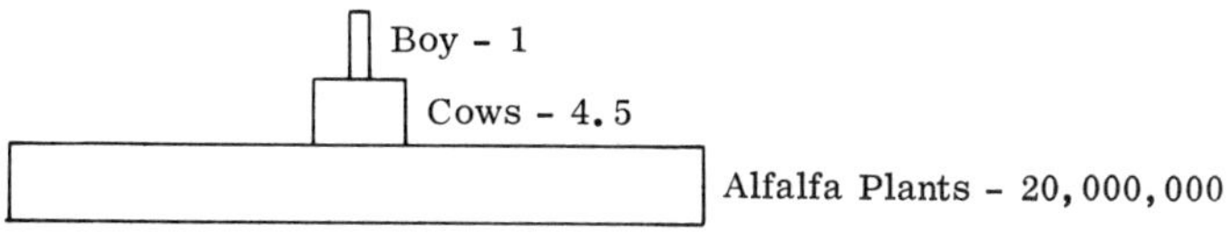

Boy – 1

Cows – 4.5

Alfalfa Plants – 20,000,000

Figure 3.27

(a) _____

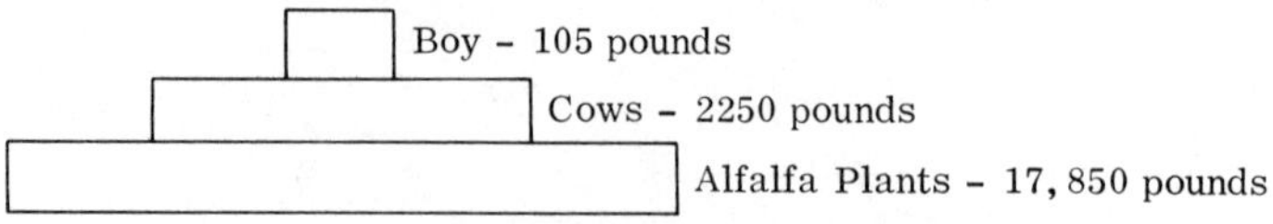

Boy - 105 pounds

Cows - 2250 pounds

Alfalfa Plants - 17, 850 pounds

Figure 3.28

(b) _____

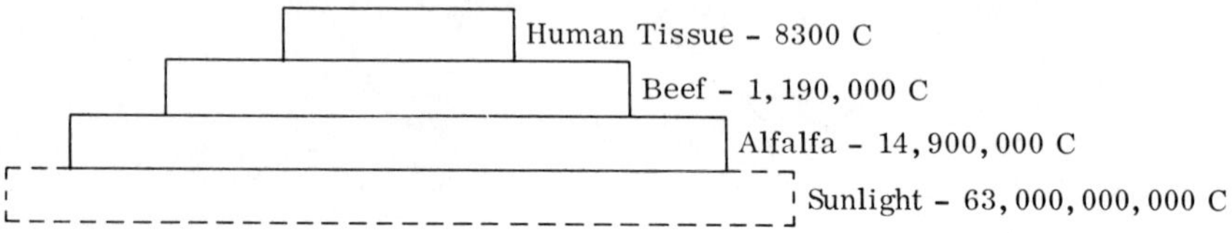

Human Tissue - 8300 C

Beef - 1, 190, 000 C

Alfalfa - 14, 900, 000 C

Sunlight - 63, 000, 000, 000 C

Figure 3.29

(c) _____

(d) What important food relationship is missing on these diagrams?

Why? _____

_____

11. Of tissue eaten by organisms on higher trophic levels, about 50 percent
is spent in respiration (and hence not passed on to any higher trophic
level). Any substance that is not involved in respiration and is stored
in body tissue and not excreted will enjoy what fate in a food chain?

(a) _____

(b) Give a common example of this. _____

ANSWERS TO SELF-TEST

Compare your answers to the questions on the Self-Test with the answers given below. If all of your answers are correct, you are ready to go on to the next chapter. If you missed any questions, review the frames indicated in parentheses following the answer. If you miss several questions, you should probably reread the entire chapter carefully.

1.   chains, webs (either order) (frame 1)

2.   (a) food chain;   (b) food web (frames 1-8)

3.   (a) 1,4;   (b) 2, 5, 6;   (c) 2, 5, 7;   (d) 3, 5 (frames 1-8)

4.   (a) incoming solar radiation;   (b) solar radiation reflected (not utilized or captured);   (c) producer or autotroph;   (d) herbivore or consumer or heterotroph;   (e) carnivore or consumer or heterotroph;   (f) heat lost in respiration—energy used in the process of living;   (g) decomposers (or heterotroph);   (h) living tissue surviving—offspring, etc., or stored organic matter passed on to other food chains (frames 1-8)

5.   (a) 1, 4;   (b) 2, 3 (frame 6)

6.   the number of steps or links in a food web that a particular organism is away from a producer, which is considered the first trophic level (frame 7)

7.   (a) 1, 2;   (b) 3, 4, 5;   (c) 8;   (d) none;   (e) 6, 7, 9, 10 (frame 7)

8.   Only about 10 percent of the energy of one trophic level can be successfully used (captured) by organisms on the next higher trophic level. (frames 9 and 10)

9.   (a) 1,240;   (b) 124;   (c) 12;   (d) 1 (frame 9)

10. (a) pyramid of numbers;   (b) pyramid of biomass;   (c) pyramid of energy;   (d) decomposers, because they are so numerous, so small, and so difficult to measure (frames 11 and 12)

11. (a) It will be passed upward through the food chain, occurring in greater and greater concentrations as it gets to higher and higher trophic levels—this is called biological concentration.
    (b) DDT, other common pesticides, strontium 90, or other "radioactive fallout" elements (frame 13)

CHAPTER FOUR
Human Energy Consumption

OBJECTIVES

When you complete this chapter, you will be able to

- define and describe man's internal and external energy consumption;

- identify man's trophic level and state its general significance;

- describe man's changing energy consumption patterns;

- define and discriminate between productivity, gross primary productivity, net primary productivity, and standing crop;

- describe the various areas of the earth in terms of their productivity capacity;

- identify man's current and future sources of external energy and indicate some of the problems inherent in them.

If you think that you have already mastered these objectives and might skip all or part of this chapter, turn to page 86 at the end of this chapter and take the Self-Test. The results will allow you to evaluate your current knowledge of this chapter's contents. If you answer all of the questions correctly you are ready to begin the next chapter. If you miss any questions, you should study the frames indicated after the answers to the Self-Test.

If this material is new to you, or if you choose not to take the Self-Test now, proceed to frame 1.

> "The human brain, so frail, so perishable, so full of inexhaustible dreams and hungers, burns by the power of the leaf."
>
> Loren Eiseley, The Unexpected Universe

1.   Human beings, like all other living things, must have energy
that ultimately came from the sun in order to maintain their
vital processes. Not being producers, humans depend upon
plants to change sunlight into energy forms that they can use.
The energy that man consumes can be divided into two types:
internal energy—used to maintain bodily processes, and external energy—used to do such things as power his machines
and maintain his culture.

A human being powers his vital processes by breaking down energy-rich
molecules during the process of respiration. To be able to release that energy, a human must first take in energy-rich foodstuffs. Hence, directly or
indirectly, man depends upon plants to capture solar energy in the photosynthetic process. All of the energy that man uses to maintain his bodily processes is called internal energy. When man first evolved, his energy consumption was limited to internal energy. But early in his development he
found that he could supplement his internal heat production by clothing his
body and using fire. From an energy point of view, these great discoveries
did not come free. The fire depended upon burning wood. Man was releasing
energy stored in a tree's tissue. The use of fur clothing was another way of
"consuming" the energy captured by another organism. Man also learned
that he could get other animals to work for him. Of course, he had to feed
those animals just as he had to feed himself.

From the simple "consumption" of fur and firewood, man learned more
complex ways of releasing the sun's energy to supplement his internal energy
consumption. He found he could use plant materials that were formed in the
distant past but which still contain energy-rich molecules that can be burned
to release energy. These materials, called fossil fuels, include gas, coal,
and oil. Elaborate and powerful machines, powered by fossil fuels, have
supplemented the use of domestic animals. All of the energy that man consumes outside his own body is referred to as external energy. With the exception of atomic energy, all of the energy that man consumes, be it internal
or external, ultimately comes from sunlight.

During the 99 percent of human history that man spent as a hunter and
gatherer, he obtained his goods and fuel from the natural assemblages of
plants and animals with which he shared the environment. Except for the
use of fire, he was just another omnivore (he ate both plants and animals).
His internal (nutritional) energy consumption amounted to about 2,000 C per
day. Another 2,000 C of external energy were probably consumed in fire
used for cooking, warmth, and protection. It has been estimated that the
earth could support only about 10 million people as hunters and gatherers
since each individual (like any top carnivore) needed a large amount of land
to find enough food. Recently the earth's potential human carrying capacity
has been greatly expanded by a succession of technological advances. These
advances include new and better ways of subsidizing nutritional energy sources
with external energy sources. Hunting man subsidized his food intake with
burning wood for heat and cooking; primitive agricultural man used animals
to make his work in the fields more productive; advanced agricultural man

used coal, water, and wind power as well as animal transport; industrial man used the steam engine which burned coal or wood to run machines.

Modern man might be called Technological Man. He uses a vast number of energy sources to run his "labor-saving," energy-expending devices varying from electric lights and toothbrushes to television sets, computers, automobiles, and spaceships. The marked increase in daily per capita energy consumption (almost exclusively due to the increase in the external energy consumed) is shown in figure 4.1. Energy subsidies including new agricultural machinery and techniques have increased food production and in turn stimulated an increase in the size of the human population. This in turn exerts more and more pressure on the food supply, forcing the human population to seek more effective means of producing even more food. This type of circular stimulation sets up a vicious cycle (positive feedback) which results in a rate of growth that is difficult to arrest.

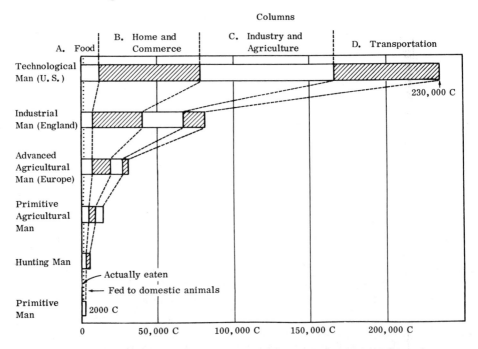

Figure 4.1 Human energy consumption (From "The Flow of Energy in an Industrial Society" by Earl Cook, Scientific American, September 1971. Copyright © 1971 by Scientific American, Inc. All rights reserved.

Examine figure 4.1.

(a) Which column(s) represents <u>internal</u> energy consumption? _____

(b) Which column(s) represents <u>external</u> energy consumption? _____

(c) The world's average human inhabitant consumes about 2,000 C/day. Has he increased his nutritional consumption over Primitive Man? _____

                                                                             yes/no

(d) Where has Technological Man's vast increase in energy consumption occurred? _____

(e) Does the fact that man has not increased his nutritional needs mean that he has no food production problems? If not, why not? _____

_____

- - - - - - - - - - - - - - - - - - -

(a) the left part of column A; (b) the right part of column A, columns B, C, and D; (c) no (More food is used to feed man's animals, but man himself eats about the same number of C/day.); (d) in external energy consumption; (e) Man has very significant food production problems because his population has increased so rapidly.

2.   Man obtains his internal energy from the food he eats. By obtaining his food from many different sources he can occupy more than one trophic level.

Figure 4.2 shows several trophic levels that man occupies at the same time because he eats plants, herbivores, and various carnivores.

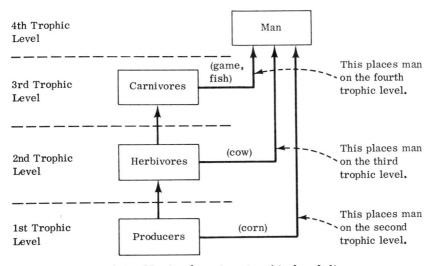

Figure 4.2   Man's place in a trophic level diagram

On the next page is a list of items eaten by the Australian aborigines. Consider that list and answer the questions which follow it.

Plants (Group 1):   29 kinds of roots, 4 kinds of fruit, 2 species of cycad nuts, seeds of several legumes, 2 kinds of mesembryanthemum, 7 types of fungus, 4 sorts of gum, 2 kinds of manna, flowers of several <u>Banksia</u> species

Plant-eating animals (Group 2):   6 sorts of kangaroos, 5 kinds of medium-sized marsupials, 9 species of marsupial rats and mice, 3 types of turtles, 11 kinds of frogs, 29 kinds of fish, all saltwater shellfish except oysters, 4 kinds of freshwater shellfish, 4 kinds of grubs

Animal-eating animals (Group 3):   2 species of opossum, dingos, 1 type of whale, 2 species of seals, 7 types of iguanas and lizards, 8 types of snakes

(a) Consumption of items from Group 1 indicates that the Australian aborigines are, in part, _____.

(b) Consumption of items from Groups 2 and 3 indicates that the Australian aborigines are also part _____.

(c) What generalization—from an energy viewpoint—can you draw from this data about the diet of the Australian aborigines?

- - - - - - - - - - - - - - - - - -

(a) herbivores; (b) carnivores; (c) The Australian aborigines occupy at least three trophic levels.

3.   The total fixed energy available for man's internal consumption directly depends upon the trophic level he chooses to occupy when he consumes.

From the Ten Percent Law, we know that more energy is available to man as a herbivore than as an omnivore (mixed diet—both plants and animals) or carnivore. As a simplified example, consider a cornfield that converts about 1 percent of its available solar energy into chemical energy. Beef cattle fed this corn will convert about 10 percent of the corn's energy into body tissue. Man in turn has a similar inefficiency in converting beef body tissue into human body tissue. As a carnivore in this food chain, man derives about 0.01 percent of the original solar energy. Ten times that would be available to him if he bypassed the cow and assumed the role of an herbivore (that is, if he became a vegetarian).

It has been estimated that 6300 C per day go to feed animals that produce the daily meat required by the average American consumer. Many people in the world subsist on about 2000 C a day (the global average is 2350 C). Three persons could be supported on the calories consumed by a meat-eating American (total U.S. per capita intake is 3100 C). Indeed, it is not hard to see why most of the world's human population is herbivorous.

It is not, however, as simple as it seems. Man does not eat food for energy alone. Food also supplies vital nutrients needed to build and repair all the tissues in the body and to construct cell components and essential enzymes needed for the body's chemical reactions. Proteins supply most of these nutrients, whereas carbohydrates (sugars and starches) and fats provide basic energy. Most starvation results from protein malnutrition, not from a lack of calories. Unfortunately, the plants with the most calories generally contain the least protein, so there is more involved in feeding the world's hungry population than shifts in trophic level consumption.

Consider two examples: (1) On the island of "Herb" the natives eat only breadfruit and coconuts. These two crops fix an average of 1,000,000 C of energy a day. (a) What percentage of this energy can men living as herbivores expect to obtain? _____ (b) If each man, woman, and child on the island is to get 2500 C per day, how many people can

live on the island? _____

(2) A second island (called "Carni") has cattle (introduced by a friendly missionary who visited the island in the 1800s). The breadfruit trees and coconuts have been cut down to allow for a meadow of grass. The field of grass fixes an average of 1,000,000 C of energy per day. (c) If a cow requires 1000 C per day, how many cows can the meadow support? (Remember

the Ten Percent Law!) _____ (d) Assuming the islanders still need 2500 C per day (and eat only meat), how many islanders

can the island of Carni support? _____

- - - - - - - - - - - - - - - - - - - -

(a) about 10 percent;   (b) 40 people (10 percent of 1,000,000, divided by 2500 = 40);   (c) 100 cows (10 percent of 1,000,000, divided by 1000 = 100);   (d) 4 people (10 percent of 100,000—total energy in cows—divided by 2500 = 4)

4.   Since the internal energy available to man depends on the amount of solar energy fixed by producers, ecologists are often concerned with the rate at which this energy is fixed. This rate is known as primary productivity or primary production.

Two types of primary productivity are usually considered.

- Gross Primary Productivity or Production: the total rate of photosynthesis, which includes energy that is fixed and then used for photosynthetic activity—respiration—as well as energy used to create new tissue in excess of the plant's respiration.

- Net Primary Productivity or Production: the rate that a plant stores energy as organic matter (tissue) in excess of that used in respiration.

(a) Define productivity (or production). _____

_____

(b) Label <u>net</u> and <u>gross</u> production in figure 4.3.

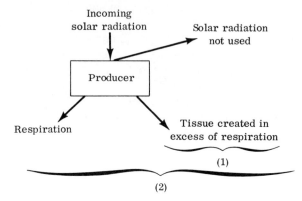

Figure 4.3

(1) _____   (2) _____

- - - - - - - - - - - - - - - - - -

(a) the rate at which organisms fix energy or accumulate biomass
(tissue);   (b) (1) <u>net</u> production, (2) <u>gross</u> production

5.   <u>Standing crop</u> is the amount of biomass present at a particular
        time. A community that has a large standing crop at a given
        time (as measured in grams of biomass) will not necessarily
        have a high rate of productivity (as measured in grams of bio-
        mass produced per year), or vice versa.

Often a highly productive area will not appear so simply because its production is rapidly consumed by herbivores. For example, consider two
fields. The grass in one field may seem taller and bushier than the grass in
a second field. But closer examination may show that the grass in the first
field is eaten less by herbivores, so the taller, bushier grass represents
virtually all of the grass produced in that year. The second field, however,
may be heavily grazed by a herbivore so that the grass, although shorter
than the first field, represents only one-tenth of the grass produced in that
year (the other nine-tenths of the grass being consumed by the herbivores).

Describe the difference between an area's productivity and its standing crop.

_____

_____

_____

- - - - - - - - - - - - - - - - - -

_____

The standing crop is the amount of biomass present in an area at a particular time, whereas the productivity of the area refers to the rate at which the area can produce biomass. Some areas produce biomass very rapidly, but, because the biomass is equally rapidly consumed, appear to have little productivity and the standing crop seems to remain constant.

6.   The earth's productivity is not randomly distributed. An area's productive capacity is severely limited by climate, the availability of nutrients, and especially by the availability of water.

Figure 4.4 shows the distribution of production on the earth's surface.

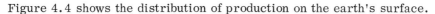
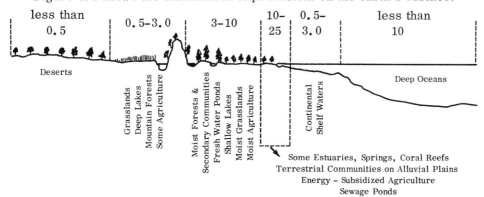

Figure 4.4 The world distribution of primary production in terms of annual gross production (in thousands of kilocalories per square meter) of major ecosystem types. (After Odum, 1971)

Where man conducts agriculture, the area is rarely as productive as the same area would be in its natural state. By using intensive, year-round agricultural techniques man is sometimes able to increase the productivity of an area over its natural level, but this increased productivity is difficult to compare with the productivity of a natural ecosystem since man uses machinery and organic matter from other areas (whose energy cost is not usually accounted for). Intensive agriculture usually causes lower productivities in adjacent or downstream areas. See figure 4.5 on the next page.

In calculating the productivity of Iowa farmland, for example, agricultural experts do not commonly subtract the decreased productivity in the river systems and oceans resulting from pesticide or fertilizer "poisoning" of the fish, bird life, etc. The problem of increasing the earth's net productivity is very complex and man's successes to date are questionable. While man has increased, perhaps even doubled, the productivity of a few areas, he has turned millions of acres of former grasslands into deserts by his poor farming practices (much of the Middle East and North Africa).

In some areas of the world, man's agricultural efforts have met dismal failure. Coral reefs and tropical rain forests, for example, are paragons of natural production. Yet when man removes the natural vegetation and re-

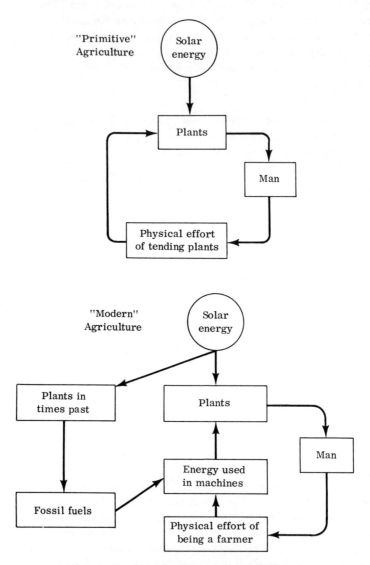

Figure 4.5 "Primitive" and "Modern"
Agricultural Systems Compared

places it with agricultural plants, the yields drop substantially, probably due to increased erosion and rapid mineral losses. Natural communities have evolved many close interrelationships which control mineral losses, thereby making high productivity possible. Man does not know enough to make these areas as productive as they are in their natural state.

(a) Examine figure 4.4. After each ecosystem listed below, indicate either HP—highly productive: 3-25 (1000 $C/m^2/yr$), P—productive: 0.5-3 (1000 $C/m^2/yr$), or NP—not very productive: less than 0.5 (1000 $C/m^2/yr$).

(1) desert _____

(2) grassland _____

(3) mountain forest _____

(4) freshwater pond _____

(5) sewage pond _____

(6) intensive agriculture (sugarcane)
_____

(7) moist agriculture (rice)
_____

(8) tropical rain forest _____

(9) deep ocean _____

(10) coastal area (continental shelf
waters) _____

(b) Wilbur, a Texas cotton grower, is proud of the fact that by using new
machines and fertilizers acreage that used to grow 10,000 units of cotton
now produces 50,000 units of cotton. Wilbur believes that his current
methods have multiplied by five the amount of energy fixed by his farm.

Is he correct? Explain. _____

_____

_____

_____

- - - - - - - - - - - - - - - - - - - -

(a) (1) NP, (2) P, (3) P, (4) HP, (5) HP, (6) HP, (7) P,
(8) HP, (9) NP, (10) P
(b) Wilbur is wrong. He is obviously growing more cotton and that cotton is obviously fixing more energy—but that's not the whole picture.
More energy is being expended to grow the cotton. The fossil fuels to
power his tractors and the machinery to extract and transport the fertilizers as well as other fossil fuels should also be taken into account.
All of this energy must be subtracted to find the true energy yield of the
acreage. It certainly isn't five times what it used to be; it might not be
an increase at all!

7. Most living organisms do not use external energy and only man
uses it in significant quantities. Looking back to figure 4.1
we can see that while internal energy consumption has remained
relatively constant throughout history (approximately 2,200
C/day[1]), external energy consumption has been increased very
markedly by Technological Man. Most of man's external energy is currently coming from fossil fuels: coal, oil, and gas.

Societies have not developed uniformly over the entire globe. A few
hunting societies (e.g., Eskimos) and primitive agricultural ones (e.g.,
New Guinea highlanders) still exist today. Much of the world has not passed
beyond the advanced agricultural stages to the industrial stage. Therefore,
there is a great disparity in today's consumption patterns. Thirty percent
of the world's population (the industrialized peoples) consume some 80 per-

1. Food fed to animals is not included.

cent of the world's energy. The United States with only 6 percent of the world's population accounts for 35 percent of the world's energy consumption! Figure 4.6 compares world and U.S. per capita annual energy consumption.

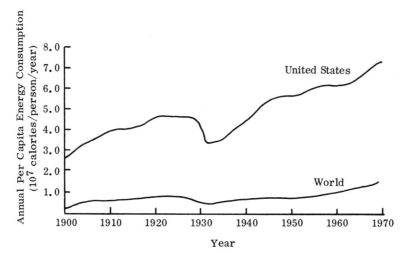

Figure 4.6   World and United States
per capita annual energy consumption

The average U.S. citizen directly or indirectly uses about 200,000 C per day while most people in the world consume energy at just barely over the food intake level of 2,000 C per day.

Complete figure 4.7 by drawing in a graph bar for yourself.

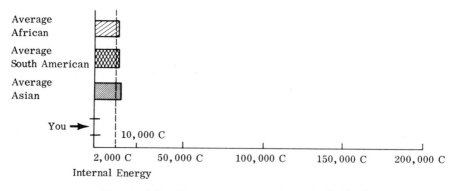

Figure 4.7   Energy consumed per individual

- - - - - - - - - - - - - - - - - - -

Your graph bar should go completely from left to right. You consume about 200,000 C/day (about 100 times the energy of any other person outside the U.S. or Western Europe).

8.   The sources of energy have changed as new ones are found
and old ones are depleted. The major future source of energy
is likely to be some form of nuclear reaction. But such a
fuel source gives off enormous amounts of heat which will certainly affect the environment by raising its temperature (thermal pollution).

The changing sources of energy in the U.S. are shown in figure 4.8. In
1850 fuel wood was the source of 90 percent of the energy and coal accounted
for 10 percent. By 2000 it is foreseen that coal will be back to almost 10 percent and that other sources will be oil, natural gas, liquid natural gas, hy-
droelectric power, fuel wood, and nuclear energy. Coal, oil, and natural
gas now account for 95 percent of the fuel consumed. The power generated
by nuclear fission, water, wood, and direct solar radiation contribute only
a small percentage to the total energy consumption. This is also true throughout the world. Present stores of fossil fuels have accumulated over the last
500 million years. At the present increasing rates of consumption, it has
been estimated that the bulk of the various fossil fuels will be exhausted in
three or four centuries. The epoch of man's exploitation of fossil fuels appears to be a relatively short-lived occurrence when placed in the perspective
of human history (figure 4.9).

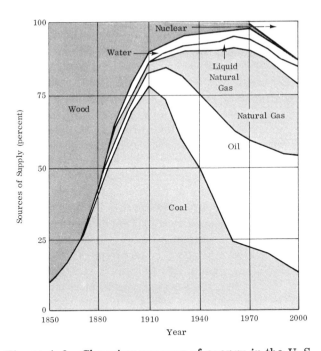

Figure 4.8 Changing sources of energy in the U.S.
(From "Human Energy Production as a Process in the Biosphere" by Fred S. Singer, Scientific American, September
1970. Copyright © 1970 by Scientific American, Inc. All
rights reserved.

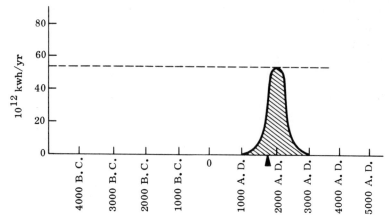

Figure 4.9   Human consumption of fossil fuels
(Modified after Hubbert, 1962)

The total energy demand in the U.S. is expected to double in the next
30 years as that of the world triples; what will replace the fossil fuels? Nuclear fission may supply up to 50 percent of our energy by then, but that too
is plagued with an exhaustible fuel supply. Uranium supplies have been estimated to last only about 30 years. By then possibly the breeder reactor,
which "breeds" more fissionable material than it consumes, will be feasible.
Perhaps controlled nuclear fusion, solar power, or geothermal power will
be developed,[2] but this is just avoiding the question. Can we or should we
expect this rapid rate of increase to continue indefinitely? What are the consequences of accommodating such growth? A consideration of the energy required to meet man's growing needs leads us to a very fundamental physical
limitation imposed by our environment. Regardless of the source and means
of generating external power, we still face the basic fact of thermodynamics
that virtually all energy generated finally ends up as heat. As G. Tyler Miller
puts it, "The limitation of energy consumption in the next 30 to 100 years does
not seem to lie in any critical shortage of resources but in the impact on the
environment of using these resources." Dissipating the heat to which all energy is eventually degraded (the Second Law of Thermodynamics) is our most
obvious problem. Several other problems resulting from rapidly increasing
power production will be treated later (e.g., the effect of CO_2 on heat balance
and the effects of heat and other wastes will be considered in Chapter 7). But
here it is important to realize that the ultimate pollutant is heat! If the amount
of heat dissipated into the atmosphere by man's activities reaches 1 percent
of the solar radiation normally received, disastrous climatic changes could
occur. At the present rate of increase (approximately 5 percent) in world

2. Controlled nuclear fusion is an atomic explosion harnessed to produce
usable power. Solar power is power derived from the direct capture of sunlight. Geothermal power is heat from the center of the earth producing usable
power. All of these methods are currently under experimentation.

energy consumption, this level will be reached in less than a century. Thus, we might say that the factor limiting future growth in the rate of energy consumption is the Second Law of Thermodynamics.

Examine figure 4.10.

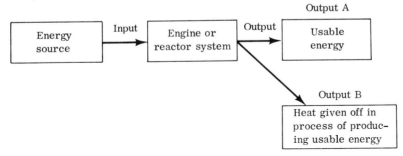

Figure 4.10

(a) It is not surprising that output B is much in excess of output A. What law does it illustrate? _____

(b) The more we increase output A, the more we will necessarily increase

   _____.

(c) Sharply increasing the rate of output B's release into the environment results in _____ pollution.

- - - - - - - - - - - - - - - - - -

(a) Second Law of Thermodynamics—In every energy transfer a large amount of it is rendered useless for work (i.e., becomes heat).   (b) output B—heat;   (c) heat (or thermal)

SELF–TEST

This Self–Test is designed to show you whether or not you have mastered this chapter's objectives. Answer each question to the best of your ability. Correct answers and review instructions are given at the end of the test.

1.   Define and describe man's need for <u>internal</u> energy. _____

_____

_____

2.   Define and describe man's need for <u>external</u> energy. _____

_____

_____

3.   What trophic level does man occupy? _____

_____

4.   Knowing what you know about trophic levels, if I tell you a population eats a lot of meat, what sort of generalization can you draw?

_____

_____

5.   Define productivity. _____

_____

_____

6.   Label figure 4.11

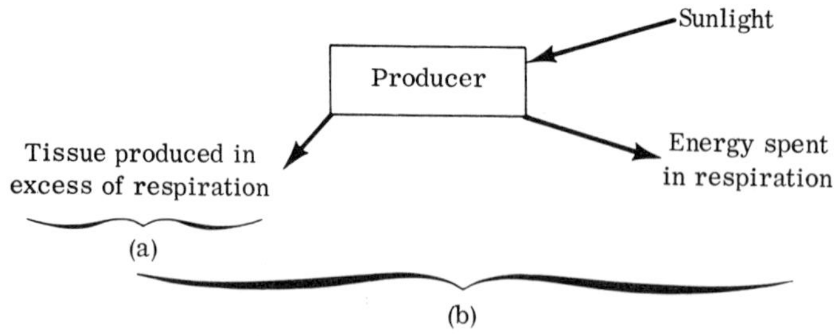

Figure 4.11

(a) _____

(b) _____

7. The standing crop is _____

    _____

8. The productivity of the earth varies. Indicate the relative productivity
    of the following areas, using high, medium, and low.

    (a) Ocean (deep) _____

    (b) Desert _____

    (c) Moist grasslands _____

    (d) Shallow lake _____

    (e) "Modern" agriculture _____

    (f) Estuaries, coastal waters _____

9. List man's major <u>current</u> sources of energy. What are the problems

    involved with these sources? _____

    _____

    _____

10. List man's likely major <u>future</u> sources of energy. What are the prob-

    lems involved with these sources? _____

    _____

    _____

    _____

ANSWERS TO SELF-TEST

Compare your answers to the questions on the Self-Test with the answers given below. If all of your answers are correct, you are ready to go on to the next chapter. If you missed any questions, review the frames indicated in parentheses following the answer. If you miss several questions, you should probably reread the entire chapter carefully.

1. <u>Internal</u> energy is food. Man needs internal energy to sustain his bodily processes. (frame 1)

2. <u>External</u> energy allows man to cope more effectively with his environment—it powers his machines. External energy is used in homes and commerce, to power industry, agriculture, transportation, and communication. Technological man uses vast amounts of external energy, especially in industry, agriculture, and transportation. (frame 1)

3. Man occupies any trophic level except the first. Most people exist on several trophic levels at the same time—they eat hamburgers on bread with lettuce and tomatoes. (frame 2)

4. They are relatively affluent. They have so much food available to them that they can afford to feed herbivores (and thus reduce the available energy by 90 percent) and still be able to get enough energy on the third trophic level to stay alive. (frame 3)

5. the rate at which organisms fix energy or accumulate biomass (tissue) (frame 4)

6. (a) net production (or net productivity); (b) gross production (or gross productivity) (frame 4)

7. the amount of biomass present at a particular time (frame 5)

8. (a) low; (b) low; (c) medium; (d) medium; (e) high; (f) high (frame 6)

9. Man's major current energy sources are coal, oil, and gas. Fossil fuels were created during the earth's early development and exist in limited quantities which are rapidly being used up. In the future they will no longer be available. (frames 7 and 8)

10. Man's major future source of energy will probably be some form of nuclear power. But it won't be the type of reactor we have today, since uranium is more limited than most fossil fuels! It might be a breeder reactor or a reactor that uses controlled nuclear fusion. Other possible future sources of energy include solar or geothermal power. In any case, the problems associated with nuclear energy production include the control of radiation and disposing of the enormous amounts of heat the reactors give off (thermal pollution). (frames 7 and 8)

PART THREE
Ecological Cycles

"By the Law of Periodical Repetition, everything which has
happened once must happen again and again and again—and
not capriciously, but at regular periods, and each thing in
its own period, not another's and each obeying its own law.
. . . The same nature which delights in periodical repetition in the skies is the nature which orders the affairs of the
earth. Let us not underrate the value of that hint."

Mark Twain

One of nature's most observable phenomena is the cyclic[1] recurrence of
events. Summer follows winter, a full moon follows a new, low tides follow
high, and night follows day. Cyclic behavior is exhibited by a multitude of
systems from the enzymes of the individual cell to the rotation of the galaxy,
and we cannot consider them all. We will only investigate some of the major
cycles that bear directly on the study of the environment.

After briefly considering the earth's motions that determine the year, the
seasons, the length of the day, and the tides, we will look at the cycles involved in the circulation of the atmosphere. The breakdown of these global
patterns of circulation contribute to local concentrations of contaminants
which are also considered in Chapter 5.

The remainder of this part considers the earth as a closed system with
regard to matter. In order to continually draw on materials in limited supply, the earth's natural systems have developed vast cycles that replenish
and recycle materials. The mobility and "cycling" of the earth's crust, and
the theories of continental drift and plate tectonics are introduced in Chapter
5. Chapter 6 discusses the water cycle, including man's water consumption
patterns and his plans for water resource development. Chapter 7 considers
the nitrogen and phosphorus cycles which are typical examples of the biogeochemical cycles that operate in all ecosystems. It also discusses the use

---

1. Although cyclic in its most restricted sense can mean recurring over a
definite time period, we are here using the term in the most general way to
refer to a series of events passing through a particular sequential pattern
over any period of time.

and distribution of elements within the biotic community referred to as nutrient budgets. Throughout Part Three we will stress man's influence on these phenomena.

CHAPTER FIVE

Astronomical and Geosystem Cycles

OBJECTIVES

When you complete this chapter, you will be able to

- identify and describe the three major astronomical cycles;

- explain the cause of the seasons;

- explain the cause, process, and results of the atmospheric cycle;

- describe the relationship between the atmospheric cycle and global air pollution;

- describe the types and causes of local atmospheric pollution problems;

- define the geological cycle and its time span.

If you think that you have already mastered these objectives and might skip all or part of this chapter, turn to page 106 at the end of the chapter and take the Self-Test. The results will allow you to evaluate your current knowledge of this chapter's contents. If you answer all of the questions correctly, you are ready to begin the next chapter. If you miss any questions, you should study the frames indicated after the answers to the Self-Test.

If this material is new to you, or if you choose not to take the Self-Test now, proceed to frame 1.

1. All of the earth's ecosystems, and the planet itself, take part in <u>astronomical</u> <u>cycles</u>. Night and day, the changing moon, and the seasons of the year are reminders of these cycles. Several great astronomical movements govern these cycles, and our measurements of time are based on the period of some of these movements:

- <u>Day</u>: the period of time it takes the earth to make one full rotation on its axis.

- Month: the period of time it takes the moon to revolve around the earth (lunar month).

- Year: the period of time it takes the earth to revolve once around the sun.

Once every 365 days the earth completes an elliptical orbit of approximately 586 million miles around the sun. Throughout this orbit the earth is rotating about its own axis which is inclined $23\frac{1}{2}$ degrees from the vertical. Thus, both the length of daylight and the angle at which the sun's rays strike the surface at any given point are constantly changing throughout the year (see figure 5.1). These two factors, taken together, explain why we have different seasons. North America experiences summer when the northern hemisphere is inclined toward the sun. At that time the sun's rays directly strike North America during an extended period of daylight. Six months later, at the opposite point of the yearly revolution, North America has a shorter day and the sun's rays arrive at a slant which is less effective in warming the surface. It is then winter. Spring and fall are transitions between these extremes.

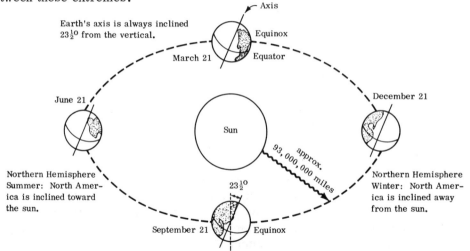

Figure 5.1   Position of the earth at each season

Another consequence of astronomical movements is the occurrence of tides. Tides result primarily from the gravitational pull on the earth of the moon and sun. The shape of the coastline and its relation to the ocean basins also influence the tides within any particular area. The water level alternately rises and falls twice daily along most coasts, reaching its high point every $12\frac{1}{2}$ hours. Twice a month the combined gravitational pull of the sun and moon causes exceptionally high tides, and twice a month the sun and moon counteract each other's gravitational pull on the earth causing exceptionally low tides.

(a)   List three astronomical cycles.   _____

_____   _____

(b) What would be the most notable result if the earth revolved about the sun with its axis in a vertical position? _____

_____

– – – – – – – – – – – – – – – – – –

(a) rotation of the earth on its axis, revolution of the moon about the earth, revolution of the earth about the sun;   (b) There would be no seasons.

2.   The earth's surface is unequally heated. This results in great motions in the atmosphere causing winds, ocean waves, and other weather conditions. These movements of air and water keep the earth's atmosphere at relatively the same temperature—an important basis for ecological developments.

Because of the spherical shape of the earth and the gaseous atmospheric envelope that encloses it, the surface of the earth is unequally heated. The areas near the poles receive less solar radiation per unit of surface area than areas nearer the equator. This is true for several reasons. First, the amount of solar energy received per unit of area at the surface of the earth is dependent on the angle at which the energy arrives. The same amount of radiation is spread over a larger area at the place of greatest curvature (see figure 5.2). Further, the radiation must pass through more atmosphere to get to the poles, and more of it is absorbed or reflected by the atmosphere before reaching the earth's surface. So it is not surprising that the tropics are warmer than the polar regions.

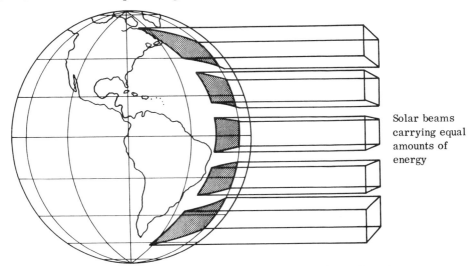

Solar beams carrying equal amounts of energy

Figure 5.2   Solar energy striking earth's surface at equinox

This differential heating sets in motion a great atmospheric "heat engine" that generates global atmospheric cycles, which move the heat toward the poles. As we saw in Chapter 2, solar radiation is radiated from the earth

as heat (wavelengths of 12 microns), which is retained by the atmosphere.
So the atmosphere is actually heated from below by the heat rising from the
earth. As the warm air rises, air currents (winds or convection currents)
are created. Because the equatorial regions receive the most solar radiation,
they radiate the most heat. Warm air rises from the equator and begins to
move toward the poles. The pattern of rising and descending air forms "tubes"
around the earth, sometimes called Hadley Cells after the English meteorolo-
gist who first proposed this scheme of atmospheric circulation. Hadley the-
orized that three cells or "tubes" exist in each hemisphere and used them to
explain the major weather patterns at the earth's surface. The poleward-
moving air tends to cool and sink at about latitude 30° North and South. From
this point the cool air is pulled along the surface, either poleward or toward
the equator where the cycle begins again. As the warm air moves north and
south through successive Hadley cells, the entire surface of the earth becomes
more evenly heated.

  If there were no atmospheric circulation, during the equinoxes, when the
sunlight comes to the earth directly at its equator, the temperatures at the
earth's poles would drop to about -270°C. And as the earth shifted, first
the northern hemisphere and then the southern hemisphere would receive
similar "cold spells." In these circumstances there would be little chance
that life could exist on earth.

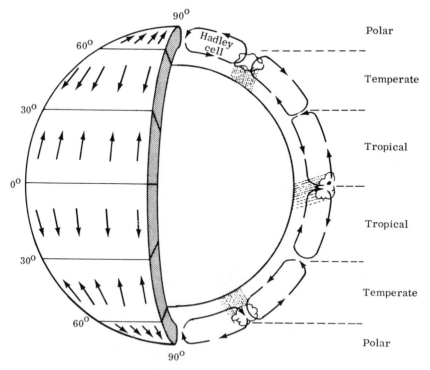

Figure 5.3   Global atmospheric cycles

From this brief discussion it should be clear that vast global patterns of atmospheric circulation (not to mention ocean circulation patterns which are partly determined by the force of winds) tie the whole world together. The northeast trade winds are not intimidated by state borders, nor do they respect national boundaries. Indeed, the atmosphere and the oceans are effective physical mechanisms for distributing various toxic substances around the world and depositing them far from their point of origin.

(a) Explain how heat "powers" the atmospheric cycle. _____

_____

_____

(b) Describe in some detail how the atmospheric cycle works. _____

_____

_____

_____

_____

_____

(c) What would the Arctic be like if there were no atmospheric circulation?

_____

_ _ _ _ _ _ _ _ _ _ _ _ _ _ _ _ _ _ _

(a) Heat radiated from the earth's surface sets up convection currents that circulate the warmed air about the earth.
(b) The spherical shape of the earth means that the earth's surface receives different amounts of solar radiation. The solar radiation is radiated to the earth's atmosphere, from below, as heat; the most heat is radiated from the earth's equator, the least from the poles. The heated air moves upward and poleward from the equator as air currents (winds). Thus, the hot air is spread toward the poles. In turn, the colder air of the polar regions is spread toward the equator. This cycle keeps the earth's atmosphere at a relatively constant temperature throughout the entire globe.
(c) very much colder!

3.   Because of atmospheric circulation, airborne particles may move great distances over the earth's surface.

Dust, bacteria, pollen, and seeds are widely distributed around the earth, borne by winds and returned to the earth in snow or rain. Islands in the middle of great oceans have life forms brought there by wind, ocean currents, and rain. Thus, atmospheric circulation plays a major role in the evolution and the distribution of organisms.

Throughout earth's history plants and animals developed ingenious ways of using atmospheric circulation to help them travel and spread their kind. Man too has used the winds in many clever ways—windmills and sailboats are fine examples. He has also managed not so cleverly to put unwanted material into atmospheric circulation.

Strontium 90, a fission product released during atmospheric testing of nuclear bombs, provides an example of the worldwide movement of unwanted particles in the atmosphere. In 1966 fallout was detected at the Brookhaven National Laboratory on Long Island nine days after a bomb test in China. A series of investigations has determined that airborne radioactive substances circle the earth (at mid-latitudes) in fifteen to twenty-five days. Rain and snow play the major role in bringing the airborne radioactive debris to the ground.

Other particles also enter global circulation patterns. Large amounts of pesticide residues, for instance, have been detected in Antarctic penguins and in Arctic Eskimos. A recent example has been reported in which DDT and its byproducts, absorbed in vapor form on dust particles, were carried 3000 miles across the North Atlantic by northeastern trade winds from Africa and Europe to the Caribbean island of Barbados. Mounting evidence suggests that considerable amounts of pesticides are circulating in the atmosphere just waiting to be precipitated back to earth.

Given the mechanisms of biological magnification (see pages 63-66) and in light of these comments, it seems that we can no longer consider pollution only a local problem. Through global processes toxic substances are transported and concentrated far from their original source.

(a)   Name some things that are carried about by atmospheric circulation.

_____

(b)   How does the atmosphere "connect the entire world with the source of

particle pollution"?   _____

_____

- - - - - - - - - - - - - - - - - - -

(a) dust, bacteria, pollen, seeds, birds, radioactive particles, pesticides;   (b) Particles put into the atmosphere are circulated and may fall wherever rain, snow, or gravity finally elect. Particles introduced at one spot may "rain down" on any other spot on the earth.

"This most excellent canopy, the air, look you, this brave o'erhanging firmament, this majestical roof fretted with golden fire, why, it appears no other thing to me than a foul and pestilent congregation of vapours. . . ."

Hamlet, act II, scene ii

4.   Although toxic wastes tend to be widely dispersed and diluted by the vast global atmosphere, local concentrations of con-

taminants do occur. Due primarily to local and regional geographic and meteorological conditions, these concentrations can reach ominous proportions and are one of the most pressing environmental problems facing technological man.

The city of Los Angeles is situated in a basin and surrounded by mountains on three sides, thus bringing together several features that create one of the worst localized air pollution problems in the world. Air movement is limited by the three mountain ranges to the northwest, northeast, and southeast; in addition, the local meteorological conditions are ideal for the formation of thermal inversions.

A thermal inversion is a condition in which a layer of warm air overlies a layer of cooler air. Normally the temperature of the air decreases with height (top half of figure 5.4); the reversed condition effectively acts as a lid, trapping in the air contaminants (bottom of figure 5.4).

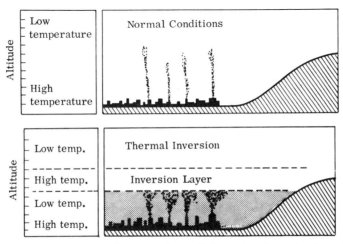

Figure 5.4   Normal thermal conditions (cooler air above)
and a thermal inversion (warm air above cooler air)

Basically there are two types of air pollution: "London smog," and "photochemical smog." London smog (smoke plus fog) contains sulfur compounds, such as sulfur dioxide and sulfuric acid. The combination of fog, a thermal inversion, and large amounts of sulfur dioxide caused the deadly 1952 London smog disaster that took 4,000 lives. Hence the name "London smog." Of course, it could just as well be called "Meuse Valley smog" after the industrialized valley in Belgium where over a thousand became ill and 60 died in December 1930, or "Donora smog" after the small mill town in Pennsylvania where 42 percent of the population became ill and 20 died in October 1948. For that matter it could be called "New York smog" because most of the atmospheric contamination in major eastern cities today is sulfur dioxide, due to the sulfur-containing fuel oils used in heating and in manufacturing of electric power.

Photochemical smog could be called "Los Angeles smog," because Los Angeles was the location of the first cited reaction and is still the most infamous example. It is not actually a combination of smoke and fog, but the term "smog" enjoys such wide usage that it would be virtually impossible to eliminate it from our vocabulary. Air pollution in Los Angeles is not caused by the primary or initial air pollutants (e.g., carbon monoxide, sulfur dioxide, nitrogen oxides, unburned hydrocarbon) but by the products formed when these compounds undergo a photochemical reaction. Ultraviolet radiation from the sun reacts with the primary pollutants to form secondary or even tertiary pollutants. The progression is shown in figure 5.5. When certain hydrocarbons (which in Los Angeles come chiefly from automobile exhausts) are exposed to sunlight in the presence of nitric oxide (NO) and nitrogen dioxide (NO$_2$) (also primarily from auto exhaust), an elaborate series of reactions takes place. The end products are mainly ozone, aldehydes, and nitrogen-containing organic compounds such as peroxyacyl nitrates (PANs for short), which can have severe physiological effects on both animals and plants. With $3\frac{1}{2}$ million cars, a mountain-formed air trap, and frequent (260-270 days a year) thermal inversions, sunny southern California is the inevitable recipient of photochemical smog and its consequences.

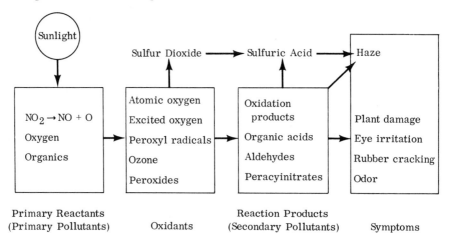

Figure 5.5   The photochemical reactions occurring
in Los Angeles smog (After Haagen-Smit, 1968)

(a) Name the two major atmospheric causes of local atmospheric pollution.

_____

_____

(b) Fill in the boxes in the following chart.

	"Regular" Smog	Photochemical Smog
Type of pollutants	Primary pollutants (sulfur compounds, etc.)	Secondary pollutants (PANs, etc.)
Main Source of Pollutants	(1)	(2)
Common Location (city)	(3)	(4)

- -

(a) limited local air circulation (geographical features, e.g., mountains) and the occurrence of thermal inversions (special meteorological conditions); (b) (1) heating and energy-generating fuels, (2) automobiles, (3) London, New York, (4) Los Angeles

5.   The geological cycle refers to the creation and the movement of that material comprising the surface of the earth. New surface is constantly being pushed up from the earth's interior through rifts in the ocean floor. The continents—great plates of hard crust—are pushed about by the pressures of the expanding ocean floor. When continent and new surface meet, the ocean floor is often pushed under, ultimately returning it to the earth's mantle. Compared with any of the other cycles we shall consider, the geological cycle has a very long time span: The simplest events are measured in millions of years.

The atmosphere is just one component of the geosystem we call earth. This geosystem is a set of interacting subsystems that includes the lithosphere —the solid earth; the hydrosphere—the zone of water cradled in the ocean basins and extending over the land surface; and the atmosphere—the gaseous envelope that surrounds them both (see figure 5.6). The earth we know today is merely the most recent in a long series of stages, which will give way to yet another stage as its major subsystems continue to interact. In this frame we will consider the lithosphere, while the next chapter is concerned with the hydrosphere. However, we will always be considering their interplay with one another and with the atmosphere.

Cycles also occur in the lithosphere, for the earth's crust is not a static, rigid arrangement of rocks, but a mobile, elastic system. The geological

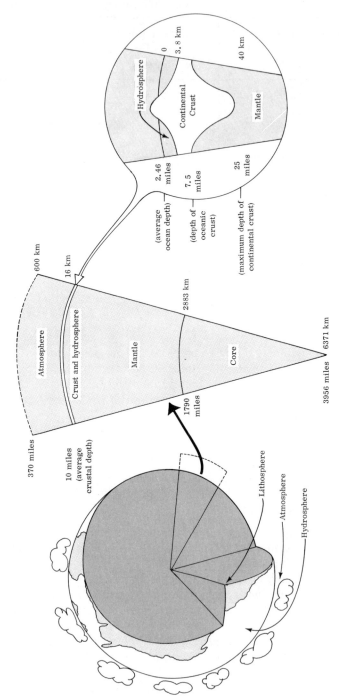

Figure 5.6   Major subsystems of the earth geosystem

cycle can only be seen from the perspective of hundreds of millions of years. Internal forces have repeatedly caused massive earth movements, resulting in the separation and uplifting of continents, the building of mountains, and the occurrence of volcanoes and earthquakes. At the same time the external forces of weathering and erosion persistently work to sculpt the face of the earth. In a never-ending battle the constructive forces work to build up the land surface and the destructive forces work to tear it down.

To imagine how the earth's surface has moved in time, we need only compare the current location of the continents to their expected original position in a gigantic continental jigsaw (see figure 5.7). In the 1920s Alfred Wegener proposed that a supercontinent—Pangaea ("all lands")—constituted the only land mass of the earth for most of our planet's history. During this time, the Panthalassa Ocean also existed as the single ocean. For decades Wegener's Theory of Continental Drift was discredited by most scientists. In the last few years, however, the evidence supporting this theory has become overwhelming.

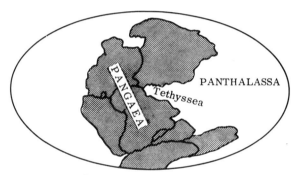

The continents were a single land mass as late as 200 million years ago.

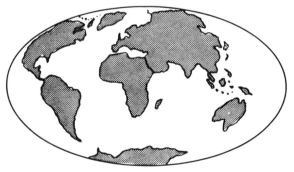

The continents as they exist today. Rifts continue to separate the continents very slowly.

Figure 5.7   Continental drift

The theory of continental drift is as follows: For reasons yet unclear, about 200 million years ago rifts began to divide Pangaea into two supercontinents: the northern continent named Laurasia and the southern continent Gondwana. Thereafter Gondwana and then Laurasia began to be broken apart by additional rifts, eventually giving rise to the continents as they exist today. The land masses of the earth are constantly moving. This continental drift, though occurring very slowly, causes environments to slowly alter. From ocean rifts new continental material is constantly emerging from the center of the earth so that the geological cycle continues even today.

The discovery of a mid-ocean ridge system some 40,000 kilometers long extending through the major ocean basins has helped to confirm the theory of continental drift. Observations have shown that the floor of the ocean is spreading at a rate of two to eighteen centimeters per year. New oceanic crust is continuously being formed as the molten material rises to fill the rifts, solidifies, and forces its way out in opposite directions from the ridge. The continents are rafted over the earth's surface as the new crustal material is produced and spread out. This concept of sea-floor spreading is only tenable if the earth is expanding, if its surface is buckling, or if other surface material is somewhere returning to the earth's interior. There is good evidence to suggest that the earth has not expanded more than 2 percent in the past 200 million years. Major buckling of the surface is only evident within some mountain belts and even then not enough to account for all of the newly formed crust. Thus it is generally held today that some crustal material is being "consumed" by downward currents at the deep oceanic trenches of the world (see figure 5.8). At the oceanic trenches the older crust sinks toward the mantle, resulting in earthquakes and volcanic activity.

Of course, it is more complicated than new crust rising and older crust sinking. There is no simple global conveyer belt and no one-to-one relation linking the sources to the sinks; and we still know very little about the lateral transfer of material at the surface and below.

The study of the lateral surface movements of the earth is called plate tectonics and has evolved from the theories of continental drift and sea-floor spreading. Plate tectonics holds that the lithosphere is composed of a number of rigid plates that are in constant relative motion. Very little geological activity occurs within them, but there is a great deal at their margins resulting in volcanoes, earthquakes, and the distribution of mineral resources. The continents resting on these plates are rafted over the surface of the globe. The plates sometimes slide past one another, sometimes move apart on opposite sides of an oceanic ridge, or sometimes converge—the edge of one plate being "consumed" at a trench.

The San Andreas fault system, for instance, lies on the boundary between the Pacific and the North American plates. In this particular instance the two plates are sliding past each other. The Pacific plate is moving north-northwest relative to the North American plate at about 5 centimeters per year. Quakes occur when enough strain has accumulated to cause the fault to give way. Initially the sliding is restricted by the friction of one plate against another, but when sufficient tension builds up, the plates adjust themselves to relieve the strain, thus causing an earthquake. Deeper earthquakes

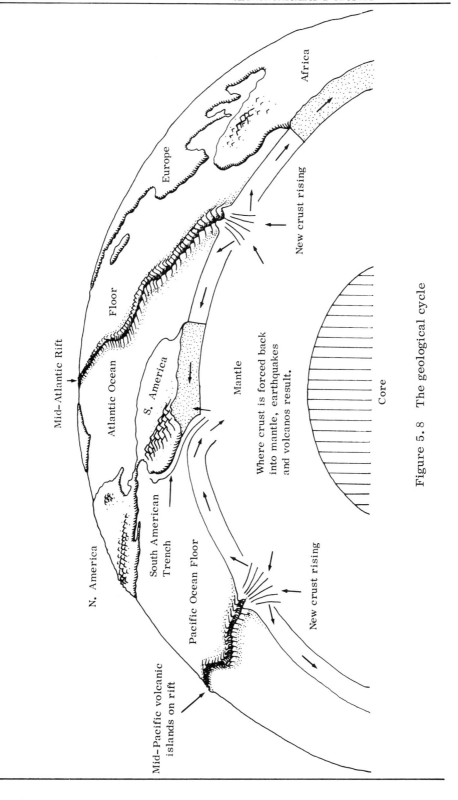

Figure 5.8   The geological cycle

and volcanic activity are usually associated with sites of downward convection currents—the deep oceanic trenches (see figure 5.8). As the crustal material begins to descend, it is crushed, bent, and distorted, giving rise to shallow earthquakes. At greater depths it encounters greater pressure and temperature and is chemically and physically transformed, producing more intense quakes. As the descending material becomes hotter, water and other volatiles are driven off. The hot gas-rock mixture rises to the surface creating volcanoes.

(a) The idea that land masses are moving apart was first expressed by Alfred Wegener in his theory of _____.

(b) Explain briefly the steps and process by which the earth's current land masses arrived at their present positions. _____

_____

_____

(c) Is the process continuing? _____
                                   (yes/no)

(d) What are some obvious signs of continuing continental stresses?

_____

_____

(e) The study of the lateral surface movement of continents is called

_____.

- - - - - - - - - - - - - - - - - -

(a) continental drift
(b) You should have included the following information: The continents started as a single land mass called Pangaea, which existed as late as 200 million years ago. Rifts broke Pangaea up into two major blocks, Laurasia and Gondwana. Gondwana and then Laurasia continued to break up, eventually resulting in the continents' present position. The process by which these continental movements occur entails the creation of new crust at the mid-ocean ridges and the "consumption" of older crust at the oceanic trenches.
(c) yes
(d) ocean floor rifts, volcanic activity, earthquakes and fault movements
(e) plate tectonics

6.   Continental drift and plate tectonics directly affect the processes by which minerals are distributed and concentrated: Geological activity constantly creates new mineral deposits by means of great movements of molten material, and continental movement slowly shifts minerals about the earth. Climate also plays a role in the formation of secondary ores.

Ores are concentrated by two main processes. Heat and pressure from magma (molten matter under the earth's crust) are responsible for concentrating the primary ores such as copper, lead, zinc, and silver. As the hot liquids and gases rise to the surface with molten rock, the various ores condense at different levels, leaving deposits of (crystallized and transformed) minerals. The formation of primary ores thus takes place at two primary locations: the oceanic trenches and the ridges. Knowledge of past and present sites of downward and rising convection currents provides very useful information in prospecting for minerals.

The secondary ores are residual deposits left in old crust by weathering and erosion processes. As surfaces are eroded, the nonsoluble residue remaining may be rich in various minerals. One example is bauxite, an aluminum-rich residue found in Arkansas and West Africa. Of those minerals going into solution, some (the heavier ones) are sorted out in transport (e.g., gold, tin), while others continue on their way in streams and rivers to be eventually deposited in basins and left after evaporation (e.g., salts, nitrates). The formation of secondary ores is largely climatically controlled, so knowledge of the location of ancient climates or more specifically the location of ancient continents with reference to tropical latitudes is an invaluable tool in locating them. For instance, most secondary ores, such as bauxite and oil, can only accumulate in large quantities in tropical latitudes. Because Europe and northern Alaska were in tropical latitudes during at least part of the last 400 million years, oil deposits have been found there. But East Africa has no oil deposits because it has entered tropical latitude only in recent geologic time.

The presence of any mineral deposit depends on the occurrence of many specific conditions that are beyond the scope of this book. Our purpose is only to introduce you to the role that the geological cycle (past and present plate movements and continental drift) has on the distribution of minerals.

What is the effect of continental drift and the geologic cycle on the existence

and distribution of minerals? _____

_____

_____

– – – – – – – – – – – – – – – – – –

As molten matter continually rises during the formation of the earth's crust, mineral deposits are concentrated and brought to the surface. Knowledge of the sites of new crust formation and consumption is helpful in locating mineral deposits. Weathering and erosion also act to expose ores.

SELF-TEST

This Self-Test is designed to show you whether or not you have mastered
this chapter's objectives. Answer each question to the best of your ability.
Correct answers and review instructions are given at the end of the test.

1. Identify and describe the three major astronomical cycles.

    _____   _____

    _____   _____

    _____   _____

2. Explain the cause of the seasons. _____

    _____

    _____

    _____

3. What is the cause of atmospheric motions? _____

    _____

    _____

4. How is it that the earth manages to remain at a pretty constant tempera-
    ture even though the equator gets more sunlight than the poles and even
    though half the earth is constantly in the dark (at night)?

    _____

    _____

    _____

5. How do particles interact with the atmospheric cycle? Where and how do

    most particles return to earth? _____

    _____

    _____

    _____

6. What are the major causes of local atmospheric pollution?

    _____

    _____

7. Name two types of local atmospheric pollution, explain the major source of pollution particles in each case, and name a U.S. city that is a good example of that type of air pollution.

    • _____

    _____

    • _____

    _____

8. Explain what the geological cycle refers to. Give some estimate of the

    time involved in this cycle. _____

    _____

    _____

9. Describe continental drift and the processes believed to cause it.

    _____

    _____

    _____

    _____

    _____

10. Name some geological implications of continental drift.

    _____

    _____

    _____

ANSWERS TO SELF-TEST

Compare your answers to the questions on the Self-Test with the answers
given below. If all of your answers are correct, you are ready to go on to
the next chapter. If you missed any questions, review the frames indicated
in parentheses following the answer. If you miss several questions, you
should probably reread the entire chapter carefully.

1. Day: the period of time it takes the earth to make one full rotation on its
    axis. Month: the period of time it takes the moon to revolve around the
    earth. Year: the period of time it takes the earth to revolve once around
    the sun. (frame 1)

2. The seasons are caused by the fact that the earth's axis is inclined $23\frac{1}{2}^{\circ}$
    from the vertical. This means that at the time in the yearly rotation
    when a particular portion of the earth (e.g., North America) is inclined
    toward the sun and hence receiving direct radiations during an extended
    daylight period, that particular portion is warmer—summer. At the
    opposite point in the yearly rotation, that portion of the earth will be in-
    clined away from the sun and hence receive the sun's rays at a consider-
    able slant. Slanted radiations are less effective in warming the earth
    —winter. Spring and fall are transitions between the extremes of summer
    and winter. (frame 1)

3. The sun's rays strike the earth and are reradiated as heat. This heat
    causes atmospheric convection currents that cause the air to move about.
    (frame 2)

4. Sunlight strikes the surface of the earth and is radiated as heat. The
    radiated heat causes convection currents in the atmosphere—causing
    wind and ocean currents that move hot air about the earth keeping the
    atmospheric temperature relatively constant. (frame 2)

5. Because of the circulation of heat in the atmosphere, particles that get
    into the atmosphere are also circulated about the earth's surface. If par-
    ticular particles get into the air in large quantities, they are distributed
    about the entire surface of the earth (DDT particles are found in the
    Antarctic!). Rain and snow play the major role in returning airborne
    particles to the surface of the oceans or land. (frames 3 and 4)

6. Limited local air circulation due to special geographical features (e.g.,
    mountains) and the occurrence of special meteorological conditions (i.e.,
    thermal inversions) (frames 3 and 4)

7. London smog, sulfur compounds (primary pollutants) caused by heating
    and energy-generating fuels, New York
    Photochemical smog, PANs (secondary pollutants) caused by the use of
    automobiles, Los Angeles
    (frames 3 and 4)

8. The geological cycle refers to the creation and movement of that material
    comprising the surface of the earth. The simplest events in the geologi-
    cal cycle are measured in millions of years. (frame 5)

9. The continents of the earth are plates of hard crust, which are pushed
    about by the pressures of the expanding ocean floor. New surface is
    constantly being created: It is forced up from the earth's interior through
    rifts in the earth—usually ridges located in the centers of oceans. The
    newly created crust expands (pushes) outward from the rift in both direc-
    tions. When new surface and a continent meet, the stronger side deter-
    mines the direction of movement and the weaker side pushes under the
    edge of the continent and forces its way back into the mantle of the earth.
    In this process some of the matter escapes and forces its way upward
    creating earthquakes, volcanoes, and mountain ranges. (frame 5)

10. The formation of mountains, earthquakes, volcanoes, and the continuing
    movement of the continents are some of the geological implications of
    continental drift. The present and future locations of minerals are re-
    lated to continental movements. (frames 5 and 6)

CHAPTER SIX

The Water Cycle

OBJECTIVES

When you complete this chapter, you will be able to

- identify the steps or elements comprising the water cycle;
- explain how the water cycle interacts with other climatic factors;
- describe some of the ways man consumes water;
- state approximately how much water the average U.S. citizen directly or indirectly "consumes" per day in food alone;
- define, describe, and discriminate between water pollution caused by cultural sedimentation, cultural eutrophication, poisons, and thermal pollution;
- explain how pollution is the change in the rate of some natural event;
- describe some of the major water problems and their implications faced by the U.S. in the near future.

If you think that you have already mastered these objectives and might skip all or part of this chapter, turn to page 121 at the end of the chapter and take the Self-Test. The results will allow you to evaluate your current knowledge of this chapter's contents. If you answer all of the questions correctly, you are ready to begin the next chapter. If you miss any questions, you should study the frames indicated after the answers to the Self-Test.

If this material is new to you, or if you choose not to take the Self-Test now, proceed to frame 1.

1.　　One of the earth's great cycles is the <u>water (hydrological) cycle</u>. Water constantly moves from the atmosphere to the earth to the oceans and then back to the atmosphere. As it moves, water

changes the surface of the earth. Because it is a universal
solvent, it is critical to the existence of life.

Water is a powerful agent of geological change. Erosion is primarily
the washing away of some portion of the global crust by running water.
While flowing over the land, water fashions buttes, canyons, and mesas.
It also transports and deposits nutrients and sediments (e.g., 2 million tons
of sediments are deposited each day at the mouth of the Mississippi River).
But this brief residence on land is only one link in the water cycle. Water
is not simply distributed among the oceans, fresh and ground water on the
land, and water vapor in the atmosphere—rather it is constantly being cycled
from one of these locations to another. This water cycle is driven by energy
from the sun and by gravity, and it provides the connection among the atmosphere, the lithosphere, and the hydrosphere that makes the presence of life
on earth possible.

Life and water are inseparable. Most living tissue is composed of water,
which acts as the medium for the chemical reactions within the body's cells.
Being a universal solvent—almost any substance will dissolve in it—water
carries most of life's essential nutrients. Plants, for example, obtain all of
their mineral nutrients by soil water intake in which the necessary substances
are dissolved. In the human body, vital water-soluble nutrients (mineral
salts, vitamins, carbohydrates, etc.) are carried through the watery media
of blood, digestive juices, and lymph. Wastes are exported from the body
dissolved in the fluids of urine and perspiration.

(a) Water, in moving from the atmosphere to the lithosphere to the hydrosphere, constitutes a _____.

(b) If there were no water or water cycle on earth, what else would be
missing? _____

— — — — — — — — — — — — — — — — —

(a) cycle; (b) life

2. Water moves from the atmosphere, where it exists as water
vapor, to the earth's surface, where it is used by organisms,
and back again to the atmosphere.

It has been estimated that the total volume of water in the biosphere
would amount to 359×10^{15} gallons.[1] About 97 percent of the total volume
is saltwater in the oceans and seas. About 2.25 percent is frozen in polar
ice caps and glaciers. Most of the remaining .75 percent is found in freshwater lakes, ground water, and other surface water (rivers, for example).

_____

1. It is convenient to express large numbers in powers of ten. 10^{15} is a
shorthand way of writing 1,000,000,000,000,000; that is, "1" with 15 zeros
after it.

A surprisingly small amount of water exists in the atmosphere as water vapor (about .001 percent).

Figure 6.1 shows the major pathways of water. Water moves from the earth's surface to the atmosphere in two ways:

- Evaporation: The sun's energy causes water to evaporate and to rise into the atmosphere as water vapor. Most evaporation occurs over the cycle's greatest reservoir, the ocean. A smaller proportion of evaporation takes place over land water such as lakes and rivers.

- Transpiration: Water stored in plant tissue diffuses through the plant membrane and enters the atmosphere as water vapor. An acre of corn transpires up to 400,000 gallons in a single growing season.

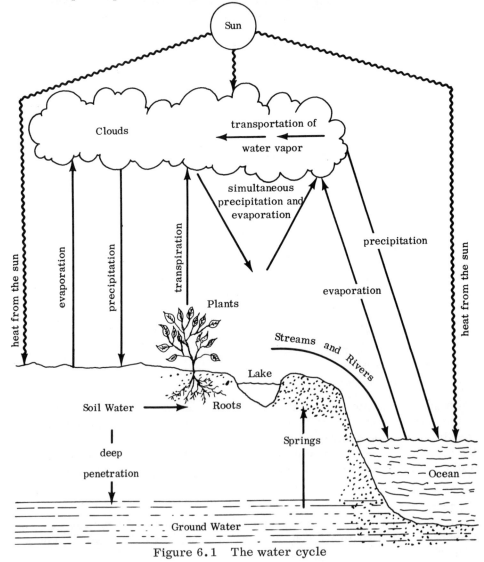

Figure 6.1 The water cycle

We have seen that air currents can transport substances for thousands of miles. Water vapor in the atmosphere is also carried great distances. When the warm air carrying the vapor cools, the vapor condenses into liquid water. We see this condensation as clouds. As the condensation continues, water droplets increase in size and begin to fall as rain or precipitation. Not all of the vapor condenses, however. Of the water vapor passing over the United States in the course of a year, only about 10 percent falls as precipitation.

Precipitation over the ocean is more than three times greater than that over land. Water precipitation may take any of several courses:

- It may be immediately reevaporated by the sun's energy. This is called simultaneous evaporation.

- It may fall into the major water reservoir, the ocean.

- It may fall onto land masses, which results in one of the following:
  △ It may infiltrate the soil to be absorbed by plant roots, used in photosynthesis, and transpired.
  △ It may run off to join streams and rivers, and eventually reach the ocean. It is this water that is primarily responsible for eroding the earth's surface.
  △ It may sink downward to join ground water reservoirs and then reappear later as springs, seeps, or lakes.
  △ It may be evaporated once again.

The use of water by land life depends upon how long the water stays on the land before it reaches the ocean. The longer water stays on land the more likely it is that it will be used. Surface and ground water provide man's freshwater supply. Vegetation also takes up significant amounts of water, thus prolonging the time water spends on land. But some of man's cities and highways tend to hasten water's return to the ocean, since water cannot penetrate paved surfaces.

On the next page, fill in the boxes in figure 6.2 with the processes occurring in the water cycle.

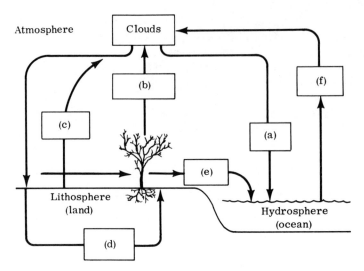

Figure 6.2

(a) _____ (b) _____

(c) _____ (d) _____

(e) _____ (f) _____

- - - - - - - - - - - - - - - - - - -

(a) precipitation; (b) transpiration; (c) evaporation; (d) soil
water (or ground water); (e) run-off, rivers, streams; (f) evaporation

3.   The distribution of precipitation depends upon the land's sur-
       face features (topography), as well as upon prevailing atmo-
       spheric conditions.

   Figure 6.3 illustrates the effect of topography on the distribution of precipitation.

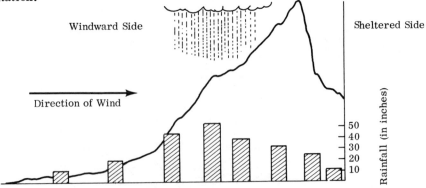

Figure 6.3   Effect of topography on precipitation distribution

Notice that the sheltered side of the mountain range receives less precipitation than its windward side. When moist air hits a mountain range, it rises, expands, and cools, which results in precipitation. As the moisture-depleted air crosses the peak of the range, it descends and becomes warm. It picks up moisture evaporated from land surfaces and releases it beyond the sheltered side of the range.

What two physical factors help determine where rain will fall and where dry areas will occur? _____

_____

— — — — — — — — — — — — — — — — — — — —

height (mountain ranges) and winds (atmospheric circulation)

4.   Evaporation is directly proportional to temperature.

The higher the temperature the greater the evaporation and consequently the less water available for the land. In some very hot areas, precipitation and evaporation occur simultaneously, and no water ever reaches the ground. In northern Australia, for example, rainfall occurs mainly in the summer when it is very hot. In this case the rainfall does not mean a good growing season, because the rainwater evaporates so rapidly and completely that none is left for use by plants.

Ecologists measure whether or not water is effectively available for living things by studying the ratio of precipitation to evaporation. This ratio, and not simply the amount of rainfall, determines if a land area will have water available for the growth of living things.

Figure 6.4 shows the relationship between rainfall and evaporation in three areas. The dotted areas in the charts ("water deficiency") indicates the season when water may be a limiting factor. Note that periods of water deficiency are only partly determined by the amount of rainfall. Rain falling during periods of high evaporation is virtually unavailable to living organisms.

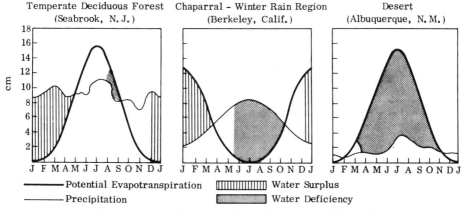

Figure 6.4   Relationship between rainfall and
evaporation (After Thornthwaite, 1955)

What is the relationship between temperature and evaporation?

_____

_____

– – – – – – – – – – – – – – – – – –

Evaporation is directly proportional to temperature; the higher the temperature the greater the evaporation.

"Till taught by pain, man really knows not what good water's worth."

Lord Byron, Don Juan

5. Technological man and his activities require enormous amounts of water, not just for drinking, washing, and flushing toilets (five gallons each time), but also for producing food, fibers, and all our modern conveniences.

We have become so accustomed to running to the tap for water and to the store for our goods that it is easy to forget that we are all drawing on the same limited supply of resources. The water available to man is almost exclusively confined to water that has reached the land and is on its way to the sea. The United States receives approximately 4,300 billion gallons of rainfall a day. Of this total, 3,000 billion gallons evaporate directly from the soil or are transpired by plants, the remainder (a little more than one-fourth —1,300 billion gallons) runs off in rivers and streams or becomes ground water.

A major entry, often overlooked in man's water budget, is the water used in food production. The amount of water passing through crops (used for both food and feed) and transpiring back to the atmosphere must be considered consumption because it is not again available until it is brought back to land by precipitation. Accounting for this transpiration brings man's water budget to staggering heights. The average American's daily food water budget is about 3,500 gallons. Georg Borgstrom has calculated the water costs of some common foods, which will give us an idea of this heavy taxation made on the water cycle.

- an orange: 90–110 gallons
- an egg: 120–150 gallons
- a 16-ounce loaf of bread: 300 gallons
- a quart of milk: 1,000 gallons
- a pound of beef: 3,500 gallons

The figures include the water needed to make the feed going into animal production. Secondary production—raising animals—is extremely costly in water terms because the water must pass first through the plants and then through the livestock. Although the animals themselves consume some water, and some is used in the dairies, factories, and farms, the major water use occurs in raising the crops to be fed to the livestock.

Man's requirements in transpired water exceed those for food alone because much of his clothing and home furnishings also come from living tissue. Borgstrom calculates that one wool suit carries a "water price tag" of 225,000-250,000 gallons. A cotton suit appears to be a bargain day special —10 to 20 times less. (Why do you suppose?)

This type of analysis can be expanded to include the water costs of industrial processes. For instance, the production of an average-size car requires 65,000 gallons of water. If a suit of synthetic fiber is more to your liking than one of wool or cotton, you should count on the manufacturing process using 1,250 gallons of water. For every ton of coal used in an electric power plant, 600 <u>tons</u> of water are needed. Nuclear power plants take even more water.

About 270 billion gallons of water per day are directly used in the U.S. (1960 figure), accounting for about 22 percent of the total run-off. Of course, most of this is reused again and again, as downstream cities receive upstream sewage discharges into their water supplies. Only an estimated 5 percent (61 billion gallons) is actually consumed per day. Thus, the U.S. would seem to have sufficient water to meet its needs.

But what of this talk of water shortages and a water crisis? This stems partially from the realities of water distribution—the people are not where the water is. Another factor contributing to shortages in the midst of plenty is the effect of our use on water quality. Our use of fresh water often leaves it unsuitable for reuse without costly treatment. Ninety-five percent of our freshwater run-off is used as a conveyor belt carrying domestic and industrial wastes including heat to the sea. Run-off from irrigated and chemically treated agricultural lands also ends up in that ultimate waste receptacle. In most of our rivers and streams we have now reached the maximum concentration of wastes that the flowing water can handle alone. The main problem then is not having enough water, but having enough that is fit for various human, industrial, agricultural, and recreational uses.

Sediments, foodstuffs, poisons, and heat are constantly and naturally entering waters. The biotic and abiotic elements of the various water ecosystems can handle certain amounts of each of these things during certain periods of time. However, if man puts in large amounts of these substances in a relatively short period of time, the water system is unable to handle the inputs and the system is changed and ultimately destroyed. Normal amounts of sediments, foodstuffs (detritus matter), poisons, or heat are not pollution. However, if they are introduced at a rate exceeding the normal rate, then they constitute pollution.

(a) List some ways human beings consume water. _____

_____

_____

(b) About how much water consumption are you responsible for, per day,

in food alone? _____

(c) What are the major problems causing water availability shortages in

the U.S. ? _____

_____

– – – – – – – – – – – – – – – – – –

(a) to drink, to "feed" animals and plants they intend to eat, to "feed" animals and plants they intend to use for clothing and shelter, to manufacture energy, to power various industrial processes, to flush wastes, and to clean houses and roadways; (b) 3,500 gallons; (c) The water isn't where people are concentrated, and the water is contaminated so it is difficult to reuse.

6. Pollution is basically a problem of excess—a problem of too much too fast. Water in natural ecosystems is always receiving certain amounts of foreign substances, which are diluted or filtered out through natural processes. When the input becomes so great that natural processes cannot control it, however, we say that pollution has occurred. A substance is not a pollutant because it is a poison; it is a pollutant because it is an amount of poison that the ecosystem can't naturally handle in a normal period of time.

There was a time when we could say that flowing water purified itself every ten miles. An increasing population with its ever-increasing per capita contribution of wastes now make this a dream of the past.

There are four basic types of pollution that commonly affect the waters of industrial societies: (1) thermal pollution, (2) cultural sedimentation, (3) poisons, and (4) cultural eutrophication.

1. We have seen that all human activity ultimately results in the formation of heat which must be disposed of. When human activity results in an abnormal increase in the heat in some part of the environment we refer to this as thermal pollution. Industrial processes use tremendous amounts of water for cooling. Power plants, for instance, give up waste heat when cool water from a river, lake, or body of salt water passes through the steam condenser. Heat from the steam is transferred to the cooling water, which returns to its source some 10-20°F warmer than when it entered. The use of natural waterways for industrial cooling poses a serious threat to fish and other organisms. Thermal pollution threatens to become an increasing problem. By 2020, the Water Resources Council predicts that electrical power plants will be heating up more than half the water in all the rivers and streams in the United States.

2. The dumping of solid wastes in water, beyond natural inputs of solid material, can be called cultural sedimentation. In this category we include nontoxic materials that accelerate the physical "filling up" of waterways by settling to the bottom and remaining there. Such materials include beverage cans, old tires, nonorganic garbage, autos, and sunken ships.

3. Most synthetic chemical compounds produced today are new to biological systems. They are not readily broken down by living organisms and may even be poisonous when present in amounts too large for the system to effectively dilute and disperse. The introduction of poisons into water systems is obviously a type of pollution. Most pesticides and many industrial wastes fall into this category.

4. Then there is the case of having too much of a good thing. Aquatic plants require nutrients such as phosphorus, nitrogen, and carbon in fixed proportions. The productivity of aquatic systems is usually limited by the level of these nutrients, particularly phosphorus and nitrogen, which only exist in limited supply in natural waters. Through a natural growth and aging process called eutrophication, aquatic systems acquire more of these nutrients and slowly "mature." This process naturally occurs over geological time but can be greatly accelerated by man's nutrient inputs. By introducing large quantities of phosphate and nitrate into water systems through sewage and run-off, man encourages algae growth. With this fertilization, the algae flourish, greatly increase in numbers, die, and bacteria begin the process of decay. Decaying organic matter sinks to the bottom, and the decay bacteria quickly use up the deep-water oxygen that fish, crustaceans, worms, insects, and larvae need to live. This process can be called cultural eutrophication. Continued breakdown of the sediment produces hydrogen sulfide gas and other foul-smelling compounds. Weeds and other plants clog the waters. By simply adding nutrients, man can change a relatively clear lake into a foul-smelling, swamplike body of water thick with algae scums and decaying vegetation.

(a) As a bear stands in a stream waiting to catch a fish, to a very slight degree his body heat causes the stream's water to become warmer. Is this an example of thermal pollution? Explain. _____

_____

_____

(b) Match these items.

_____ 1. thermal pollution	(A) filling a swamp with trash
_____ 2. cultural sedimentation	(B) pouring large amounts of water with detergents into a stream
_____ 3. poisons	(C) pouring large amounts of lead arsenic into a stream by an industrial plant
_____ 4. cultural eutrophication	(D) using water to cool a nuclear power plant and thereby raising the water's temperature

- - - - - - - - - - - - - - - - - -

(a) No, the bear's heat is not in excess of the amount or rate of heat the stream ecosystem can easily handle. (Pollution only occurs when the input is in excess of the natural input capacity of the ecosystem.)

(b) 1. (D); 2. (A); 3. (C); 4. (B)

7.   Because of insufficient usable run-off, we are now overusing
        ground water.

Ground water—water in the saturated zone beneath the ground surface—
accounts for sixty times more water than in lakes and streams. But a problem arises when the water is withdrawn faster than the recharge rate (the
rate at which water seeps into the earth from the surface). The water table
in the U.S. in continually dropping wherever we are drawing on our under-
ground water "capital."

In addition, as contaminated water infiltrates into ground water reservoirs,
these subsurface waters also become contaminated. Our rate of withdrawal
is currently exceeding twice the recharge rate. So ground water levels are
receding and water must be pumped to the surface from ever greater depths.

If man were to decontaminate his streams and rivers and thus rely less on
ground water (say, use half as much), what would happen?

_____

_____

_ _ _ _ _ _ _ _ _ _ _ _ _ _ _ _ _ _ _

    The ground water would remain at its current level, neither rising nor
    receding, since man's withdrawals and the natural recharge rate would
    be in balance.

SELF-TEST

This Self-Test is designed to show you whether or not you have mastered this chapter's objectives. Answer each question to the best of your ability. Correct answers and review instructions are given at the end of the test.

1. Fill in the boxes in figure 6.5.

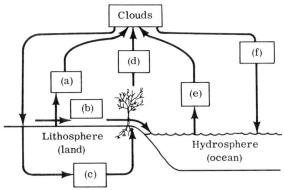

Figure 6.5

(a) _____ (b) _____

(c) _____ (d) _____

(e) _____ (f) _____

2. Explain how each of the following abiotic factors interacts with water.

   (a) topography _____

   _____

   (b) temperature _____

   _____

3. Name a few of man's uses of water. _____

   _____

   _____

4. Approximately how much water does the average U.S. citizen "consume" per day in food alone? Explain your answer. _____

   _____

   _____

5. Describe the following types of water pollution.

   (a) cultural sedimentation _____

   _____

   (b) cultural eutrophication _____

   _____

   (c) poisoning _____

   _____

   (d) thermal pollution _____

   _____

6. What do we mean when we say that pollution is just "too much too fast"?

   _____

   _____

   _____

7. What is involved in the deepening U.S. water table (ground water)?

   _____

   _____

   _____

ANSWERS TO SELF-TEST

Compare your answers to the questions on the Self-Test with the answers given below. If all of your answers are correct, you are ready to go on to the next chapter. If you missed any questions, review the frames indicated in parentheses following the answer. If you miss several questions, you should probably reread the entire chapter carefully.

1. (a) evaporation; (b) run-off, rivers, and streams; (c) soil water (or ground water); (d) transpiration; (e) evaporation; (f) precipitation (frames 1 and 2)

2. (a) The distribution of precipitation is dependent upon surface topography, especially mountains. (frame 3)
    (b) Evaporation is directly proportional to temperature. (frame 4)

3. drinking; washing; flushing wastes; production of food, fibers, wood; cooling houses and industrial machines; manufacturing processes (frame 5)

4. About 3,500 gallons. Not only do we directly consume water (drink it), but we use it to grow plants and to water and feed animals that we intend to eat. Each item we eat is an indirect consumption of water. (frame 5)

5. (a) waste material dumped in the water by man in excess of natural inputs of solid materials; (b) nutrient materials dumped in the water by man in excess of natural inputs of nutrient materials; (c) poisons dumped in the water in excess of the system's ability to effectively dilute and disperse them; (d) heating of the water to a higher than normal temperature (frame 6)

6. Normal amounts of sediments, foodstuffs (detritus matter), poisons, or heat are not pollution. If they are introduced at a rate exceeding the normal rate, they constitute pollution. (frames 5 and 6)

7. Because there is insufficient surface water available for the current needs of the U.S., the ground water is being withdrawn at an accelerating rate. Ground water is currently being used at greater than the normal replenishment rate; hence to get more ground water (to reach the water table), we must go even deeper into the ground. (frame 7)

CHAPTER SEVEN

Biogeochemical Cycles and Nutrient Budgets

OBJECTIVES

When you complete this chapter, you will be able to

- list the major characteristics of a biogeochemical cycle;
- identify and discriminate between gaseous and sedimentary cycles;
- explain how elements commonly pass through the biotic components of an ecosystem;
- identify and describe the major steps in the nitrogen cycle;
- identify and describe the major steps in the phosphorus cycle;
- explain the relationship between the flow of energy, the water cycle, and the biogeochemical cycles;
- explain the concept of a nutrient budget;
- explain the difference between the internal and external nutrient budget viewpoints.

If you think that you have already mastered these objectives and might skip all or part of this chapter, turn to page 140 at the end of the chapter and take the Self-Test. The results will allow you to evaluate your current knowledge of this chapter's contents. If you answer all of the questions correctly, you are ready to begin the next chapter. If you miss any questions, you should study the frames indicated after the answers to the Self-Test.

If this material is new to you, or if you choose not to take the Self-Test now, proceed to frame 1.

"Time, to an atom locked in a rock, does not pass. The break came when a bur oak root nosed down a crack and began prying and sucking. In the flash of a century, the rock decayed, and X was pulled out and up into the world of living things. He helped to build a flower, which became an acorn, which fattened a deer, which fed an Indian, all in a single year."

Aldo Leopold, "Odyssey" of Atom X

1. The late Aldo Leopold, a great naturalist and writer, traced the pathway of Atom X from the abiotic environment through the biotic and back to the abiotic in his classic book, A Sand County Almanac. He was describing a biogeochemical cycle. The term biogeochemical is derived because the cycling of elements involves biological organisms ("bio"), their geological environment ("geo"), and chemical change. These elements circulate through the air, land, sea, and living systems along intricate pathways using the water cycle, the geological cycle, and the ecological cycles of the opposing processes of photosynthesis and respiration.

Living organisms require from 30-40 elements for normal development. The most important are carbon, hydrogen, oxygen, nitrogen, sulfur, and phosphorus. Since there is only a finite supply of each, their continued availability depends on some cycle that leads to the reuse of the elements. Vast biogeochemical cycles make these elements available for reuse by transforming and circulating them through the atmosphere, hydrosphere, lithosphere, and biosphere.

For an ecologist, the most important feature of a biogeochemical cycle is that the biotic components and the abiotic components are tightly intertwined with one another. All biogeochemical cycles involve organisms—without life, the biogeochemical cycles would cease, and without the biogeochemical cycles, all life would cease. A biogeochemical cycle has the following characteristics:
- Movement of the nutrient element from the environment to organisms and back to the environment;
- Involvement of biological organisms (plants and/or animals, especially microorganisms);
- A "geological" reservoir (atmosphere or lithosphere);
- Chemical change.

(a) If the elements needed by living organisms did not recycle, what would happen? _____

(b) What are the four main characteristics of a biogeochemical cycle? (You may write your answer in the space on the next page.)

_____

_____

_____

_____

— — — — — — — — — — — — — — — — —

(a) The elements would eventually be used up and life would cease.
(b) movement of the nutrient element from the environment to organisms
and back to the environment; involvement of biological organisms; a
"geological" reservoir; chemical change (in any order)

2.   Biogeochemical cycles can be divided into two basic types:
        (1) gaseous nutrient cycles, and (2) sedimentary nutrient
        cycles. In gaseous cycles the reservoir where the nutrient
        collects is the atmosphere. There is little or no loss of the
        nutrient element during the relatively quick cycling process.
        In sedimentary cycles the nutrient reservoir is sedimentary
        rock. These cycles are slower and tend to exert a more
        limiting influence on living organisms.

During a major phase of the relatively "closed" <u>gaseous cycle</u>, the element is widely distributed in the atmosphere, which serves as the nutrient's major reservoir. Typical gaseous nutrient cycles include the carbon cycle, the oxygen cycle, and the nitrogen cycle.

In a <u>sedimentary cycle</u>, sedimentary rocks are the major reservoir. For the element to reach an organism such as a plant, these rocks have to be weathered and later transported to the soil. In this process, most of the element is washed away and eventually deposited in the sea as sediment. The element tied up in these new sediment deposits is thus unavailable to organisms until the uplift of the continents once again exposes them to weathering. Thus sedimentary nutrient cycles are much slower than gaseous cycles. Further, since the sedimentary reservoirs are relatively unavailable to organisms, nutrients involved in sedimentary cycles are more likely to exert a limiting influence on organisms than elements in gaseous nutrient cycles. In other words, significant shortages are more probable among the sedimentary nutrients than among the gaseous nutrients. Typical sedimentary cycles include the phosphorus cycle and the sulfur cycle.

(a) Complete the chart on the next page by writing "yes" or "no" in the first two columns of blanks and naming the major reservoirs.

	Gaseous Cycle	Sedimentary Cycle
Experiences little or no loss of the element		
Occurs relatively quickly		
Major reservoir		

(b) Match the following:

_____ (1) gaseous cycle

_____ (2) sedimentary cycle

A has a major gaseous phase
B major reservoir: sedimentary rock
C nitrogen cycle
D sulfur cycle
E hydrogen cycle
F phosphorus cycle
G oxygen cycle

(c) Read the following about the <u>carbon</u> cycle:

Carbon is widely distributed in the atmosphere in the form of carbon dioxide gas (CO_2). Carbon dioxide is used directly by plants in photosynthesis to produce carbohydrates (complex carbon compounds). Plants are eaten by animals. Carbon dioxide gas is returned to the atmosphere by <u>respiration</u> (the reverse of photosynthesis). Thus its concentration is maintained.

Now answer the following:

(1) The carbon cycle is a _____ cycle.

(2) Why? _____

_____

_____

- - - - - - - - - - - - - - - - - - -

(a) Gaseous Cycle   Sedimentary Cycle
    yes   no
    yes   no
    atmosphere   sedimentary rocks
                    in lithosphere

(b) (1) A, C, E, G; (2) B, D, F; (c) (1) gaseous nutrient; (2) The atmosphere is the major nutrient reservoir and it experiences no loss (CO_2 concentration in the atmosphere is maintained).

3.   In biogeochemical cycles, nutrient elements usually enter the
        living systems through vegetation.

Animals are unable to free and absorb the nutrient elements from the
soil or the atmosphere as plants can. Plants easily absorb nutrients along
with soil water through their root system. Animals also cannot synthesize
proteins by producing amino acids (basic protein building blocks) from these
inorganic molecules. An ecosystem depends on plants not only to supply the
necessary nutrients to maintain the flow of energy but also to fix the solar
energy.

How are elements brought into the <u>bio</u> phase of biogeochemical cycles?

_ _ _ _ _ _ _ _ _ _ _ _ _ _ _ _ _ _

        by plants, when they use the elements

4.   The <u>nitrogen cycle</u> is a typical gaseous nutrient cycle. The
        major reservoir of nitrogen is the earth's atmosphere. Atmo-
        spheric nitrogen is combined (fixed) with other chemicals into
        organic compounds used by plants and animals. It is a vital
        component of proteins which are necessary to all living things.
        When plants and animals die, their bodies are broken down by
        bacteria (decomposers) into ammonia, a nitrogen compound.
        Other bacteria change the ammonia to nitrates. Still other
        bacteria break down the nitrates and release the nitrogen as
        gas back into the atmosphere, completing the cycle.

Nitrogen is absolutely necessary for the existence of life as we know it.
It is an essential ingredient of proteins, which are vital to the chemistry of
all living organisms. Luckily, the earth's atmosphere is 79 percent nitrogen.
However, most organisms cannot use nitrogen in its gaseous form—nitrogen
must first be converted from a gas to nitrate compounds, which plants use to
make proteins. Animals get their nitrogen already fixed in the plant tissue
they eat.

Examine figure 7.1 on the next page, and go through the cycle, referring
to the numbers in the figure.

(1) The major reservoir of nitrogen is the atmosphere, where nitrogen
exists as a gas.

(2) Nitrogen is changed from a gas into nitrate compounds by means of a
process called nitrogen fixation. There are three ways nitrogen fixation can
occur:
   • <u>Biological fixation</u> is accomplished by nitrogen-fixing bacteria that
     either live free in the soil or in nodules attached to the roots of plants
     called legumes (e.g., peas, beans, clover, redbud trees, locust trees)
     and also by certain blue-green algae that live in the oceans.

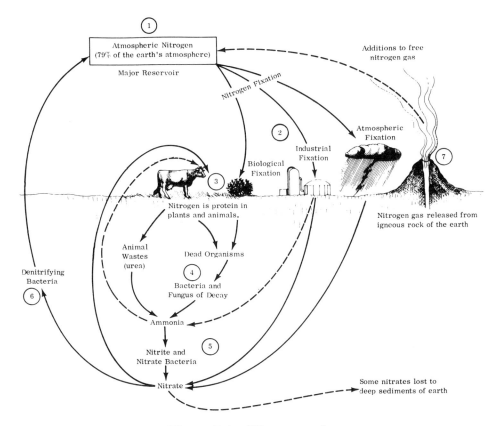

Figure 7.1 Nitrogen cycle

- Atmospheric <u>fixation</u> is accomplished by a physio-chemical process that occurs when lightning converts atmospheric nitrogen into nitric acid. This acid is dissolved in rain and carried to the earth. Plants acquire it when they absorb water and other minerals through their roots.
- Industrial <u>fixation</u> is accomplished by the Haber-Bosch process which is a physico-chemical process based on the same principle as atmospheric fixation.

(3) Plants acquire nitrogen compounds from the soil through their roots. Animals acquire nitrogen compounds from plant tissue. In both cases the nitrogen is used to build protein molecules.

(4) Nitrogen compounds are returned to the soil when plants and animals die or when animals give off waste products (urea). Bacteria and fungus of decay break down the tissue of dead organisms, ultimately reducing it to amino acids. Other bacteria change amino acids into inorganic ammonia in a process called aminification.

(5) Still other bacteria change ammonia into nitrites and then into nitrates. Some nitrates are reabsorbed by plant roots in a subcycle of the overall ni-

trogen cycle. Other nitrates are carried in streams and rivers to the ocean, where, with other nitrates that escape the oceanic food chains, they become part of the deep ocean sediments and are lost to the nitrogen cycle.

(6) Most nitrates, however, are altered by denitrifying bacteria that live in the soil, and the nitrogen is released as gas back into the atmosphere in a process called denitrification.

(7) The gas from volcanoes is rich in nitrogen, hence some new nitrogen is constantly being added to the atmosphere.

The four special processes involved in the nitrogen cycle are summarized below.

- Nitrogen fixation [(2) in figure 7.1]
    1. converts atmospheric nitrogen to nitrates
    2. accomplished physio-chemically and by nitrogen-fixing bacteria

- Aminification [(4) in figure 7.1]
    1. converts nitrates to ammonia and ammonia compounds
    2. accomplished by bacteria and fungus of decay

- Nitrification [(5) in figure 7.1]
    1. converts ammonia compounds and ammonia to nitrates
    2. accomplished by nitrite and nitrate bacteria

- Denitrification [(6) in figure 7.1]
    1. converts nitrates to atmospheric nitrogen
    2. accomplished by denitrifying bacteria

(a) Bacteria play a very important role in linking one step in the nitrogen cycle to the next. Starting with nitrogen fixation, name the groups of bacteria involved and the product they produce.

Bacteria	Product
(1) _____	usable nitrogen in soil _____
(2) _____	_____
(3) _____	_____
(4) _____	gaseous nitrogen _____

(b) A diagram of the nitrogen cycle is reproduced in figure 7.2 on the facing page; describe the steps in the spaces below.

(1) _____   (2) _____

(3) _____   (4) _____

(5) _____   (6) _____

(7) _____   (8) _____

- - - - - - - - - - - - - - - - - - -

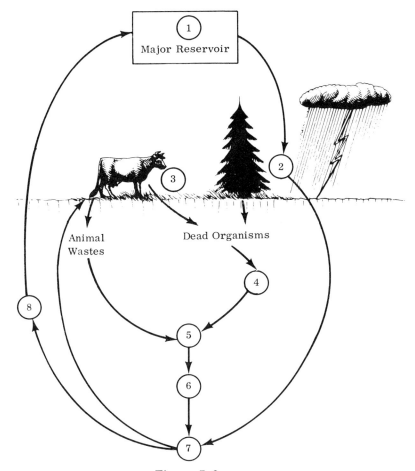

Figure 7.2

(a) (1) nitrogen-fixing bacteria   usable nitrogen in soil
     (2) decay bacteria   ammonia
     (3) nitrite and nitrate bacteria   nitrates
     (4) denitrifying bacteria   gaseous nitrogen
(b) (1) atmosphere; (2) nitrogen fixation, accomplished in large part by
nitrogen-fixing bacteria; (3) Nitrogen in protein in plants and animals;
animals eat plants. (4) bacteria and fungus of decay; (5) ammonia;
(6) nitrite and nitrate bacteria; (7) nitrate; (8) Denitrifying bacteria
release nitrogen as a gas into the atmosphere.

5.   The phosphorus cycle is a typical sedimentary nutrient cycle.
       The major reservoir of phosphorus is sedimentary rock,
       which is only available to the basic cycle in small amounts
       as a result of weathering. The cycle does not have a major
       gaseous phase and therefore moves at a very slow pace.
       Phosphorus is a vital component of DNA, RNA, and ATP

(genetic and energy-producing molecules, respectively) and
therefore necessary to all living cells. The basic phosphorus
cycle begins with dissolved phosphates. These are absorbed
by plants through their roots and incorporated into all cells in
complex molecules. Animals get their phosphorus from
plants. When plants and animals die or excrete waste products,
the dead organic compounds are broken down by phosphatizing
bacteria into inorganic dissolved phosphates, completing the
basic cycle.

Phosphorus is essential in DNA and RNA molecules, which transmit
genetic information, and in ATP molecules, which are involved in the energy
transactions of every cell. Phosphorus exists primarily as inorganic phosphate compounds which are bound up in sedimentary rocks.

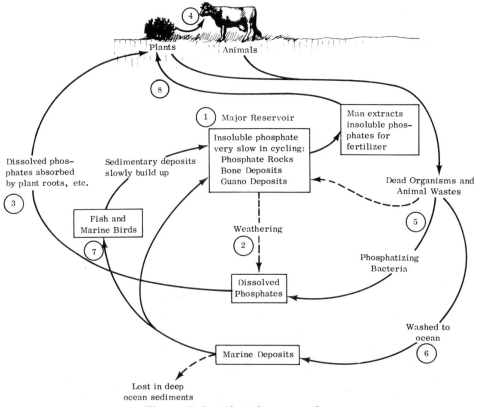

Figure 7.3   Phosphorus cycle

Here is a brief description of the entire cycle. Each number corresponds
to the numbered step in figure 7.3.

(1) The phosphate deposits in the lithosphere represent the <u>major reservoir</u>.

(2) These phosphates are weathered and later transported to the soil by wind
and water, where they exist as inorganic dissolved phosphates.

(3) Phosphates in the soil are absorbed by plants for use in making their own tissue.

(4) Plants are eaten by animals.

(5) Decay bacteria break down the tissue of dead animals and plants. Phosphatizing bacteria further break down these products and return phosphates to the soil. Phosphates are also returned to the soil by animal wastes.

(6) Much of the phosphate in the soil is washed away by run-off water and eventually reaches the ocean. In the ocean, some of the phosphates precipitate as shallow marine sediment.

(7) Small amounts of phosphate are returned to land surfaces by fish harvesting and fish-eating sea birds. The guano deposits near the coast of Peru are sea-bird excrement. The amount of phosphorus brought back to land surfaces, however, does not balance the loss to the deep sea. These deep sea deposits may eventually be uplifted to land surfaces by geological processes and join the major reservoir; however, this would take thousands of years, so for all practical purposes, phosphates deposited deep in the ocean are considered lost to the cycle.

(8) Man mines phosphate rocks and imports fish and guano for use as fertilizer, thereby speeding up the otherwise slow weathering process that usually limits the speed of the cycle.

A diagram of the phosphorus cycle is reproduced in figure 7.4 on the next page. Describe the steps in the cycle in the spaces below, referring back to figure 7.3 if necessary.

(1) _____   (2) _____

(3) _____   (4) _____

(5) _____   (6) _____

(7) _____   (8) _____

- - - - - - - - - - - - - - - - - -

(1) Phosphorus in all living tissue, animals eat plants.   (2) phosphatizing bacteria;   (3) dissolved phosphates;   (4) dissolved phosphates absorbed by plant roots, etc.;   (5) sedimentary phosphate rock and guano deposits;   (6) weathering;   (7) washed into ocean;   (8) marine deposits;   (9) via fish and marine birds, bones, guano

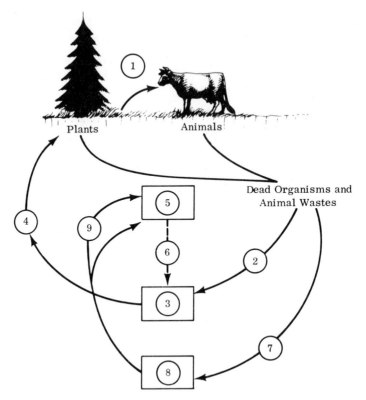

Figure 7.4

6.   The phosphorus cycle has fewer steps than the nitrogen cycle,
       but in other ways it is more complex. For example, it de-
       pends on a more delicate balance since phosphorus is not near-
       ly as common as nitrogen and its major reservoir holds onto
       its supply much more vigorously than the atmosphere holds
       onto nitrogen.

     Phosphorus and nitrogen exist on earth in a ratio of 1 to 23. Yet for or-
ganisms to carry on their life processes, phosphorus must be much more
abundant in all living tissue than nitrogen. Consequently, phosphorus is the
most likely element to limit the production of biomass in any ecosystem.

     Intensive agriculture rapidly depletes available dissolved phosphate sup-
plies. Fifty years of cultivation in temperate zones can easily reduce available phosphates by more than one-third, thus very severely limiting the land's
fertility (cultivation is much more destructive of available phosphate reserves
in tropical climates). Much of the land in the ancient near east and India was
once fertile but later failed, because it simply ran out of phosphate. To overcome this problem man has learned to use fish and animal wastes as fertilizer to replenish phosphates in the soil. Modern man mines and therefore
"artificially weathers" insoluble phosphate to use as fertilizer.

As we discussed previously (see page 118), run-off of agricultural fertilizer as well as run-off from houses that use common household detergents
(which are very rich in phosphates) increase the rate of eutrophication in
rivers and streams.

In interfering with the nitrogen cycle, we said that man didn't really increase
the amount of nitrogen available for circulation, he just changed the rate of
the cycle. What sort of interference is man undertaking in the case of phos-

phorus? _____

_____

_____

– – – – – – – – – – – – – – – – – – – –

He is mining phosphorus from sedimentary rock and using guano and
fish for fertilizer. He has <u>increased</u> <u>the</u> <u>amount</u> of phosphorus in circulation as well as increased the rate of circulation.

7.   All biogeochemical cycles are closely tied to the water cycle
        and the flow of energy through the biosphere. Water in one
        form or another is the principal means of nutrient circulation.
        And sunlight, as captured by plants, provides the energy nec-
        essary to allow plants to carry on the "pumping" and tran-
        spiration needed to keep the nutrient cycles moving.

Obviously the water cycle plays a vital role in all biogeochemical cycles.
Dissolved nutrients are carried from the earth's surface either into the
ground or into the oceans. Atmospheric nutrients are often brought to the
earth's surface in rainwater. Nutrients held in rock are gradually released
by weathering accomplished by rains, by erosion through flowing water, and
by the freezing and defrosting of ice. Nutrients are usually dissolved in
water when they are absorbed into the roots of plants. And water is critical
in accomplishing the various chemical changes that nutrients experience as
they pass through the <u>bio</u> phase of their cycle.
    Less obvious, but equally important, is the role of energy flow in facili-
tating biogeochemical cycles. On a gross level it is energy from the sun
that (1) keeps the earth warm enough so that chemical reactions are possible,
(2) makes it possible for living organisms to carry on their vital processes,
and (3) powers the atmospheric, geological, and water cycles.
    On a more subtle level, plants expend energy to "pump" water, and con-
sequently extract dissolved nutrients from the soil. Otherwise, the nutrient
cycle would stop since the nutrients would simply stay in the soil. Furthermore, bacteria require considerable energy to carry out their vital processes
and thereby change nutrients from one form to another and, in some cases,
release nutrient elements as gas. All of these vital plant processes require
that plants first capture sunlight in complex chemical molecules so that later
when these chemicals are broken up, energy will be available to power other
chemical reactions.

Figure 7.5 is a model showing some of the interactions between the energy, water, and biogeochemical cycles. The sun's heat causes atmospheric currents and hence powers the precipitation and evaporation of the water cycle. The sun's energy powers living organisms (especially plants) that "pull" nutrients from their reservoirs and into the biogeochemical cycles. And biogeochemical cycles require the flow of water to maintain themselves.

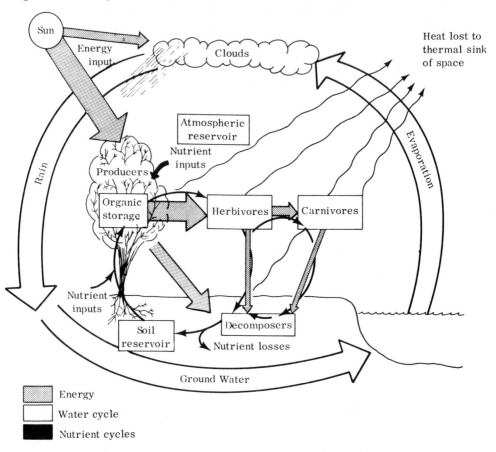

Figure 7.5 A model showing the flow of energy, the cycling of water, and the association of biogeochemical cycles with both

Briefly summarize the relationship between the flow of energy, the water cycle, and the biogeochemical cycles. _____

_____

_____

_____

‒ ‒ ‒ ‒ ‒ ‒ ‒ ‒ ‒ ‒ ‒ ‒ ‒ ‒ ‒

_____

Biogeochemical cycles depend upon the flow of energy and the water cycle: Water carries nutrients in dissolved form from place to place. Plants absorb nutrients from the soil dissolved in water. Energy powers the water cycle and this causes atmospheric circulation, as well as providing plants with the energy to "pump" nutrients from the soil and bacteria with the energy they need to chemically transform the nutrient elements from one compound to another.

8. Cycles usually refer to nutrient exchanges between several different ecosystems on a global scale. On the other hand, a study of nutrient flow within and through an ecosystem is called a nutrient budget. Nutrient budgets are divided into two categories. External nutrient budgets concentrate on the nutrient inputs and outputs of an entire ecosystem. Internal nutrient budgets concentrate on nutrient exchanges between the subsystems or components of a particular ecosystem.

Until now we have been studying the broad pathways of the biogeochemical cycling of the gaseous and sedimentary nutrients. We have paid little attention to what happens to nutrients inside the ecosystem. Nutrient budgets are studies of the quantity and availability of nutrients in an ecosystem and its parts. Even though nutrient budget studies concentrate on specific nutrients, their conclusions can be applied to the movement of all essential nutrients. In nutrient budget studies, the emphasis is on quantitative information, as well as on the description of general nutrient pathways.

Internal and external nutrient budgets are two ways of viewing the passage of nutrients within and through an ecosystem. These two viewpoints are presented graphically in figures 7.6 and 7.7 on the next two pages.

External nutrient budgets concentrate on the input and output of an entire ecosystem. Figure 7.6 shows how an ecologist looks at the external nutrient budget of an ecosystem. The input (by way of precipitation) and the output (by way of water run-off) of calcium (Ca), magnesium (Mg), sodium (Na), and potassium (K) have been studied in six New England watersheds. The input of nutrients in each watershed was determined by measuring the volume of rainfall (rainwater contains Ca, Mg, Na, and K). The output was determined by measuring the volume of water leaving the system (run-off) using a gauging device (run-off water dissolves material from the soil). The rainwater and the run-off water were then analyzed for their calcium, magnesium, sodium, and potassium contents. In order that a system be maintained, a net loss of any element must be compensated for by decomposition of the underlying soil material.

Internal nutrient budgets (figure 7.7) concentrate on nutrient input and output through particular biotic components within an ecosystem. Internal nutrient budgets have been studied using radioactive substances as "tracers" or "tags" to follow the movement of materials. One experiment was performed by inoculating the trunks of white oak trees with a very small but known amount of radioactive cesium 134 (^{134}Cs). The movement of ^{134}Cs to the different parts of the trees (trunks, leaves, and branches), as well as

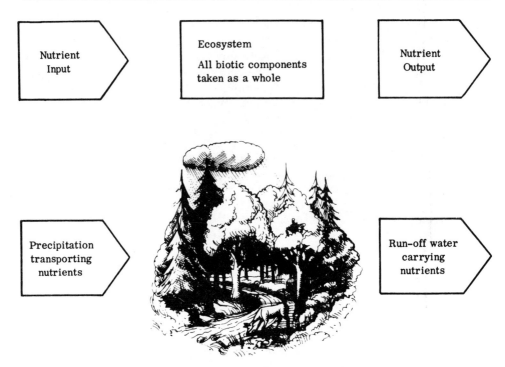

Figure 7.6   External nutrient budgets

its transfer from the trees to the soil, was followed for two years. This type of study provides the ecologist with some insight into how essential nutrients are recycled within a specific biotic component (in this case, white oak trees) of an ecosystem.

Nutrients enter an ecosystem in a variety of ways. Gaseous nutrients such as nitrogen and carbon dioxide are taken in by plants either directly (carbon dioxide) or indirectly (nitrogen) from the atmosphere. Sedimentary nutrients are generally brought into the soil of an ecosystem in the form of compounds which are carried by wind, rain, dust, or running water.

Match the following:

_____ (a) nutrient budgets

_____ (b) internal nutrient budgets

_____ (c) external nutrient budgets

(1) concerns the quantity and availability of nutrients in an ecosystem and its parts

(2) concerns the quantity and availability of nutrients moving into and out of particular components of an ecosystem

(3) concerns the quantity and availability of nutrients moving into and out of an entire ecosystem

- - - - - - - - - - - - - - - - - - -

(a) 1;   (b) 2;   (c) 3

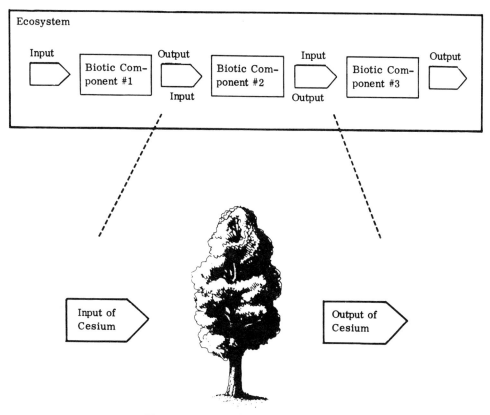

Biotic Component #2: White Oak Trees

Figure 7.7   Internal nutrient budgets

SELF–TEST

This Self–Test is designed to show you whether or not you have mastered
this chapter's objectives. Answer each question to the best of your ability.
Correct answers and review instructions are given at the end of the test.

1. What are the major characteristics of a biogeochemical cycle?

    _____

    _____

2. Match the following:

    _____ (a) gaseous nutrient   (1) involves a major gaseous phase
              cycle   (2) occurs relatively slowly
                                        (3) little or no loss of the nutrient
    _____ (b) sedimentary nutrient   element
              cycle   (4) uses the atmosphere as a major
                                            reservoir
                                        (5) uses sedimentary rock as a major
                                            reservoir
                                        (6) phosphorus cycle
                                        (7) nitrogen cycle

3. Most cycling nutrient elements commonly enter the bio phase of their

    biogeochemical cycle through _____.

4. A diagram of the nitrogen cycle is reproduced in figure 7. 8 on the facing
    page. Write the labels for the steps of the cycle in the spaces below.

    (a) _____   (b) _____

    (c) _____   (d) _____

    (e) _____   (f) _____

    (g) _____   (h) _____

    (i) This biochemical cycle is a typical example of a _____
         nutrient cycle.

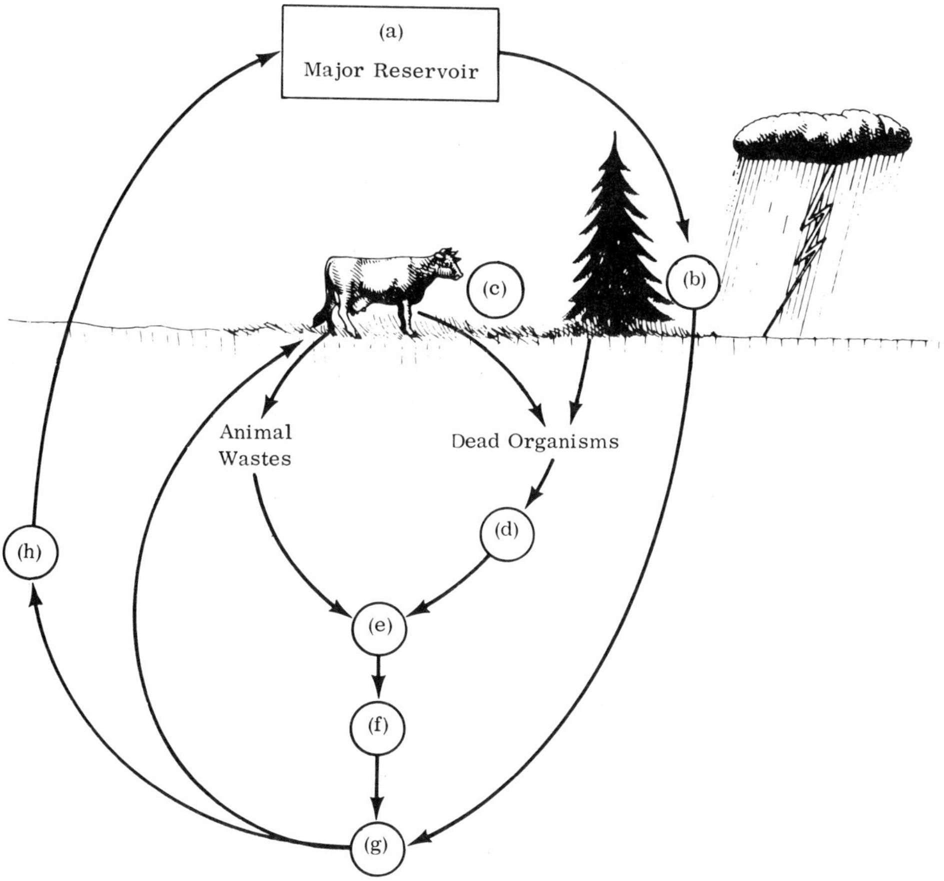

Figure 7.8

5. A diagram of the phosphorus cycle is reproduced in figure 7.9 on the next page. Write the labels for the steps of the cycle in the spaces below.

(a) _____   (b) _____

(c) _____   (d) _____

(e) _____   (f) _____

(g) _____   (h) _____

(i) _____

(j) This biogeochemical cycle is a typical example of a _____ nutrient cycle.

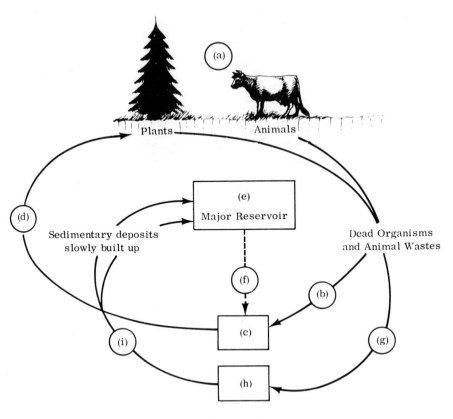

Figure 7.9

6. What is the relationship between the flow of energy, the water cycle, and biogeochemical cycles? _____

_____

_____

_____

7. What is a nutrient budget? _____

_____

8. Match the two diagrams in figure 7.10 to the appropriate labels.

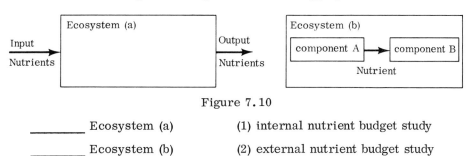

Figure 7.10

_____ Ecosystem (a)   (1) internal nutrient budget study

_____ Ecosystem (b)   (2) external nutrient budget study

ANSWERS TO SELF-TEST

Compare your answers to the questions on the Self-Test with the answers given below. If all of your answers are correct, you are ready to go on to the next chapter. If you missed any questions, review the frames indicated in parentheses following the answer. If you miss several questions, you should probably reread the entire chapter carefully.

1.   movement of the nutrient element from the environment to organisms and back to the environment; involvement of biological organisms; a geological reservoir; chemical change (frame 1)

2.   (a) 1, 3, 4, 7 (frames 2 and 4)
     (b) 2, 5, 6 (frames 2 and 5)

3.   plants (plant roots) (frame 3)

4.   (a) atmosphere;   (b) nitrogen fixation, accomplished in large part by nitrogen-fixing bacteria in the soil and in nodules on legume roots;   (c) nitrogen is protein in plants and animals; animals eat plants;   (d) bacteria and fungus of decay;   (e) ammonia;   (f) nitrite and nitrate bacteria;   (g) nitrate;   (h) denitrifying bacteria release nitrogen as a gas into the atmosphere;   (i) gaseous (frame 4)

5.   (a) phosphorus in all living tissue, animals eat plants;   (b) phosphatizing bacteria;   (c) dissolved phosphates;   (d) dissolved phosphates absorbed by plant roots, etc.;   (e) sedimentary phosphate, rock, bone deposits, and guano deposits;   (f) weathering;   (g) washed into ocean;   (h) marine deposits;   (i) via fish and marine birds, bones, guano;   (j) sedimentary (frame 5)

6.   Water carries nutrients in dissolved form from place to place. Plants absorb nutrients from the soil dissolved in water. Energy powers the water cycle and this causes atmospheric circulation, as well as providing plants with the energy to "pump" nutrients from the soil and bacteria with the energy they need to chemically transform the nutrient elements from one compound to another. (frame 7)

7.   A nutrient budget is a quantitative study of the flow of nutrients into and out of or within a particular ecosystem. (frame 8)

8.   (a) 2;   (b) 1 (frame 8)

PART FOUR
Ecology of Populations

In Part Three we considered some of the broad forces that make up the dynamic physical "background" against which all biological systems must interact. We could view an ecosystem as a theater production. The atmosphere, land, water, incoming solar energy, and all the other abiotic elements provide the background—the sets, the lighting, and the structure of the theater itself. The play must be presented within the limits of this theater. We are now ready to see the actors play out their roles. In this analogy, the actors are the individual populations of living organisms. How these actors interact with each other determines the final play that is presented. The success or failure of each individual population depends upon its ability to accommodate itself to the "set" in which it appears, as well as the role it must play relative to the other members of the cast.

In this part we study these actors of the ecological theater. To study populations, we must look at a new level of biological organization. Individual organisms must be considered as a part of a larger, more complex scheme. Just as we cannot understand what an individual human being is like from a detailed study of his digestive, nervous, and muscular systems, so we cannot understand what a population is like simply from studying its individual members. This new level of organization—the population level—has characteristics not possessed by the individual organisms that make it up.

A population is a group of individuals of the same species that occupy a given area and interbreed with each other. Much of the existing ecological research was conducted using the population as the basic research unit. Indeed, ecology itself has been defined as the study of the distribution and abundance of populations, and although this may be a rather narrow definition, it does pinpoint some of ecology's most interesting questions. What factors influence when, in what numbers, and where particular organisms will occur? How do you measure these occurrences? Why do some populations suddenly disappear? Such questions concern the population ecologist, and they are considered in the following three chapters.

In Chapter 8 we consider the characteristics and behavior of populations that make them a unique level of organization. We discuss population growth and some of the simple means of measuring it. Chapter 9 concerns the various factors suspected of affecting population size. We consider various external factors, including abiotic factors such as climate and topography and

and biotic factors such as the impact of one population on another. Finally, the chapter concludes with a brief consideration of those intrinsic factors generated within the population itself (e.g., territoriality, social stress) that affect population growth. Chapter 10 considers how these basic principles have affected and are reflected in today's human population.

CHAPTER EIGHT

Population Characteristics and Dynamics

OBJECTIVES

When you complete this chapter, you will be able to

- define population;
- explain the processes of evolution, natural selection, and differential reproduction;
- explain the relationship between biotic potential, environmental resistance, population growth, and population density;
- explain the demostat model using the terms set point, positive feedback, and negative feedback;
- identify and explain the tendencies implicit in an S-shaped population growth curve;
- identify and explain the tendencies implicit in a J-shaped population growth curve;
- explain growth rate, rate of change, birth rate, and death rate for a population;
- describe and explain survivorship curves;
- explain fertility rate and its importance;
- explain age pyramids and their significance.

If you think that you have already mastered these objectives and might skip all or part of this chapter, turn to page 169 at the end of the chapter and take the Self-Test. The results will allow you to evaluate your current knowledge of this chapter's contents. If you answer all of the questions correctly, you are ready to begin the next chapter. If you miss any questions, you should study the frames indicated after the answers to the Self-Test.

If this material is new to you, or if you choose not to take the Self-Test now, proceed to frame 1.

1.   When an ecologist talks about changes in living organisms of
        an ecosystem, he is using a population as his unit of reference.
        A population is a group of interbreeding individuals of the
        same species that occupy a specific area. Evolution is the
        process by which species populations change their character-
        istics in the course of time. These changes occur as a result
        of natural selection. Taken as a whole, a population possesses
        certain characteristics which none of its individual members
        possess. An individual member of a population may be born,
        grow, and die, but only a population can have a birth rate, a
        growth rate, a death rate, and a pattern of dispersal in time
        and space.

The process of evolution is a fundamental biological principle and will be
related to several ecological concepts throughout the remainder of this book.
A complete explanation of the process is beyond the scope of this book, but
we will give a general explanation.

Evolution is the process by which species populations change their characteristics (genetic makeup) in the course of time. Individual organisms
have the traits they have because of the genetic material they received from
their parents. In the process of reproduction, the parents' genetic material
can come together in different combinations resulting in offspring different
from each other and from their parents. In addition, outside influences such
as radiation, heat, and chemicals can cause specific changes in the genetic
material—mutations. The various combinations of genetic material inherited
from parents, coupled with mutations, guarantee that each of the individuals
comprising a single population will be slightly different. This variation in
genetic makeup is the raw material of evolution.

Some individuals within a population have traits that allow them to be
particularly successful in coping with the environment (adaptive traits).
These individuals usually are also most successful in breeding. Those individuals who have traits that are disadvantageous in coping with the environment usually have fewer offspring. Thus, in the long run, a population comes
to be composed of those individuals with the more adaptive traits. In one generation those individuals whose genetic material and/or mutations make them
most successful in dealing with the environment produce more offspring and
their traits tend to predominate in future generations of the population. We
refer to this process as differential reproduction.

The environment "selects" in the sense that some traits give their pos-
sessor an edge in surviving and producing offspring. This is the essence of
the process called natural selection. Those individuals possessing traits
that make them better able to survive and reproduce are said to be "selected
for" by natural selection. Evolution occurs as a result of natural selection
where changes in a population's collective genetic material (gene pool) is
altered over the course of time (see figure 8.1 on the next page). These
genetic changes are ultimately expressed as differences in the functioning
and structure of the individual organisms.

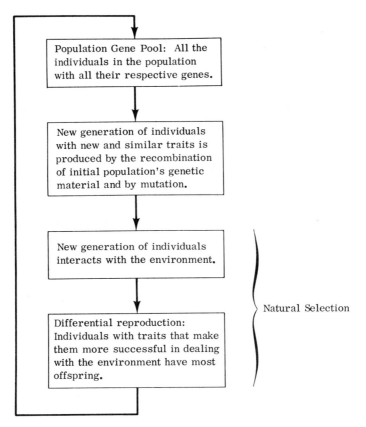

Figure 8.1   Natural selection, differential
reproduction, and the evolutionary process

Consider this example taken from the evolution of the horse.   Early
horses were small—about the size of dogs.   A few individuals, by chance
combinations and by mutations, turned out to have slightly larger bodies.
This increased body size gave their possessors an advantage in rapid travel
and in seeking food, avoiding injury, and ultimately in finding mates.   Thus,
they had a better chance of having offspring.   They reproduced more successfully than the individuals with smaller bodies.   By the process of differential
reproduction, individuals with larger bodies became more common in future
generations of the population.   The new generation had individuals with an
even larger body size, and they, in their turn, were also more successful
at breeding.   Hence a horse with a still larger body came to be common in
still later generations.   Because the horse with the larger body size was
most successful in coping with the environment (as judged by his reproductive success), we say that among horses the environment "selected for"
successively larger body size.   Thus the relatively large modern horse has
developed as a result of natural selection.

We have been considering how one population of individuals changes from generation to generation to become more successful in coping with its environment. In our discussion we have acted as if the environment were always the same; in fact, it is always changing. The geological cycle, climate, and other species as they evolve, all change the environment. Hence the criteria by which organisms within a population are selected constantly shift. A good adaptation in one generation in one environment may prove useless or even harmful to a later generation that finds itself in a new set of environmental circumstances. Because of the constant and dynamic shifts in the relationships between the various evolving and interacting populations and the abiotic environment, some populations are unable to successfully obtain their needed resources and become <u>extinct</u>. Those populations that survive, on the other hand, are constantly evolving better ways of dealing with the problems of the changing environment.

The key things to remember about evolution are:

- Evolution is the process by which species populations change their characteristics in the course of time. The main cause of evolution is natural selection.

- Natural selection results in the differential reproduction of traits that give individuals an advantage in coping with their environment.

- Individuals do not evolve—populations evolve, because evolution only refers to a change in the population's collective genetic material (gene pool) from generation to generation. Because the changes from one generation to another are usually small, major evolutionary change takes a very long time.

- In the case of individuals or populations as a whole, success is judged by the number of breeding offspring produced.

- To survive, populations must be constantly evolving since their environments are constantly changing.

(a) Examine figure 8.2 in order to answer the questions on the next page. The figure shows 30 generations of population X.

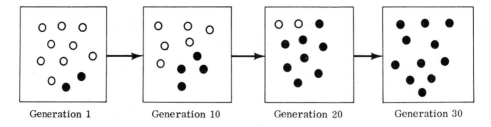

| Generation 1 | Generation 10 | Generation 20 | Generation 30 |

O = individuals with trait A

● = individuals with trait B

Figure 8.2

Assume the environment was constant during all 30 generations. Explain in general terms what happens in each box.

(1) Generation 1: _____

_____

_____

(2) Generation 10: _____

_____

_____

(3) Generation 20: _____

_____

_____

(4) Generation 30: _____

_____

_____

(b) Define evolution. _____

_____

_____

(c) Briefly describe natural selection. _____

_____

_____

(d) When a population ecologist asserts that in a population of organisms, the whole is greater than the sum of its parts, what does he mean?

_____

_____

- - - - - - - - - - - - - - - - - - -

(a) (1) Most of the individuals making up population X have the A trait. Because of a chance combination of genetic material or a mutation, however, two individuals have the B trait. (2) In generation 10, 4 of the 10 individuals comprising the population have trait B. Trait B must give the individual possessing it an advantage since type B individuals, relative to their numbers, are outbreeding type A individuals. The environment can be said to be selecting for the B trait. (3) Differential reproduction continues and individuals with trait B now make up the majority of the population. (4) Population X is now composed only of individuals with the B trait. The population has evolved so that it now displays the B rather than the A trait. All individuals with the A trait have become extinct in this population.

(b) Evolution is the process by which species populations change their
characteristics in the course of time.

(c) Natural selection is the process by which those individuals possessing
traits that give them a competitive edge in their environment survive and
flourish. This results in the differential reproduction of the individuals
with those traits that give them an advantage in coping with their environment.

(d) He means that the whole—the population—has characteristics that are
not possessed by any of its individual members and could not be reasonably studied by studying those individuals separately.

2.　　Biotic potential refers to the ability of organisms to reproduce
themselves under optimal conditions. Environmental resistance
refers to the biotic and abiotic factors that keep organisms from
reaching or continuing at their biotic potential. Population
growth is the increase or decrease in the total number of organisms in a population due to the interplay between biotic potential
and environmental resistance. This process can be viewed as a
cybernetic system, with negative feedback tending to keep the
population in some sort of balance. The feedback process is
based on the fact that as population density increases, environmental resistance increases, which in turn decreases subsequent population density.

Reproduction at a maximum rate in an unrestricted environment would
lead to incredible numbers because unrestricted population growth is exponential—the population increases by a constant percentage of the whole in a
constant time period. (Recall our discussion of exponential growth in the Introduction.) Two common houseflies, for instance, in a year's time would
give rise to 6 trillion individuals. Charles Darwin once calculated that at the
end of 750 years a pair of elephants would be represented by 19 million des-
cendants. Of course, these are theoretical calculations that assume all offspring survive and reproduce offspring that in turn survive and reproduce,
and so forth. Reproduction is clearly an example of positive feedback: Offspring produce offspring that produce more offspring. Much like the com-
pounding of interest in the bank, the interest itself becomes capital earning
interest of its own. The positive feedback of unopposed reproduction, like
any other runaway feedback, cannot be maintained for long in a world of limited resources. Actual populations are restricted from realizing the positive
feedback of their biotic potential by the negative feedback of environmental
resistance. A cybernetic system of population control exists, which is shown
in a demostat[1] model, which can be compared to the thermostat system discussed in Chapter 1. This demostat model is illustrated in figure 8.3.

1. The word is a play on thermostat. A similar model was first proposed by
Garrett Hardin (1966) which applied only to human populations (see page 215);
we have generalized it here to apply to any population of organisms.

A tendency away from a set point caused by increases in the number of individuals comprising the population is opposed by various components of environmental resistance, which include starvation, disease, and competition. Each of these factors acts to decrease reproduction and individual survival, thereby checking population growth when it approaches "overpopulation" proportions and ultimately returning the population to the environment's set point. In the case of "underpopulation" the restraining influence of environmental resistance is lifted and the population returns to the set point through increased reproduction and survival. You may want to refer to this model as we discuss more fully these rather abstract terms of set point, overpopulation, and environmental resistance.

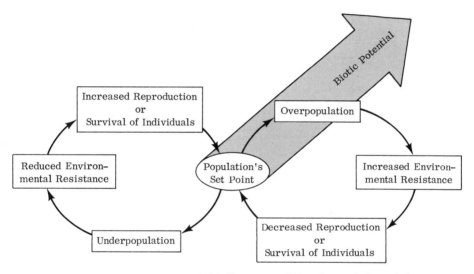

Figure 8.3 Figure-eight diagram of the demostat model

Given a population's potential for exponential growth (its biotic potential), any factor that affects a constant percentage of the population cannot effectively "control" its growth. A truly "regulatory" system requires that the intensity of the limiting factors vary with the size of the population. In other words, the components of environmental resistance must operate more severely when the population is large (density is high) and less severely when its size diminishes (density is low). In the next chapter we will focus on some specific kinds of environmental resistance. The rest of this chapter considers the nature of population growth.

(a) The two factors that interact to determine population growth are

_____ and _____

(b) In the demostat model (figure 8.3), what is the positive feedback element?

_____

(c)   A population that grows 50 percent every day is exhibiting _____

_____ growth.

(d)   On the chart below (figure 8.4), draw a line connecting two of the four
points (A, B, C, D) to show the general relationship of environmental
resistance and population density.

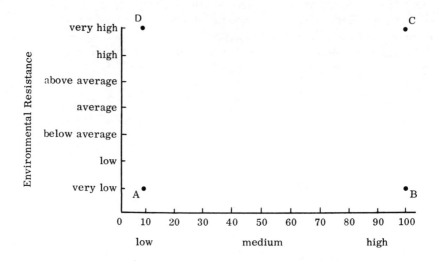

Figure 8.4   Environmental resistance and population density

— — — — — — — — — — — — — — — — — — — —

(a) biotic potential, environmental resistance;   (b) biotic potential;
(c) exponential;   (d) You should have drawn a line connecting points
A and C to indicate that when population density is low, environmental
resistance is also low, and that when population density increases, environmental resistance also increases.

3.   A common population growth pattern is the S-shaped curve.
This is typical of an organism in a new environment. This
curve begins with a slow rate of growth (the lag phase), experiences very rapid exponential growth (the logarithmic
phase), and then levels off (the equilibrium level).

If individuals of a population are introduced into an area suitable for their
growth and reproduction, we can reasonably predict an increase in their numbers as time passes, and we can determine several characteristics descrip-
tive of that growth. Population growth can be plotted on a graph as a curve
relating the numbers of individuals to the passage of time. The best curves
result from laboratory populations that are easy to grow and have a very
short life cycle. For example, figure 8.5 on the next page shows a study of
the growth of yeast cells.

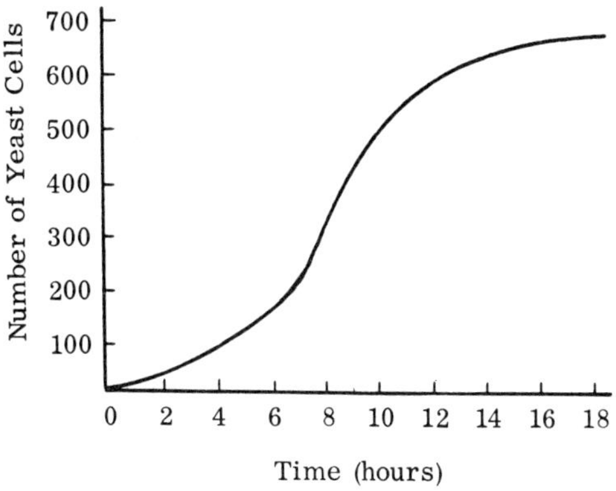

Figure 8.5 S-shaped growth curve of
yeast cells in a laboratory setting

This growth curve takes the form of an S and is thus called an S-shaped
curve. This is a very typical growth pattern for any organism in a new and
favorable environment. The curve clearly has three phases:

> lag phase: a slow initial phase of growth in which the organisms are
> acclimating to a new environment (1-4 hours on figure 8.5)

> logarithmic phase: a period of rapid exponential growth following the
> lag phase (called logarithmic because it would appear as a straight line
> on a logarithmic graph) (4-10 hours on figure 8.5)

> equilibrium level: a phase of gradual leveling off at some set point
> (10-18 hours on figure 8.5)

The curve tells us the total number of organisms in the population at any
given time on the graph. It can also tell us something about the rate of population growth. The steeper the curve, the faster the population is growing.
Thus, the rate of growth is greater between the sixth hour and the eighth
hour than it is between the second hour and the fourth hour. After the four-
teenth hour, the population levels off at about 650 individuals. Its growth
rate at this point is zero.

At the equilibrium level, we say the population has reached the maximum
density that the environment can support. This is usually referred to as the
carrying capacity of the environment and is the environmental "set point" of
the demostat model. Of course, this is really an oversimplification—a population almost never really levels off and maintains a static size. Rather,
it tends to vary around the set point as we would expect when we consider the
interaction and time lag between the elements of the demostat. Figure 8.6
on the next page shows the growth curve of sheep introduced to Tasmania in
the 1800s and illustrates the oscillations one can expect in a natural population. An S-shaped curve is followed by a rough equilibrium.

Figure 8.6   The growth curve of sheep following their
introduction into Tasmania (After J. Davidson, 1938)

If the environment changes, the carrying capacity may also change. Figure 8.7 shows the response of three water flea populations to three different temperature conditions. Notice that all three populations show the typical S-shaped curve and all reach different equilibrium levels (different set points).

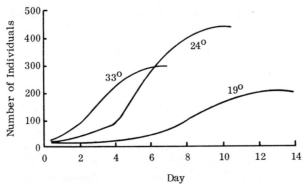

Figure 8.7   Growth of the water flea, Moina
macrocopa, at three different temperatures
(After A. Terao and T. Tanaka, 1928)

Figure 8.8 is an ideal growth curve of a single species population.

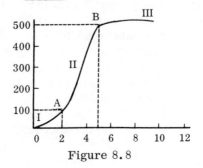

Figure 8.8

(a) The curve in figure 8.8 is called a(n) _____ growth curve.

(b) The horizontal axis represents _____.

(c) The vertical axis represents _____.

(d) Part I of the curve is the _____ phase.

(e) Part II of the curve is the _____ phase.

(f) Part III of the curve is the _____ phase.

(g) Population is growing fastest during which phase? _____

(h) Where on the curve is there zero population growth (ZPG)? _____

(i) The equilibrium phase describes the maximum density that the environment can support and therefore defines the _____ of the environment.

_ _ _ _ _ _ _ _ _ _ _ _ _ _ _ _ _ _

(a) S-shaped; (b) time; (c) numbers of individual organisms; (d) lag; (e) logarithmic; (f) equilibrium; (g) the logarithmic phase; (h) III; (i) carrying capacity

4.   The S-type of growth pattern is not universal to all populations. A J-shaped curve shows more dynamic growth and never levels off long enough to define a carrying capacity.

J-shaped growth curves are typical of many insect populations which produce only one generation of offspring per year. Plankton algae species that quickly replace each other in lake and ocean waters and bacteria in various solutions also show a J-shaped pattern. The early part of the growth curve in figure 8.9 on the next page shows some similarities to the previous S-shaped curve. Both the S and J curves have a similar phase of slow initial growth. Both proceed to a phase of rapid increase. But the final phase of the S-shaped curve is characterized by a gradual leveling off, while the J-shaped curve is marked by a sharp decline once a maximum value is reached.

One explanation for J-shaped curves is that many species have very specific environmental requirements. When the environment changes unfavorably, perhaps because of the population's own growth (accumulation of toxic waste products or exhaustion of food resources, for example), the population cannot continue to survive. A few individuals may persist (perhaps in some dormant state like an egg or spore), but the majority of the members making up the population dies. When conditions again become favorable, any survivors will start to grow. Organisms having a J-shaped growth curve usually have tremendous biotic potentials. From a systems point of view, the J-shaped curve represents an imperfect regulatory system in which adequate corrective (negative) feedback is absent, weak, or overly slow in responding.

The ideal S-shaped and J-shaped growth curves shown here are of the type generated in a laboratory under experimental conditions. Natural populations show growth patterns that are generally the same, but usually more complex because of the greater variety of environmental factors.

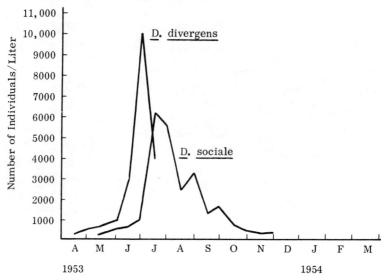

Figure 8.9 J-shaped growth curves of two
species of golden-brown algae, Dinobryon di-
vergens and D. sociale (After Stankovic, 1960)

Match the following:

_____ (a) population size

_____ (b) growth rate curve

_____ (c) J-shaped growth curve

_____ (d) growth rate

_____ (e) S-shaped growth curve

_____ (f) carrying capacity of the
environment

(1) shows rate of change over time
(2) number of individuals in a population
(3) change in population size per unit
of time
(4) population size at equilibrium level
(5) rapid population growth, then a leveling off at a more or less constant level
(6) sudden population drop to zero
(7) typical of species that have a big
burst of reproductivity at one
time during the year

- - - - - - - - - - - - - - - - - - -

(a) 2; (b) 1; (c) 6, 7; (d) 3; (e) 5; (f) 4

5.   The Rate of Population Change (called the Population Growth
Rate if the population is increasing) is calculated by subtracting the death rate from the birth rate and then adding
or subtracting the net migration rate. In human populations,
this rate is often calculated relative to 1000 members of the
population (called a "crude" rate) or calculated relative to
100 members of the population (called a percent rate).

We have been looking at growth curves (S-shaped curves, J-shaped curves), which plot the number of individuals on one axis and time on the other axis. Growth curves give us a picture of a population's size at any given time as well as showing us how it has changed with the passage of time. Although we can estimate from the curves how rapidly a population's size has changed, the curves do not show the specific rates of change.

We now want to consider the rate of population change—the change in the number of individuals making up a population over some specified period of time. If the overall number of individuals increases, we refer to the rate of population change as a growth rate.

Any natural population is constantly changing. The population gains new individuals by births and by immigration (individuals migrating into the area from another area). The population loses members by deaths and by emigration (individuals migrating out of the population's area). The rate of population change is the balance of these various effects.

RATE OF POPULATION CHANGE = BIRTH RATE minus DEATH RATE plus or minus NET MIGRATION RATE

When we refer to Rate of Population Growth, we are talking about a period of time in which the birth rate plus immigration exceeds the death rate plus emigration. Let's examine each of the components of population change. In doing so we will define the terms as they are used in the study of human populations.

Crude Birth Rate refers to the number of babies born in one year for each 1000 persons in a population at the midpoint of that year:[2]

$$\text{CRUDE BIRTH RATE} = \frac{\text{Number of births per year}}{\text{Total population}} \times 1000$$
(calculated at midpoint of year)

Crude Death Rate refers to the number of deaths in one year for each 1000 persons in a population.[3] This rate is also conventionally based on the size of the population taken at the midpoint of the given year:

$$\text{CRUDE DEATH RATE} = \frac{\text{Number of deaths per year}}{\text{Total population}} \times 1000$$
(calculated at midpoint of year)

Net Migration Rate refers to the difference between the number of people who enter a country (immigration) and the number who leave (emigration), per year per 1000 persons in the population:

---

2. The term Natality Rate is also used and is approximately synonymous, but is a more general term covering the production of new individuals whether by birth, hatching, germination, or by asexual reproduction. Birth rate is the term used in demography, the study of human populations.
3. Mortality Rate and Crude Death Rate are synonymous.

$$\text{NET MIGRATION RATE} = \frac{\text{Immigration} - \text{Emigration}}{\text{Total population}} \times 1000$$

(calculated at midpoint of year)

Net Migration can be either positive (with more immigrants than emigrants), or negative (with more people leaving than entering).

Obviously from these definitions, the rate of population change (or population growth rate if the change is positive as it usually is with human populations) is relative to 1000. Conventionally this figure is then divided by 10 to yield a _percent_ growth rate (the rate per 100 instead of the rate per 1000). Thus, in the United States in 1972, the Crude Birth Rate was 17.3 (per 1000). The Crude Death Rate was 9.3 (per 1000). The Net Migration Rate was 2.0 (per 1000). Thus the rate of population change (growth) can be calculated:

RATE OF POPULATION CHANGE = Birth Rate − Death Rate + Net
Migration Rate

$$= 17.3 - 9.3 + 2.0$$

$$= 10 \text{ (per 1000)}$$

When we divide 10 by 10 we get the U.S. percent growth rate of 1.0.

Complete the following formulas.

(a) Rate of Population Change = _____

_____

(b) Crude Birth Rate = _____

_____

In Mexico in 1972, the Crude Birth Rate was 43, the Crude Death Rate was 10, and the Net Migration Rate was 0.

(c) What was the rate of population change in Mexico in 1972?

_____ (per 1000)

(d) What was Mexico's percent growth rate? _____

- - - - - - - - - - - - - - - - - - - -

(a) Birth Rate minus Death Rate plus or minus Net Migration Rate;
(b) Number of babies born in one year for each 1000 persons in the population, or

$$\frac{\text{Number of births per year}}{\text{Total population}} \times 1000;$$

(c) 33;
(d) 3.3

6.   <u>Survivorship</u> <u>curves</u> help us study the number of organisms
     in a population that survive to any particular age (usually ex-
     pressed as survivors per 1000 members of a population).

The statistics we have been discussing are called "crude" for a reason.
We all know, for instance, that the probability of dying varies with many
things, especially age. Yet the <u>Crude</u> Death Rate is expressed as so many
deaths per 1000 members of a population regardless of their age or sex. To
further dissect a population's crude death rate, ecologists use life tables.
Patterned after insurance companies' actuarial tables, life tables state the
probability of dying by, and the life expectancy at, the end of a series of age
intervals. The details of these tables are clearly beyond the scope of this
book, but we should look at one interesting tool derived from them. Because
ecologists are interested in the survival as well as the death of organisms,
mortality can also be expressed as a <u>survivorship</u> <u>curve</u>. Using data from
the life table, a survivorship curve expresses the number of survivors expected from a given sized population (usually 1000) at the end of various age
intervals. It is assumed that all the individuals are of the same age and
equally healthy. These curves take on several basic forms which supply us
with much information on the organisms' life history.

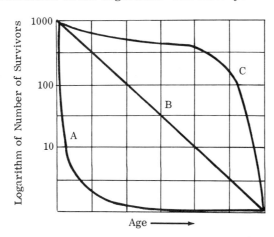

Figure 8.10   Three different survivorship curves

Figure 8.10 shows three survivorship curves. Survivorship curve A is
typical of many invertebrate and plant populations and reflects a very high
mortality rate during the embryonic, infant, and juvenile stages of life followed by a very low mortality rate once the organism reaches adulthood. An
oyster is a good example of this type. Until a larva attaches itself on a rock
it is very likely that it will die, but once attached it has a very high probability of surviving to a relatively old age.

The straight line relationship of curve B represents a situation in which
the mortality rate remains constant throughout the organism's life span.
This pattern rarely occurs in nature but if it did the Crude Death Rate would
not be a bad approximation.

The pattern shown by curve C is typical of many large mammal populations in which most individuals are able to live out their physiological life span. Starved fruit flies in the laboratory and mountain sheep of Alaska are classic examples of populations that show this right-angle curve. Perhaps most interesting to us, however, is that this survivorship curve is typical of industrialized man. Mortality in infants, juveniles, and elderly humans of fifty and sixty has been reduced in industrialized society so that a higher and higher percentage of individuals are realizing their potential life span.

One common fallacy prevalent today is that the wonders of modern medicine have drastically increased the duration of human life. Although the average life span (life expectancy) of industrialized man has been raised, there is no evidence of a substantial increase in his physiological life span. Because more people are surviving to the age of 70 and 80, more deaths are concentrating around the life span limit, thus raising the average age of death. But we are still and probably always will be searching for that fountain of youth to expand man's potential life span.

(a) Survivorship curves give us a way to study _____

_____.

(b) Describe industrialized man's survivorship curve in general terms.

_____

_____

(c) Examine this very hypothetical survivorship curve for population R.

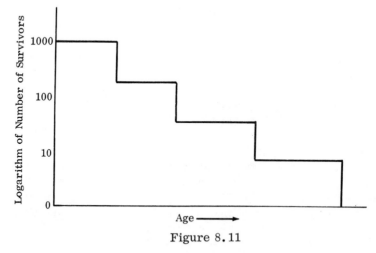

Figure 8.11

Describe what's happening in figure 8.11—in general terms.

_____

_____

- - - - - - - - - - - - - - - - - - -

_____

(a) the number of organisms of a population that survive to any particular age;

(b) a few fatalities in the early years, followed by a period when nearly everyone survives, followed by a period when everyone dies in a relatively short time (curve C on figure 8.10);

(c) Population R is surviving by steps. Every so often a large portion of the population dies and thereafter the survivors live until another sharp death toll occurs. (A real population that might show such a pattern might be a farmer's population of frying chickens, which he kills and sells at fixed periods.)

7.   Fertility rate describes the births per 1000 female members of a population who are capable of giving birth to young (ages 15-45).

Ecologically speaking, an organism's life has three periods: pre-reproductive, reproductive, and post-reproductive. The relative lengths of these periods vary from species to species. In human beings, the pre-reproductive period (birth to about 15 years) takes up about 21 percent of a 70-year mean life span. The reproductive period (15-45 years) takes up about 42 percent, and the post-reproductive period takes up about 37 percent. Any human reproductive rate depends on (1) the birth rate of females in the reproductive age group, and (2) the proportion of women in a particular population who are in the reproductive (childbearing) period of their lives. The fertility rate is a more refined indicator of birth trends than the birth rate because it describes the birth rate of only those within a population who are actually capable of bearing young.

Define fertility rate. _____

_____

- - - - - - - - - - - - - - - - - -

Fertility rate describes the birth rate of the female members of a population who are actually capable of bearing young.

8.   Populations are not composed of individuals of equal age as in the theoretical populations of life tables. In reality, generations overlap, so that populations display an age structure. This structure is described by the percentage of the population in different age classes, usually shown as age pyramids. Based on proportions, these pyramids provide an easy means of comparing different populations' age structures.

The typical age pyramids for expanding, stable, and declining populations are shown in figure 8.12 on the following page. A population that has maintained a high birth rate for some time acquires the age structure of pyramid A in which each succeeding generation is larger than the preceding one. If the rate of population growth decreases and approaches zero (ZPG), a stabi-

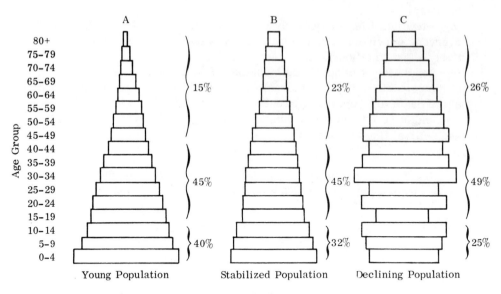

Figure 8.12   Age pyramids comparing young,
stabilized, and declining human populations

lized structure develops in which the pre-reproductive and reproductive age
groups become more or less equal in size, as in pyramid B. Declining populations occur when the birth rate continues to fall until the proportion of
reproductive and post-reproductive segments of the population are higher
than the pre-reproductive.

The age structure of a population is important if we want to predict future
population trends. Projections based on only crude growth rates can be quite
misleading. For example, there has recently been some rather naive and/or
optimistic heralding of the end of the population explosion in the United States.
The basis of this optimism is the steady and substantial drop in the birth rate
through the 1950s and 1960s. It is true that in 1968, after a steady decline
of 25 percent since 1959 (see figure 8.13), the crude birth rate hit a record
low of 17.5 (the previous low was 18.4 in the depression in 1936). You may
wonder if this decrease is due primarily to a smaller number of women in
their peak childbearing years or to a smaller number of children being born
to each woman in the reproductive group. For example, a population could
have a crude birth rate of 18 as a result of a fertility rate of 120 with the females from 15-45 years making up 15 percent of the population ($120 \times 15\%$ =
18) or a fertility rate of 60 with women 15-45 equaling 30 percent of the population ($60 \times 30\%$ = 18). A thorough investigation of the U.S. birth rate un-
covers that the recent decreases have resulted from both. The fertility rate
has been on a downward trend since the mid-1950s and was 85 in 1968 (figure
8.14). It rose to 87 in 1970. At the same time, the percentage of the population in childbearing years dropped to 20 percent in 1968, compared to 24
percent in 1936. The fertility rate in the depression was well below 80; so it

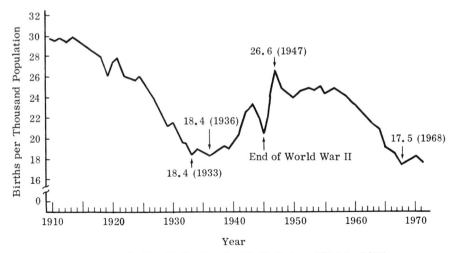

Figure 8.13   U.S. Crude Birth Rate, 1910 to 1971

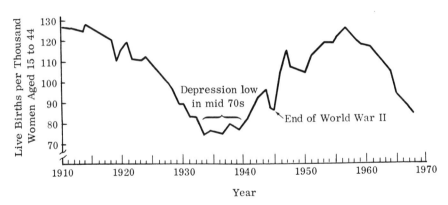

Figure 8.14   U.S. fertility rate, 1910 to 1968

is mainly the smaller proportion of U.S. females in their prime reproductive years that has caused the recent decrease in the U.S. birth rate.

Future growth is affected by the age structure of a population. Figure 8.15 on the next page shows the age structure of the U.S. population in 1960. The large "bulge" in the 0-14 age class represents the age group that will be reproducing in the 1970s and 1980s. The accompanying table shows the increasing number of women in their peak reproductive years in 1970 and 1980. It is obvious therefore that a hope of subsiding population growth is indeed premature. Given the normal consequences of the population's age structure, unless a really drastic reduction in the fertility rate occurs (or a considerable increase in the death rate), we are destined to experience an increase in the growth rate of the United States population for some time to come. Indeed, if every U.S. couple began tomorrow to only replace themselves (an average of about 2 children per family), the population would be 70 years in reaching equilibrium at 300 million. Figure 8.16 on page 167 helps explain the mo-

Number of U.S. women in
peak reproductive years
(ages 20-29) between 1930-1980

Year	Numbers in Millions
1930	10.0
1940	11.5
1950	12.1
1960	11.0
1970	15.5
1980	20.1

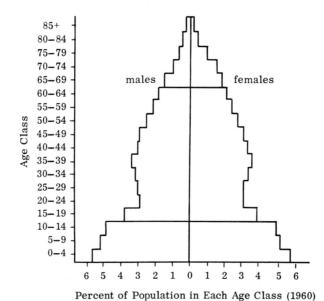

Percent of Population in Each Age Class (1960)

Figure 8.15   Age composition of the U.S. population
in 1960   (After Thompson and Lewis, 1965)

mentum, which is primarily due to the fact that 29 percent of the U.S. population is under 15 years of age. The world situation is even more alarming because approximately 37 percent of the world's population comprises the base of the population pyramid. They are future parents—the fuel for the future population explosion.

1. An average of 2 children per family would slow population growth, but would not stop it soon because the number of people of childbearing age is increasing . . .

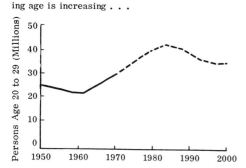

2. . . . so even if family size drops to a 2-child average . . .

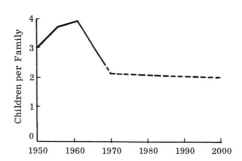

3. . . . the resulting births will continue to exceed deaths for the rest of this century . . .

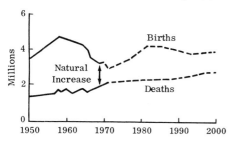

4. . . . so the population will still be growing in the year 2000, but at a decreasing rate.

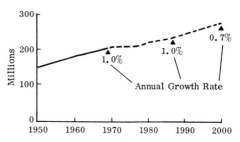

Figure 8.16   Why the U.S. population will keep expanding even with the 2-child family (From Interim Report of the President's Commission on Population Growth and the American Future, 1971)

Examine the three actual population pyramids in figure 8.17 on the next page, so that you can answer the questions below.

(a) Identify the countries in the blanks below.
   (1) typical underdeveloped country, very rapid growth rate

   _____

   (2) typical older developed country, low birth and death rates for several decades _____

(b) Assuming (they don't actually) that all three countries had the same size populations and the same food resources available, which would reach a food crisis sooner? (1) _____ Which would be best able to handle its food problems? (2) _____

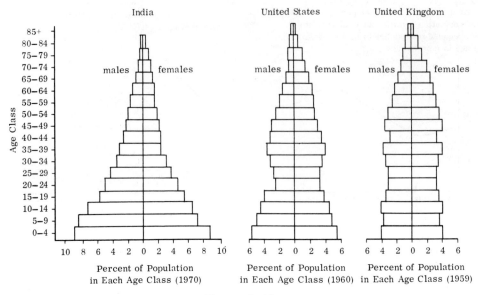

Figure 8.17

(c) Combining what we learned about <u>fertility rate</u> and population pyramids, assuming that all three countries had the <u>same fertility rate</u>, would that mean they faced equally bright or dim futures? _____

Why? _____

_____

(d) There has been much in the news lately about the U.S. population reaching zero population growth (ZPG). The average number of children per U.S. family has fallen from 2.9 in 1965 to 2.3 in 1971, but we are still a long way from a sustained ZPG. Why? _____

_____

_____

- - - - - - - - - - - - - - - - - - - -

(a) (1) India, (2) United Kingdom; (b) (1) India, (2) U.K.; (c) No, a set fertility rate would produce about the same numbers of births in the U.K. over the next few years, but in the U.S. births would increase (numbers reproducing × fertility rate) as the next generation began reproducing. In India, the results will obviously be tragic. (d) because of the momentum built into the population's age structure: The number of people of childbearing age is due to increase for some time to come.

SELF-TEST

This Self-Test is designed to show you whether or not you have mastered this chapter's objectives. Answer each question to the best of your ability. Correct answers and review instructions are given at the end of the test.

1. Define population. _____

    _____

    _____

2. Define evolution and explain its relation to the process of natural selec-

    tion and differential reproduction. _____

    _____

    _____

    _____

3. Define and explain the relationship between biotic potential, environmental

    resistance, and population growth. _____

    _____

    _____

    _____

4. Explain the relationship between population density and environmental re-

    sistance. _____

    _____

5. Examine the unlabeled diagram of the demostat model in figure 8.18.

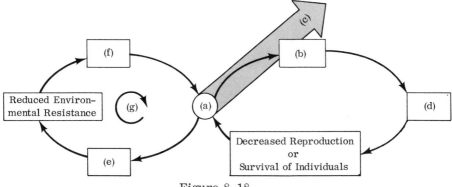

Figure 8.18

On the next page, identify and explain each of the numbered components.

(a) _____

_____

(b) _____

_____

(c) _____

_____

(d) _____

_____

(e) _____

_____

(f) _____

_____

(g) The entire loop is _____ .

6. Examine figure 8.19 below. Identify it and explain what it implies about a population. What part of the curve relates to carrying capacity?

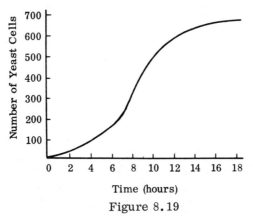

Figure 8.19

_____

_____

_____

_____

7. Examine figure 8.20 on the next page. Identify it and explain what it implies about population.

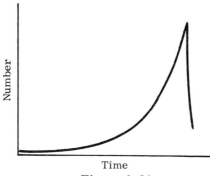

Time

Figure 8.20

_____

_____

_____

_____

8. Define rate of population change. _____

_____

_____

9. What is the relationship between rate of population change and the rate of population growth? _____

_____

10. Examine the survivorship curves in figure 8.21 and answer the questions which follow.

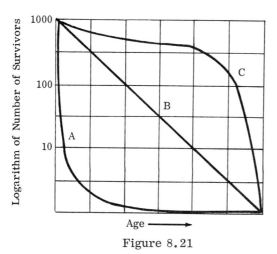

Figure 8.21

(a) What does a survivorship curve show? _____

_____

_____

(b) Explain curve A. _____

_____

(c) Explain curve B. _____

_____

(d) Explain curve C. _____

_____

11. Define fertility rate and explain its importance. _____

_____

_____

_____

12. Examine the age pyramid in figure 8.22

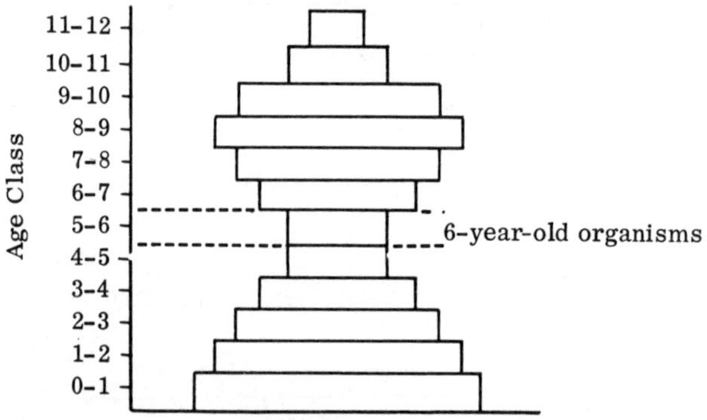

Figure 8.22

(a) What does an age pyramid show? _____

_____

(b) Explain the age pyramid in figure 8.22. Indicate roughly what sort
of change will occur in the 6-year-old age group in about four years.

_____

_____

_____

_____

ANSWERS TO SELF-TEST

Compare your answers to the questions on the Self-Test with the answers given below. If all of your answers are correct, you are ready to go on to the next chapter. If you missed any questions, review the frames indicated in parentheses following the answer. If you miss several questions, you should probably reread the entire chapter carefully.

1. A population is a group of interbreeding individuals of the same species that occupy a specific area. (frame 1)

2. Evolution is the process by which species populations change their characteristics in the course of time. Natural selection is the process by which adaptive traits are selected for, resulting in the differential reproduction of those traits that give individuals an advantage in coping with their environment. (frame 1)

3. Biotic potential refers to the ability of organisms to reproduce themselves under optimal conditions. Environmental resistance refers to the biotic and abiotic factors that keep organisms from reaching or continuing at their biotic potential. Population growth is the increase or decrease in the total number of organisms in a population due to the interplay between biotic potential and environmental resistance. (frame 2)

4. As population density increases, environmental resistance increases. (frame 2)

5. (a) set point—zero population growth—the average number of a population in a given area averaged over a number of years
    (b) biotic potential—reproduction—positive feedback—the tendency of a population to increase its numbers rapidly
    (c) overpopulation—an increase in population that is subject to negative feedback control mechanisms (i.e., within the system's homeostatic plateau)
    (d) increased environmental resistance—a negative feedback mechanism that goes into action to reverse the tendency of the population to increase its numbers
    (e) Severe, abnormal environmental resistance results in underpopulation—a tendency away from set point that results in decreased numbers of organisms (another example of positive feedback).
    (f) increased reproduction or survival of individuals resulting from a reduction in environmental resistance—a movement of population numbers back toward the set point
    (g) a negative feedback loop
    (frame 2)

6. It is an S-shaped curve. It shows a population growing slowly at first (lag phase), then increasing rapidly (logarithmic phase), and then leveling off around some set point (the equilibrium phase or level). The equilibrium level is assumed to represent the carrying capacity of the environment. (frame 3)

7. It is a J-shaped curve. It shows a population that is experiencing very rapid growth. The population is growing at an exponential rate—it will sooner or later outstrip some limited resource and then the population will collapse. This curve does not have an equilibrium level. Populations that experience this positive feedback situation usually end up extinct or with very few surviving members. (frame 4)

8. The rate of population change equals the birth rate minus the death rate plus or minus the net migration rate; thus:
   Rate of pop. change = birth rate − death rate ± net migration rate
   (frame 5)

9. When the rate of population change is positive it is called the rate of population growth. (frame 5)

10. (a) A survivorship curve shows the number of organisms that are surviving at any particular age.
    (b) Survivorship curve A shows a population whose members die rapidly at a young age. Those few organisms that survive to "middle age," however, live a long time.
    (c) Survivorship curve B shows a population whose members die at a steady rate from birth to death.
    (d) Survivorship curve C shows a population with a low infant mortality rate, whose members live a long time and then all die at some older age. (frame 6)

11. Fertility rate is the birth rate per 1000 female members of a population who are capable of reproducing. Fertility rate is a more refined indicator of birth trends because it describes the rate of the childbearing members of a population. (frame 7)

12. (a) An age pyramid shows the percentage of a population in different age classes.
    (b) The age pyramid shows a population with a large number of young members, relatively fewer 4, 5, 6, and 7-year-old members, and a large number of older (8, 9, 10-year-old) members. In four years the 6-year-old age group will be much larger as the presently large group of 2-year-olds become 6-year-olds. (frame 8)

CHAPTER NINE
Factors Affecting Population Size

OBJECTIVES

When you complete this chapter, you will be able to

- describe environmental resistance, extrinsic environmental resistance (factors), and intrinsic environmental resistance (factors);

- explain the Law of Tolerances;

- identify and discuss some of the abiotic factors that can limit an organism;

- define symbiotic relationship;

- identify and cite possible examples of each of the following terms: cooperation, amensalism, competition, predation, commensalism, parasitism, and mutualism;

- discriminate between intraspecific and interspecific competition;

- explain the Competitive Exclusion Principle and the process of niche differentiation;

- discuss territory and nucleated territory;

- describe how stress from increasing social density may operate as a factor of intrinsic environmental resistance.

If you think that you have already mastered these objectives and might skip all or part of this chapter, turn to page 207 at the end of the chapter and take the Self-Test. The results will allow you to evaluate your current knowledge of this chapter's contents. If you answer all of the questions correctly, you are ready to begin the next chapter. If you miss any questions, you should study the frames indicated after the answers to the Self-Test.

If this material is new to you, or if you choose not to take the Self-Test now, proceed to frame 1.

1.　　Environmental resistance refers to all of the biotic and abiotic factors in an environment that tend to decrease the fertility and survival of the individuals in a population. The two general types of environmental resistance factors are (1) extrinsic factors (affecting a population from outside itself), and (2) intrinsic factors (affecting a population from within).

We have discussed the growth patterns of populations just establishing themselves in a new habitat or recovering from some major disaster. Most populations, however, have already established themselves and are varying about their set point, the degree of fluctuation depending on the efficiency of the negative feedback mechanisms. Later we will discuss the working of these mechanisms, but first let us look at some of the factors that make up the negative feedback element of environmental resistance.

The factors that operate to decrease fertility and survival of the individuals comprising a population have been a major concern of population ecologists for many decades. The major controversy in the field has centered around the relative importance of two types of factors making up environmental resistance:

- Extrinsic Factors: those factors that operate on the population from outside it. Examples: climate, predation, available food supply, disease

- Intrinsic Factors: those factors that are generated within the population itself. Examples: territoriality, social stress

(a) Define environmental resistance. _____

_____

_____

(b) A deer wandering onto a highway and being killed is an example of what kind of environmental resistance? _____

– – – – – – – – – – – – – – – – – – – –

(a) those extrinsic and intrinsic environmental factors that operate to decrease the fertility and survival of individuals comprising a population, some of these factors being abiotic and some biotic

(b) extrinsic environmental resistance

2.　　If environmental conditions become extreme, certain organisms will perish. This general concept is called the Law of Tolerances: For each abiotic factor, an organism has a range of tolerances within which it can survive. Toward the upper or lower extreme of this tolerance range that abiotic factor tends to limit the organism's chance of survival.

We will begin our consideration of environmental resistance by looking at the effects of certain abiotic factors on the presence and the breeding success of organisms in certain locations. Remember, however, that the effect of any of these abiotic factors on an organism or population may be considerably altered by the presence of one or more biotic factors.

The Law of Tolerances evolved primarily from the work of two men, Justus von Liebig, a German organic chemist, and V. E. Shelford, an American ecologist. In 1840, von Liebig formulated what is called the Law of the Minimum. He stated that the growth of a plant was dependent on that foodstuff which was available to it in the minimum quantity. That is, an organism has many requirements, and if any one of them is in short supply, that one will limit the organism's development, regardless of the abundance of other needed foodstuffs. In 1913, V. E. Shelford expanded this concept into the Law of Tolerances by adding the idea that too much of something may be just as limiting as too little. Thus, the Law of Tolerances recognizes that organisms have an ecological maximum, as well as a minimum. They can live and grow only within a tolerance range defined by the extremes of the abiotic factors upon which they are dependent.

The wider an organism's tolerance range for a given factor, the more likely that the organism will be able to survive environmental variations of that factor. Through his technology, man has artificially broadened his tolerance to many factors so that he can survive almost anywhere on (or in the case of astronauts, off) the planet.[1] Some fish, on the other hand, have such a narrow tolerance for temperature change that a deviation of more than a few degrees will eliminate an entire population.

As an organism's upper or lower tolerance limit for a particular abiotic factor is approached, that factor is said to exert a limiting influence upon the organism. Suppose, for example, that a farmer plants corn in a field containing too little phosphorus. Even though the corn crop's requirements for water, temperature, and other nutrients are met, the crop will continue to grow only until it has used up the available phosphorus. The corn's growth, in this situation, is said to be limited by phosphorus.

Not only do organisms have a tolerance range, they also have a smaller optimum range within which they function best. This optimum range may vary from one season to another and from one stage of an organism's development to another. Human infants, for example, have a much narrower tolerance range for temperature than adult humans. An organism's tolerance range can also vary at different developmental stages. For example, adult blue crabs can tolerate fresh or brackish (partly salty) water with a high chloride content, and they are often found in rivers far from the ocean. The blue crab larvae, however, cannot live in fresh water, so the blue crab can never reproduce there. Because of its wider tolerance range, the adult blue crab is more widely dispersed than the blue crab larvae.

Generally speaking, the wider an organism's tolerance range, the more widely dispersed the organism will be. The converse of this statement is also generally true, that is, organisms will always tend (conditions permit-

---

1. Actually we could say that man's tolerances remain unchanged, but that man has circumvented the limits by wearing clothing and so forth.

ting) to disperse themselves across an area that meets the requirements of their tolerance limits.

Figure 9.1 summarizes our discussion of abiotic factors and the Law of Tolerances. We have seen that an organism's tolerance range determines its ability to function under varying conditions. The geographic distribution of various limiting factors will determine, to a certain extent, where the organisms will be found. The geographic distribution of the optimum range will largely determine in what locations the organism will occur in the greatest numbers.

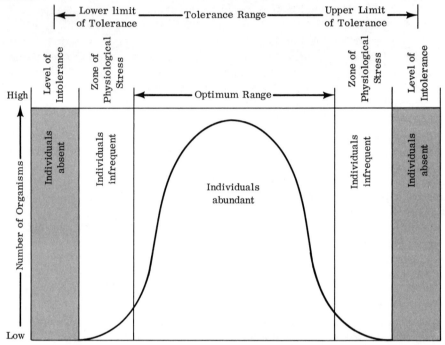

Figure 9.1   Distribution of a population
throughout its tolerance range

We expect any organism's reproduction to be curtailed and his survival threatened in the presence of conditions falling near either its high or low tolerance limit. Likewise, organisms will usually be most abundant in their optimum range. But the environment is always changing, and at any given moment it is possible that one or more physical variables are transcending some organism's optimum range and thereby decreasing the number of individuals present.

(a)   Define the Law of Tolerances. _____

_____

_____

_____

_____

(b) Organism A needs food, a temperature between 75° and 90°F, and nutrients X, Y, and Z. Examine figure 9.2, which graphically describes an environment E.

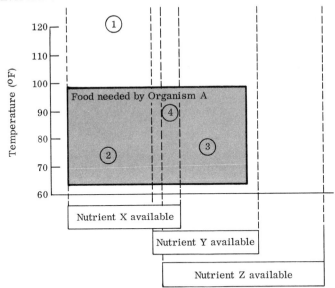

Figure 9.2 Graphic representation of environment E

(1) Could organism A live at point ①? What factors would limit him here, if any? _____

(2) Could organism A live at point ②? What factors would limit him here, if any? _____

(3) Could organism A live at point ③? What factors would limit him here, if any? _____

(4) Could organism A live at point ④? What factors would limit him here, if any? _____

— — — — — — — — — — — — — — — — — — —

(a) For each abiotic factor, an organism has a range of tolerances within which it can survive. As an organism approaches the upper or lower extreme of its tolerance range for a particular factor, that factor exerts a limiting influence on the organism's survival.

(b) (1) no, temperature, food, and nutrients Y and Z; (2) no, nutrients Y and Z; (3) no, nutrient X; (4) yes, none

3. Climatic change is one extrinsic factor of environmental resistance. Many factors contribute to what we call climate; two major factors are temperature and moisture. Usually they interact. In very hot or cold areas, for example, it is difficult for organisms to obtain moisture. On the other hand, the presence of large quantities of moisture tends to make the tempera-

ture less extreme. Organisms have evolved many complex
ways of extending their tolerances of climatic conditions.

All organisms live within a range of temperature tolerance. Few species
can exist for great lengths of time in temperatures below 32° Fahrenheit or
above 130° Fahrenheit. As temperature decreases, the speed of all chemical reactions, including the life functions, slows down. Hence, plants are
not productive and certain animals hibernate in winter temperatures. Animals
cannot live at very high temperatures, because when temperature increases
to about 150° Fahrenheit it destroys the enzymes essential for life.

Different organisms have different temperature tolerance limits; moreover, the optimum temperature for any organism may vary during its development. For example, the most favorable range for brook trout is between
57° and 62°F, but brook trout eggs develop best at 46°F. Similar variations
in temperature tolerance exist in the plant kingdom. Some cereal seeds,
for example, do not sprout unless they are chilled by winter temperatures.
Consequently, seeds sown in early spring, rather than in the fall, will not
sprout.

The way a species deals with temperature variations depends on its physiology. The body temperatures of most invertebrates, including most fish,
reptiles, and amphibians vary with external conditions. They have no internal
temperature regulating mechanism. These cold-blooded (poikilothermal) animals become inactive at temperatures outside the range of 43° to 108° Fahrenheit. Warm-blooded (homeothermal) animals have internal cybernetic
mechanisms for keeping body temperature constant regardless of the outside
temperature. (See frame 8, Chapter 1.) Birds and mammals are warm-
blooded organisms and most are generally active throughout all seasons.
Should the internal regulatory mechanism fail, the organism dies.

Moisture is another climatic factor. Since water is the major ingredient
in living tissue, it is required by all living things. Many desert plants overcome their dry environment by having a short life cycle—they grow during
the rainy season, and survive the dry weather by remaining in dormant seed
form. Other desert plants, such as cacti, draw in water when available and
conserve it through the dry season. Desert animals overcome the problem
of dryness by being active only between sunset and sunrise, the coolest part
of the day—thus decreasing their demand for water. What water they do need
is obtained through the breakdown of the food they eat (metabolic water) and
retained through adaptations that concentrate urine and reuse "waste" water.

Aquatic animals also have problems with water supply. The salt concentration of fresh water is lower than the concentration in the bodies of freshwater fish. Because of this difference, external fluids tend to pass through
the tissue membranes of freshwater fish, diluting the internal body fluids.
Freshwater organisms must therefore remove this excess water that enters
their bodies. Saltwater fish have the opposite problem—the high salt concentration in the surrounding water causes a water loss and a resulting higher
salt concentration in the bodies of the fish. Thus, regulatory mechanisms
of animals in the open sea work to excrete excess salts and retain water.

Because temperature and moisture are easy to measure, the tendency in the past has been to study them as separate influences on the ecosystem. In reality, the interaction between the two determines the effect on an organism. Lack of moisture, for example, is a greater problem when temperatures are either high or low. Similarly, an animal's resistance to high or low temperatures is affected by the moisture in the air.

We must also consider the effect of temperature on the availability of water. Evaporation, the loss of water vapor to the air, is a function of temperature as we saw in Chapter 6. The higher the temperature the more water escapes into the air from the land surfaces. Thus the ecological effectiveness of rainfall varies with the temperature that prevails during the rainy season. For example, only part of the rain falling during the summer is available to land organisms, since much of it quickly evaporates. But in winter, when evaporation is minimized, downpours are largely left for use on land. In extremely cold areas water that exists only in a frozen state is largely unavailable to organisms. The seasonal variation in the interaction of just these two factors indicates the complexity of environmental influences, which should caution you against the simplified approach of isolating one factor at a time and then assuming that the total effect is merely the sum of all the individual factors.

(a) Climate is composed of many factors. Name two. _____

_____

(b) Warm-blooded animals usually have much wider temperature tolerances than cold-blooded animals. Would you expect the animals of the Arctic

to be warm-blooded or cold-blooded? _____

(c) Explain how two climatic factors could interact to make a desert a difficult environment for you. _____

_____

_____

— — — — — — — — — — — — — — — — — —

(a) temperature, moisture; (b) warm-blooded; (c) In the desert the high temperatures evaporate moisture quickly. The scarcity of water would also hinder your ability to cope with higher temperatures, since water is needed for cooling.

4. Nutrients are abiotic substances that are necessary for the growth and reproduction of plants and animals. The supply of nutrients is maintained by their movement within biogeochemical cycles from the nonliving to the living parts of an ecosystem and back again. The most important nutrients are classified as either: (1) macronutrients—required in relatively large quantities, or (2) micronutrients—required in relatively small quantities.

Because certain nutrients are essential to organisms, they are potential extrinsic limiting factors. An acre of grassland must supply seven grazing sheep with 0.01 ounce of cobalt per year. If cobalt is in short supply, the sheep become anemic and eventually die. Other nutrients such as sulfur are limiting in oversupply as well as undersupply. Vegetation exposed to an overconcentration (one part per million) of sulfur in the air die. We have also seen the disastrous effects that excessive concentrations of sulfur-laden smog can have on human beings.

Figure 9.3 lists many important nutrients and the amounts of each required to grow 100 bushels of corn. The table does not show all of the important nutrients nor all of the known uses.

Nutrient	Number of pounds needed to grow 100 bushels of corn	Function
• Macronutrients		
Nitrogen (N)	160	Structural component of amino acids and many hormones
Phosphorus (P)	40	Structural component of ATP
Potassium (K)	125	Maintenance of ionic balance between the cell and its surroundings
Sulfur (S)	75	Structural component of some amino acids, vitamins, enzymes
Magnesium (Mg)	50	Structural component of chlorophyll
Calcium (Ca)	50	Influences chemical flow through body
Iron (Fe)	2	Structural component of some enzymes

Nutrient	Number of pounds needed to grow 100 bushels of corn	Function
• Micronutrients		
Manganese (Mn)	0.3	Needed in cellular respiration and photosynthesis
Boron (B)	0.06	Function unknown
Chlorine (Cl)	0.06	Maintenance of balance between cellular and extra cellular fluids
Sodium (Na)	0.06	
Zinc (Zn)	Trace	Necessary for synthesis of some of the amino acids
Copper (Cu)	Trace	Structural component of many enzymes
Molybdenum (Mo)	Trace	Structural component of the enzyme that reduces nitrate to nitrite; essential for fixation of nitrogen by nitrogen-fixing bacteria

Figure 9.3 Amount and function of some Macronutrients and Micronutrients needed to grow 100
bushels of corn (Adapted from Keeton, 1967)

(a) What are nutrients? _____

_____

(b) Why do nutrient supplies continue to be available after organisms have

been using them for so many millions of years? _____

_____

(c) Name three important nutrients. _____

_____

– – – – – – – – – – – – – – – – – – – –

(a) substances necessary for the growth and reproduction of plants and animals (organisms); (b) They are constantly cycling (renewing themselves). (c) Any nutrient listed in figure 9.3 is acceptable.

5.　　　Whenever one population interacts with another, one or both of them will change in their ability to grow and survive. If the population benefits from an interaction, its growth rate will tend to increase. If it is harmed, its growth rate will tend to decrease. Thus, interacting species act as biotic extrinsic limiting factors for each other. All relationships between organisms are referred to as symbiotic (living together) relationships.

Some interactions between species are mutually helpful, some have mixed effects, and some are mutually harmful. The following table lists the different types of interactions that can occur between two single species populations.

Type of Interaction	Immediate Effects of Interaction (Pop. 1/Pop. 2)	Definition
1. Cooperation	+/+	Each population benefits. The interaction is optional for both species.
2. Mutualism	+/+	Each population benefits. The interaction is necessary for the survival and growth of each species.
3. Commensalism	+/0	One population benefits; the other is unaffected.
4. Amensalism	-/0	One population is inhibited; the other is unaffected.
5. Competition	-/-	One population eliminates another; in the process both suffer.
6. Predation 7. Parasitism	+/-	One population benefits. The interaction is necessary for the survival of the predator or the parasite.

The first column names the type of interaction. The second column shows the general effects of the interaction on both populations. This is represented by a combination of two of three possible symbols: a positive sign, a negative sign, and a zero. A + indicates that the population's growth rate is increased, a - indicates that the growth rate is decreased, and a 0 indicates no effect. The third column defines the type of interaction.

The interactions that have a negative effect (to oppose the positive feedback of reproduction) on one or both of the interacting populations are probably the most effective in determining long-term stability in a community. For this reason, although we will consider all seven types of interactions, we will concentrate on the last three types (competition, predation, and parasitism), emphasizing their important role as extrinsic environmental resistance factors.

(a)   Match the following:

   _____ (1) cooperation   A. (-/0)

   _____ (2) amensalism   B. (+/+)

   _____ (3) competition   C. (-/-)

   _____ (4) predation   D. (+/0)

   _____ (5) commensalism   E. (+/-)

   _____ (6) parasitism

   _____ (7) mutualism

(b)   All relationships between organisms may be referred to as _____

   _____ relationships.

(c)   Because one species population serves as environmental resistance for another when they interact, we can say that species interaction is one

   type of _____.

(d)   Which of the following are true? The interaction of two populations:

   _____ (1) affects only organisms in the ecosystem outside of the population involved.
   _____ (2) affects only the populations involved.
   _____ (3) is necessary for the survival of both populations involved.
   _____ (4) has an influence on the growth and survival of both populations involved in the interaction and also affects the stability of the ecosystem as a whole.

- - - - - - - - - - - - - - - - -

(a) (1) B;   (2) A;   (3) C;   (4) E;   (5) D;   (6) E;   (7) B;   (b) symbiotic;   (c) extrinsic environmental resistance, clearly a biotic extrinsic factor;   (d) (4)

6.   In cooperation (+/+), both species benefit. However, they
      are not dependent on one another, and the interaction is not
      necessary for their survival. Each is able to survive sep-
      arately, but cooperative interaction increases both of their
      growth rates.

An example of cooperation is the relationship between crabs and coelenterates such as hydra or sea anemone. The coelenterates live on the top side
of a crab's body and serve as camouflage for the crab's protection. When the
crab eats a captured animal, bits of this food are made available to the coelenterates.

Several examples of cooperation occur in the African savanna, where herds
of browsing and grazing animals (impalas, gazelles, giraffes, baboons, etc.)
mix together, each providing its own unique warning system to the association.
Any one population, however, could survive without associating with any of
the others.

An old woodsman is fond of a chipmunk that lives near his cabin. Occa-
sionally he throws out bread crumbs for it. When it is going to rain, the old
woodsman knows because the chipmunk chatters a lot.

(a) What kind of relationship is this? Explain. _____

_____

(b) How is it symbolized? __(/)__

— — — — — — — — — — — — — — — — — —

   (a) It is a type of cooperation. Both species benefit but neither is dependent upon the other.   (b) (+/+)

7.   In mutualism (+/+), both species benefit. In this relation-
      ship, however, the two species are so dependent upon each
      other that they cannot live apart. The interaction is the re-
      sult of a long evolutionary history and has become a necessity
      for the survival of both populations.

An example of mutualism is the interaction between nitrogen-fixing bacteria and leguminous plants. The nitrogen-fixing bacteria produce nutrients
called nitrates, which are used by the plants. The plants, in turn, provide
the bacteria with organic material needed for growth. Neither organism can
survive without the other.

Another mutualistic relationship exists between some species of algae and
fungi. The two species are commonly joined together in a single "organism"
known as a lichen. The photosynthetic algae provide the fungus with organic
material needed for growth. The fungus supplies structural support and also
absorbs from the environment the water and minerals that are needed by the
algae. This relationship is so successful that lichens are often found in environments where neither fungi nor algae could possibly survive alone.

Termites have protozoa living in their intestine. Without the protozoa,
the termites are unable to digest wood—and hence would starve to death.

Likewise, the protozoa have become so specialized that they cannot survive in any environment other than the termites' intestine.

What kind of species interaction is this? Explain your answer. _____

_____

_____

- - - - - - - - - - - - - - - - - -

Mutualism; both the protozoa and the termite have evolved to the point where they are dependent upon each other.

8.   In commensalism (+/0), one species benefits from the rela-
        tionship and the other is unaffected. Commensalism is usually
        necessary for the survival of the benefiting species—the com-
        mensal.

An example of commensalism is the association between remora fish and sharks. The dorsal fin of the remora fish is highly modified into a suction disc with which the fish attaches itself to the belly of a shark. The remora is carried around by the shark and obtains scraps of the shark's food. The remora benefits while the shark is unaffected except for perhaps some slight loss of speed.

Many vertebrates have formed commensal relationships with man. The concentration of man into cities and towns provides many new habitats and sources of food for a variety of animals. The house sparrow, pigeon, house mouse, and house cats are all prime examples of animals that have benefited through human association.

This may be a good time to note that there are no precise lines between these different types of interrelationships. Symbiotic relationships are not static relationships. They are dynamic, selective forces that contribute to the evolutionary adaptation of the populations involved. We should always expect that the nature of the relationship between two populations will change with time. For example, man originally domesticated dogs to help him hunt and to warn him of danger. Some dogs still do this and thus have a coopera-tive relationship with man. Other dogs are just pets, however, and exist in a strictly commensal relationship to man. Agricultural plants are another good example. The domestication of plants (and farm animals too, for that matter) developed as a form of cooperation. Ten thousand years ago man did not have to depend on farming and animal husbandry to live. As his pop-ulation grew, however, his survival began to depend on the new found means of productivity and the relation evolved into one of commensalism (man be-came a commensal). The present relationship is probably a form of mutual-ism, since most of the human population could not survive without domesti-cated plants and animals. Likewise, the genetically specialized high yield grains as well as meat and dairy animals would soon perish without the con-stant care of the farmer.

The hermit crab often protects itself by using a shell discarded by some other species. What type of interaction is this? Explain your answer.

_____

_____

_____

- - - - - - - - - - - - - - - - - - -

Commensalism: the hermit crab benefits from the shell. The mollusk, whose shell it had been, died before the crab came along, and hence was completely unaffected by the relationship.

9.   Amensalism (-/0) is the opposite of commensalism. In amensalism, one species inhibits the growth and survival of another while remaining unaffected itself. The species that is inhibited is called the amensal.

In a forest, for example, as the large trees grow older and produce a fuller and thicker leaf canopy, the plants on the forest floor receive less and less sunlight, thus their growth, reproduction, and survival are inhibited. The trees are relatively unaffected by the fate of the plants, which are the amensals.

In most examples of amensalism, one species produces a substance that is toxic to another species. For example, tremendous numbers of fish are killed by "red tides," which result from a toxic chemical produced by large numbers of microorganisms in the sea. The microorganisms are not affected by the death of the fish.

The study of one amensal relationship led to the development of antibiotics. It was found that the mold penicillin secretes a substance that inhibits the growth of various species of bacteria. The human use of the antibiotics penicillin, streptomycin, and aureomycin all represent man's application of his knowledge of amensalism.

Fewer and fewer brown pelicans are breeding successfully in the Gulf of Mexico. DDT from midland U.S. agricultural uses is washing into the Gulf. As a top carnivore, the pelican concentrates so much DDT that it is unable to make adequate eggshell material.

What kind of relationship exists between pelicans and human beings? Explain.

_____

_____

- - - - - - - - - - - - - - - - - -

Amensalism: the pelican is becoming extinct and man is essentially un-affected.

10.   Competition (-/-) occurs when two populations vie for such
        limited environmental resources as food, nutrients, sun-
        light, and living space. During competition both populations
        are affected, but sooner or later one species predominates,
        takes the limited resource in question for itself, and elimi-
        nates the other species (a process called competitive exclu-
        sion).

Competition can occur between individuals of two different species—interspecific competition, or it can occur between members of the same species
—intraspecific competition. Interspecific competition is a form of extrinsic
environmental resistance and will be considered in this frame. Intraspecific
competition is a form of intrinsic environmental resistance and will be taken
up in frame 15.

The resources of the environment are always limited. If two species
populations need the exact same resource, then each will serve as a check
on the other's growth rate. Each population will be able to grow only if it
manages to get more of the limited resource. When one of the competing
populations "wins" the competition, its numbers increase rapidly until it
takes all of the limited resource (and the other population decreases as less
and less of a vitally needed resource is available). The intensity of the competition between two populations depends on the degree to which the two species share common resource needs.

In the first clear demonstration of interspecific competition, the Russian
biologist Gause grew two closely related species of protozoa separately, and
then together (see figure 9.4 on the next page). Since the food of the species
used (a bacterial medium) was kept the same, the change in their growth
rates when they were grown together indicates the degree to which their competition for the same food inhibited each from its normal growth pattern.
Ultimately one protozoan (Paramecium aurelia) proved most successful in
getting the food and the other protozoan population was eliminated.

As a result of Gause's work, ecologists derived a basic ecological principle: if two populations compete for some resource that is necessary for
the survival of each and is in short supply, one of the populations will be
eliminated. This principle is commonly known as the Competitive Exclusion
Principle. It has been demonstrated for a variety of organisms. It should be
noted, however, that the competitive advantage of one species over another
depends on the specific environment. The same species would not necessarily
have the same advantage over another in even a slightly different environment.
In another part of Gause's experiment, the two species were placed in a non-
bacterial instead of a bacterial medium. In this case, the other species of
paramecium had the advantage and achieved a higher growth rate, therefore
eliminating Paramecium aurelia.

In 1961, Connell successfully demonstrated interspecific competition
under natural conditions in a study of the interaction between two populations
of barnacles in Scotland. Barnacles are exceptionally good for this type of
study, since once the larval forms attach themselves to a rock they live the
rest of their lives in the same position. As you can see in figure 9.5 on page
191, the larvae of the two species attach themselves to overlapping areas.

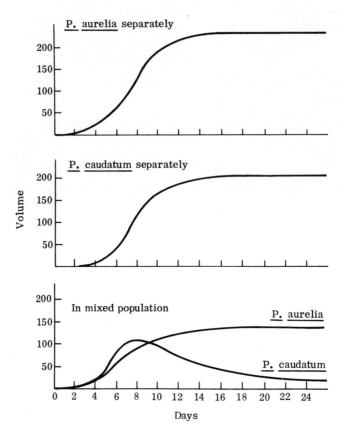

Figure 9.4 The growth of two closely related pro-
tozoans, Paramecium aurelia and P. caudatum,
when grown separately and in mixed culture demon-
strating the competition and then elimination of P.
caudatum (After Gause, 1934)

Thus, the distribution of the adult barnacles shows the result of the competition between the two species. The lower range of Chthamalus was determined by the more vigorously growing Balanus, which either overgrew or
dislodged the young Chthamalus.

(a) Species X and species Y live in exactly the same area and require exactly
the same limited source of food. Neither species is doing as well as it
has been observed when occupying the area alone. This is an example

of what sort of symbiotic interaction? _____

Give a symbol for it. _____

(b) Can this interaction go on forever? _____ Explain. _____

_____

_____

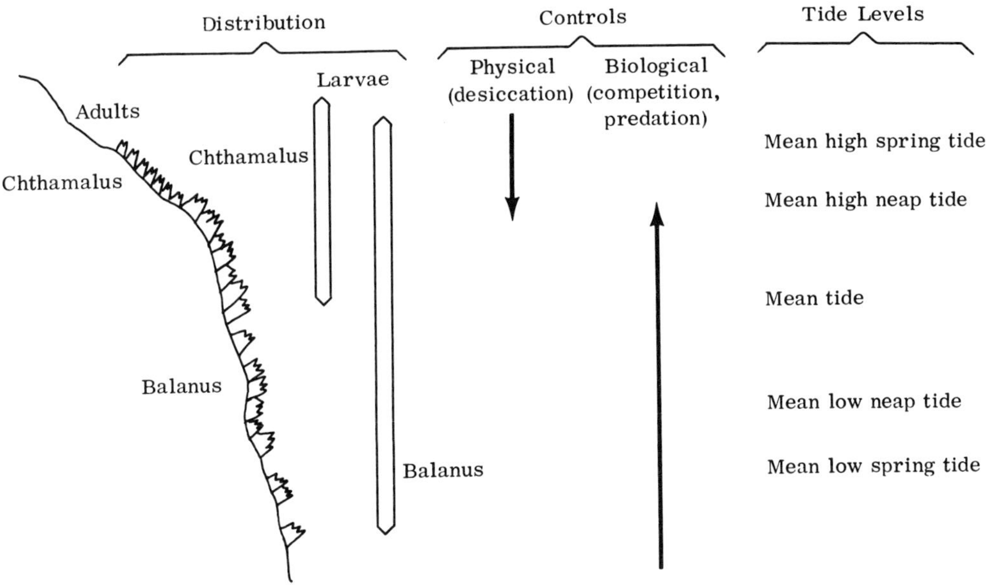

Figure 9.5   Interspecific competition between two species of barnacles, Chthamalus stellatus and Balanus balanoides, in the intertidal zone. Desiccation is the primary controlling factor in the upper part of the zone for Balanus; competition with Balanus is the primary controlling factor in the lower part of the upper half of the zone for Chthamalus; predation by the whelk, Theis lapillus, and intraspecific competition are the primary controlling factors in the lower part of the zone for Balanus. (After Connell, 1961)

(c)   This explanation is based on what principle? _____

_____

_ _ _ _ _ _ _ _ _ _ _ _ _ _ _ _ _ _ _

(a) competition, (-/-);   (b) No. If two populations compete for some limited resource that is necessary for the survival of each and is in short supply, one of the populations—sooner or later—will be eliminated. (c) Competitive Exclusion Principle

11.   A niche is a set of characteristics that describe the precise resources an organism needs to survive. No two species can occupy exactly the same niche—have precisely the same environmental requirements and tolerances—but their niches may overlap, in which case the two species will compete for a specific resource. Niche differentiation is said to occur when a species switches its resource requirements (and hence its niche) to reduce direct competition.

All of the conditions that an organism needs combine to form its niche.[2] The niche of every existing species is, at least in part, the result of competition it has overcome in the course of its evolutionary development. Current competition helps to determine the future niche of the species. Extinction is not always the outcome of competition between two populations. Niche differentiation may occur when some shift in one population's requirements minimizes its interaction with a competing species. In other words, a species may evolve a new set of niche characteristics—it changes its niche.

Minor shifts in food preferences may evolve, for example. By eating different parts or different developmental stages of the same plant, competition for the same food source can be alleviated. For example, in East Africa, several species of browsing and grazing herbivores occupy the same range of savanna, feeding on the same limited numbers of grasses. They do this without competing and displacing one another. Indeed, research on the plains of Serengeti has shown that the principal migratory species, such as wildebeest, zebra, and Thompson's gazelle, have developed a degree of interdependence. Each seeks different tissues of the same grasses and herbs. Changes in the availability of these specific tissues determine the order of the animal migrations. The first migrational group (the zebra) opens up the dense stands of grass, and later populations select food from the lower levels of the herb layer. This may imply that the reduction of one population would lead to the decline of another species. Each species seems to depend on the others to prepare or leave specialized food for it. Possibly a relationship of cooperation or even mutualism has evolved from one of competition by slight shifts in the food preference of these migrating species.

The concept of competition has widespread implications for the human species. Probably the most obvious example concerns our rivals in the insect world, with whom we are constantly competing for a larger portion of the world's food crop. We will discuss some other examples later in this chapter.

Answer the following questions in one or two sentences.

(a) State the Competitive Exclusion Principle in terms of niche. _____

_____

_____

_____

---

2. The term "niche" is used in a variety of ways in ecology. (For example, E. P. Odum defines it as an organism's role or status in the community.) We are using the term in a very comprehensive sense to represent a volume in space where all the environmental conditions under which a species population could exist and reproduce are found. It refers to the totality of biotic and abiotic factors to which a given species is uniquely adapted.

(b) The cormorant and the shag are two fish-eating species of birds. They both occupy the same waters. The cormorant is a bottom feeder that eats flounder and shrimp. The shag feeds in the upper waters on free-swimming fish and eels. In terms of the niche concept, explain how it is possible for these two species to coexist in the same habitat.

_____

_____

_____

_____

- - - - - - - - - - - - - - - - - - - -

(a) If the niches of two species overlap, there will be competition until one species is eliminated from the area of overlap. You might also have said that ultimately only one species can occupy one niche.
(b) The two species can coexist because they are in different niches. (They feed on different things at different places.)

12.   Predation (+/-) is a type of interaction in which one species (the predator) attacks and kills another species (the prey). The predator population benefits by obtaining food; the prey population is inhibited.

Everyone is familiar with such common examples of predation as the lion and the antelope, or the hawk and the field mouse. The dynamics of predation and the possible benefits of predation to both the predator and the prey are less well known. Predation is not necessarily "bad" for the prey population, even though it inhibits its growth rate. On the contrary, predation may be very important to the prey population's general welfare. Predation often operates as a natural method of quality control by culling out the diseased or otherwise less fit individuals. In addition, predation may act as an important means of keeping the prey population within the limits of its food supply.

For example, in tundra areas where both reindeer and wolves live, reindeer herds do not exceed the carrying capacity of the environment. In 1944, however, members of the U.S. Coast Guard transported 29 reindeer to St. Matthew Island. This island had a typical tundra climate but no wolves. The reindeer herd was soon growing exponentially. By 1966 they had destroyed the 128 square mile island's winter forage crop of reindeer moss, and the reindeer population had suffered a sharp decline (see figure 9.6 on the next page). This study, and others, suggest that unless some predator exerts an extrinsic check on the reindeer's population growth rate, they increase until they destroy the range, and themselves.

In natural systems, the J-shaped curve is uncommon for either predator or prey populations. In theory (based primarily on mathematical models) a series of cycles evolves, in which the rise in the predator population results in a subsequent decline in the prey population, as the predator consumes a progressively larger number of prey. With the decline in the numbers of prey, the predator is left with less and less food, and its population conse-

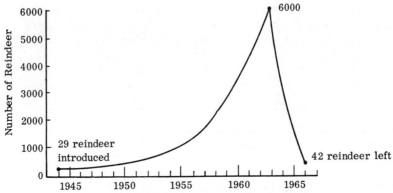

Figure 9.6   Reindeer population's growth on
St. Matthew Island when there were no wolves
to inhibit the growth by predation (After Klein,
1968)

quently declines, allowing for a resurgence in the numbers of the prey population. If the prey is never quite destroyed by predation, and the predator
never completely eliminated by starvation, this cycle may continue indefinitely. For a predator-prey relationship to persist for any length of time in nature this must be the common pattern.

These cycles can be graphed in a simplified form—see figure 9.7. According to figure 9.7, when the prey population density is high (point A) the predator population has an adequate food supply and can increase (from point B to
point B'). But this increase causes the predators to deplete the supply of
prey (A to A'), which in turn decreases the predator population density (B' to
B'').

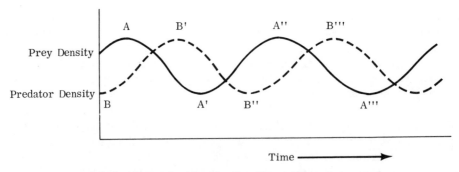

Figure 9.7   An idealized pattern of predator and
prey population interactions over a period of time

One common natural example of this series of cycles involves the snowshoe hare and the lynx. By plotting the number of animals trapped over a
period of years, the Hudson Bay Company obtained the data shown in the
graph in figure 9.8 at the top of the next page. This graph does not show the
simple curves shown in figure 9.7. It can be seen, however, that the increase

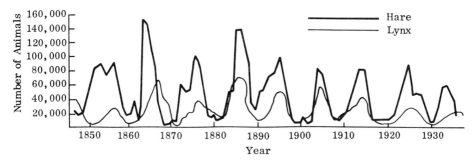

Figure 9.8   Alterations in populations of the
snowshoe hare and lynx. Data is based on pelts
purchased by the Hudson Bay Company. (Adapted
from MacLulich, 1937)

in the lynx population generally occurs slightly after the increase in the hare
population and probably triggers a decline in the hare population.

Such predator-prey cycles are generally found when a single predator
population feeds on a single prey population. The process becomes more
complex for predators that feed on several types of prey. In those instances,
the predator can feed on a more available prey while another, less available
prey is increasing in number. So a predator population may not always decline following a decrease in prey population.

Human populations, especially those in developed countries, have almost
completely eliminated their predators. But, as a predator himself, man's
efficiency and ferociousness is unmatched in the animal kingdom. Americans
have caused the Eastern Woods bison and the passenger pigeon to become extinct. More current examples of man's predatory capacities include the
California and East Asian sardine fisheries, the Atlantic and Pacific tuna,
anchovies off California, and the world whale populations. In all of these
cases formerly large populations have been reduced to dangerously low levels
by man's very efficient predation.

The idealized predator-prey situation can be diagrammed as an integrated
cybernetic system that regulates both populations. The positive feedback of
the predator's reproduction is opposed by the negative feedback of its decreasing food supply, while the positive feedback of the prey's reproduction is
countered by the negative feedback of increasing predation. The magnitude
of the fluctuations will be dependent on the lag between the feedback and the
severity of the corrective response.

(a)   Examine the complex double figure-eight diagram in figure 9.9 on the
next page. The set point is for both the prey and the predators (though,
of course, it's a different number for each). In the space allowed below
the figure explain what is happening in the numbered boxes in the diagram.

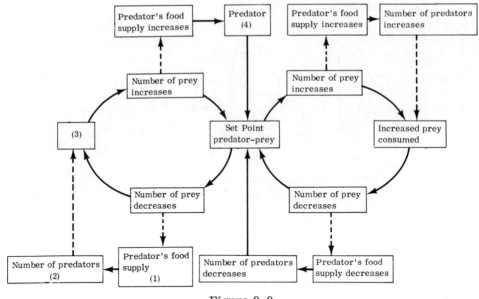

Figure 9.9

(1) _____

(2) _____

(3) _____

(4) _____

(b) When moose first arrived on Isle Royale in 1913 their population quickly grew. It grew to such numbers that it damaged the range, and then it swiftly declined because of the lack of food. The population violently fluctuated for many years until a pack of wolves arrived from the mainland. Since then the numbers of moose and wolves have remained relatively stable on Isle Royale. Explain what might have happened on Isle

Royale. _____

_____

_____

_____

- - - - - - - - - - - - - - - - - - - -

(a) (1) predator's food supply decreases; (2) number of predators decreases; (3) number of prey increases; (4) number of predators increases

(b) The wolves from the mainland may have acted as an extrinsic environmental resistance factor, keeping the prey population (moose) within the limits of its food supply. The moose and wolf populations might be acting as checks on each other through an integrated cybernetic system of population control.

"Little fleas have lesser fleas upon their backs to bite them
Lesser fleas have smaller fleas and so on ad infinitum. "
Jonathan Swift

13.   Parasitism (+/-) is an interaction between two species in which one species (called the parasite) nourishes itself at the expense of the other (called the host). Such an interaction is necessary for the survival of the parasitic species. This relationship sometimes indirectly causes the death of the host.

The parasite does not directly kill the host, but death of the host may result indirectly from the effects imposed by the parasite (for example, stunted growth, weakness, or sterility). The parasitic species is at an advantage as long as the interaction continues. It is, therefore, in the best interests of the parasite that its host remain alive. By killing its host, the parasite loses its own means of survival. Through a long period of evolving together, parasite and host populations adjust to one another.

Human beings are hosts to many parasites, including intestinal worms, protozoa, parasites of the blood, ectoparasites (living outside the body of the host, such as ticks, mosquitoes, and fleas), and many infectious microorganisms, such as bacteria and viruses. All of these human parasites extract some nutrients from human cells. Some of these organisms are pathogenic (cause an "unhealthy" condition), and some are not. As with any other host, the harm done depends on the human's ability to adjust to the parasite. Where both the host and parasite populations have had sufficient periods of time to adapt, the parasites have little or no pathogenic effect on the human host. In tropical Africa, for example, over 80 percent of the population is infected with both hookworm and malaria.

The relation of the tropical African populations to malaria is a good example of evolutionary adaptation. Some of the normally round-shaped red blood cells in these populations have been replaced by a sickle-shaped blood cell. Sickle cells offer some resistance to the protozoan causing malaria that reproduces in normal red blood cells. On the other hand, sickle cells have less capacity for carrying oxygen, so some hosts develop sickle cell anemia. Over a long period of time a balance has been struck between the resistance of people with some sickle cells to malaria and their susceptibility to sickle cell anemia. Of course, without the presence of malaria, the sickle cell trait is a definite liability. This is the case in the United States, where the incidence of sickle cell anemia is almost exclusively confined to people of African descent who acquired the sickle cell traits (genes) from their ancestors.

Interactions in which parasitism causes the host's debilitation and subsequent death usually indicate a recently established host-parasite relationship. Most recent cases of the introduction of a "new" parasite (one to which the host is not adapted) are the work of man. A classic example involves the parasitic fungus Endothea parasitica and the chestnut tree. In its native China, Endothea is a parasite of the Oriental chestnut, which has apparently evolved adaptations to cope with the infestation. But the introduction of the parasite into the United States in 1904 has resulted in the virtual elimination of the American chestnut, since it had evolved no such resistance.

When European cattle were exported to Africa, they quickly succumbed to a sleeping sickness caused by a parasitic protozoa. African cattle, however, were not affected. Explain why this might have happened.

_____

_____

_____

_____

- - - - - - - - - - - - - - - - - -

    The African cattle had probably adapted to the parasite over a long period of time. The European cattle had never been exposed to the parasite before and so had not evolved any resistance.

If you wish to take a break, this is a good point in the chapter to pause.

14.   Intrinsic environmental resistance occurs when members of a population compete with each other. It is now believed that in most cases intrinsic, or intrinsic plus extrinsic, environmental resistance plays a much greater role in controlling population growth than any form of extrinsic environmental resistance by itself.

    We began this chapter by saying that environmental resistance could be divided into extrinsic factors and intrinsic factors. We said that extrinsic factors affected a population from outside itself and we have briefly considered such examples as climate (especially temperature and moisture), nutrient availability, and various forms of symbiotic relationships.

    We now want to briefly consider some intrinsic factors. These factors are generated within a single species population and affect that population's ability to survive and reproduce. Until recently, greater emphasis was given to extrinsic environmental resistance. Sometimes extrinsic factors clearly do constitute a population's major environmental resistance. In most cases, however, evidence suggests that extrinsic factors, acting by themselves, are too inconsistent to be the sole regulating or balancing forces. This new evidence, which we will consider in the next few frames, suggests that behavioral interactions within a single species population, either alone or in league with extrinsic factors, play a major role in regulating population growth.

In discussing competition we said that a species could either compete with other species or with members of its own species.

(a)   If a species competes with another species, this is an example of

_____ environmental resistance.

(b)   If members of the species compete with each other, this is an example

of _____ environmental resistance.

_ _ _ _ _ _ _ _ _ _ _ _ _ _ _ _ _ _

(a) extrinsic;   (b) intrinsic

15.   Intraspecific competition tends to be more intense than interspecific competition because the members of the same species must compete for nearly the same resources.

We have already described competition as a type of interaction in which different organisms vie for the same resource. We said that the intensity of competition depended upon the degree to which the organisms' niches overlapped. For this reason, intraspecific competition tends to be much more intense than interspecific competition. Members of the same species population obviously share nearly the same niche—they all need about the same resources. Hence, as population density increases, for example, all deer find themselves competing for the same food plants. In these circumstances the subtlest differences in individual members of a single population help to determine which individuals survive and bear young.

We can generalize and say that when intense interspecific competition occurs, the members of a population will develop more limited niches (i.e., resource needs) so as to avoid the competition of the other species. When intraspecific competition occurs, the members of a population will tend to develop more diverse resource needs so they can use resources not available to other members of the same population. Figure 9.10 shows the effects of interspecific and intraspecific competition on niche size. A represents the situation when the species population is exposed to competition from closely related species—there is selection for more limited niches. C represents the situation when members within a population compete—the overall range of the species widens.

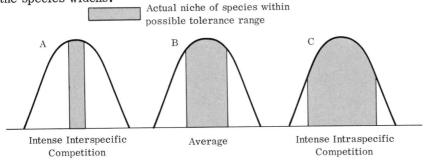

Figure 9.10   The effect of inter and intraspecific competition on niche size

Not all intrinsic environmental resistance springs from intraspecific competition, but much of it does. As man has eliminated various forms of interspecific competition, he has become particularly prone to this more intense battle for resources. As Garrett Hardin has said in <u>Nature</u> <u>and</u> <u>Man's</u> <u>Fate</u>:

> As a species becomes increasingly "successful," its struggle
> for existence ceases to be one of struggle with the physical
> environment or with other species and comes to be almost ex-
> clusively competition with its own kind. We call that species
> most successful that has made its own kind its worst enemy.
> Man enjoys this kind of success. Intraspecific competition
> may be as crude as cannibalism or infanticide, as "romantic"
> as chivalrous jousting or dueling, or as subtle as Stephen
> Potter's "one-upmanship," but it all has the same end in
> view: the securing of advantage to one's self at the expense
> of one's neighbor in a world that is not, and cannot be, large
> enough for the continuously "successful" species. No activity
> of man is without competitive uses. Even tact is a competitive
> weapon. From a humane point of view, we may prefer one
> weapon to another, but let us not deceive ourselves as to their
> ultimate effect. We are at one with the rest of the living
> world; either we must struggle with other living species, or
> we must compete with ourselves. . . .

Examine the two simple diagrams in figure 9.11. One of these diagrams can be thought of as representing a typical interspecific competition situation, the other a typical intraspecific competition situation. (Each circle refers to an individual organism. The shaded area indicates the degree to which two organisms' niches—resource needs—overlap. You are not being told if the organisms are of the same or different species populations—that's what you are supposed to figure out.)

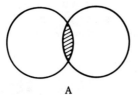 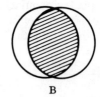

A   B

Figure 9.11

_____ (1) two individual organisms in intraspecific competition

_____ (2) two individual organisms in interspecific competition

_____ (3) two individuals most likely members of the same species pop-
               ulation

_____ (4) two individuals most likely members of separate species pop-
               ulations

_____ (5) an example of extrinsic environmental resistance

_____ (6) an example of intrinsic environmental resistance

_____ (7) the situation with the most intense competition

_____ (8) two species with the greatest degree of niche differentiation

- - - - - - - - - - - - - - - - - - - -

(1) B,   (2) A,   (3) B,   (4) A,   (5) A,   (6) B,   (7) B,   (8) A

16.   <u>Territory</u> refers to an area that an organism will defend
against other members of its own species.[3] Territoriality is
therefore a form of intraspecific competition. It is a social
behavior mechanism that exerts intrinsic environmental resistance on a population by restricting a given area's food
supply and sexual partners to the limited number of individual
members who are able to defend that area against others.

A group of organisms usually confines its activities to a particular area.
The area in which the members of a population freely interact with others
and wander in search of food is called their <u>home range</u>. That part of the
home range that one organism defends against intruders of the same species
is called its <u>territory</u>. <u>Territoriality</u> is the behavior a species displays in
defending its territory; it has been observed in many species of birds, mammals, lizards, fishes, and social insects. Territoriality is a mechanism of
social behavior that seems to regulate a population's size by limiting the
access of individual members to specific habitats, food supplies, and sexual
partners. Only individuals possessing a territory can get a mate. Surplus
individuals are forced into poorer habitats where their chances of survival
and reproduction are greatly reduced.

Social primates (e.g., baboons) and some hunting-gathering human societies (e.g., Australian aborigines) have a <u>nucleated territory</u>. Specific
geographic boundaries are not defended, but the area currently occupied by
the group is defended against an intruder.

Territory size varies with the favorability of the habitat. When food is
scarce, territory size tends to be larger. Thus, in unfavorable times, a
particular area will support fewer organisms. When food is abundant, smaller territories are defended, thereby allowing more individuals to inhabit a
given area. The size of the nucleated territory of a group of Australian aborigines, for example, has been observed to vary in size depending on rainfall (see figure 9.12 on the next page).

_____

3. Individual organisms will defend their breeding and feeding areas against
intrusion by individuals of other species as well as by members of their own
population. The defense of an area against other species, however, is not
commonly included in the concept of territoriality.

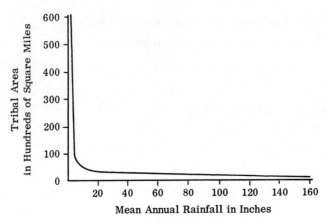

Figure 9.12   Correlation between the mean
annual rainfall and the territory size for Australian aborigine tribes (After Birdsell, 1953)

Five males have divided an area among them, and none will accept less territory. Ten females occupy the same area. One male will only breed with two
females each year. New males or females, having no resources, either
leave the area or are killed. Is this a form of intrinsic environmental re-

sistance? How? _____

_____

_____

– – – – – – – – – – – – – – – – – – – –

Yes, new males or females have no room: they can't get food or mates,
and hence they can't affect the population occupying the area, which will
begin each breeding season with a population of 15 individuals.

17.   Individual organisms need a certain amount of personal
space. If they are crowded, they are put under a degree
of stress. A set of bodily reactions (called a stress syndrome) is activated that can eventually result in a decline
of the reproductive capacity or even in the death of the individual organism. As a population's density increases,
its social density increases (more intrusions occur on the
individual's personal space) and stress becomes a factor
in intrinsic environmental resistance.

In addition to exhibiting territoriality an animal may possess an individual
distance, within which the presence of another produces various adverse reactions. Social encounters that increase with population size have been shown
to produce definite quality changes in the organisms, and these changes in
turn can affect their ability to both survive and reproduce. These encounters

do not necessarily have to be direct physical contacts in which the organism is wounded or scarred. The fear of physical harm or the recollection of past harm may induce a similar reaction. When processed through the higher brain centers, any number of sensory inputs (the smell of another organism, noise, etc.) may construct mental images that are just as capable of triggering a stress response.

Stress is a specific series of reactions that an organism undergoes in response to many different stimuli (called stressors). Physical and mental stressors (e.g., temperature extremes, trauma) produce a common set of radical adjustments of the body's processes through the endocrine glands and nervous system. This general plan of defense has been called the General Adaptation Syndrome (G.A.S.). Under prolonged stress the organism may develop some resistance to the initial stimulus while becoming less able to cope with another.

The numbers of social interactions between individuals in a given area has been called the social density. This can be contrasted to the population density, which is simply the number of organisms per unit of area. One could expect that at any given time in any given area the social density will be greater and increasing faster than the population density.[4] It has been shown that all aspects of reproductive activity are inhibited by increasing social density. In addition, the stress caused by these social encounters also may increase the organism's vulnerability to normal mortality factors. Decreased resistance and increased susceptibility to disease have been shown to accompany increasing social density. It is clear then that a portion of the encounters included in the concept of social density are harmful to the organisms involved and through the stress they produce are factors of intrinsic environmental resistance.

(a) A recently impregnated female mouse smells a strange male mouse and the pregnancy is terminated.

(b) In mouse populations of higher density, fewer healthy young are born per female.

(c) Experimental populations subjected to crowded conditions show a higher percentage of infectious disease than normal.

The examples above show how social encounters can adversely affect an

organism. What mechanism might be working here? _____

_____

_____

4. The number of possible contacts, as well as the number of actual contacts per individual, will increase much more rapidly than the number of individuals in a population. The number of possible contacts can be computed by the formula for numbers of two-body interactions (i.e., in a population of size N there are $N(N-1)/2$ possible two-body interactions). Realizing that at various phases of growth a population itself can grow exponentially, you can see how quickly adverse contacts between individuals might increase.

- - - - - - - - - - - - - - - - - -

Any stimulus perceived by the organisms as stressful can produce a stress response (G.A.S.). Odor, physical contact, or sight of another can cause the body to respond to meet the stressful assault. If the stress persists or if another arises, the organism's ability to reproduce and resist other stresses (such as disease) will decrease.

18.   It is quite likely that no universal cause of population regulation will be found. At any given time, an increase in mortality
or a decrease in fertility may be triggered by a shortage or
quality change in food supply, a climatic change, disease,
predation, or the organism's own social behavior.

No one factor predominates at all times and places; rather, a population is more likely regulated by a whole complex of environmental factors (both extrinsic and intrinsic). A "population regulation system" would need to include many interacting components such as weather, predation, disease, and food supply acting through the animal's own behavior and physiology. Figure 9.13 on the facing page outlines such a proposed system. Admittedly it is incomplete and is just an attempt to picture the interdependence and inter-relatedness of these components.

Figure 9.13 visualizes a system of population regulation with negative feedback loops, where an increase in population density first results in an increase in social density. The increasing number of social encounters acts as stressors along with many other external stimuli. The "stressor" component of this model is meant to include all the extrinsic factors (i.e., food, predation, weather) and intrinsic factors (i.e., behavioral, physiological, genetic) that are capable of producing the stress response (General Adaptation Syndrome) in the organism. Together, all of these factors operate to debilitate the animal, increasing its susceptibility to other mortality factors and decreasing its reproductive activity through effects (i.e., decreased fertility, decreased infant survival, inadequate lactation, etc.) known to accompany the G.A.S. The resultant decrease in reproduction and increase in mortality contribute to a decrease in population density, which, in turn, decreases social density, thus alleviating the stress on the animal. Reproductive activity and resistance to external insult thus return to normal in the organism.

Many factors in addition to increased social density are shown to lead to the G.A.S., which in turn may make the organism more vulnerable to other stresses. As an example, a bad winter or short food supply may weaken the organisms of a population to the point where their resistance is lowered and some die of disease.

Another example of interacting factors includes food supply and predation. If a large population overgrazes the vegetation that is both its food and its cover, it may very well fall victim to predators. Although the predators ultimately cause the deaths, the overgrazing (or more properly the lack of food-cover) would also be a contributing factor.

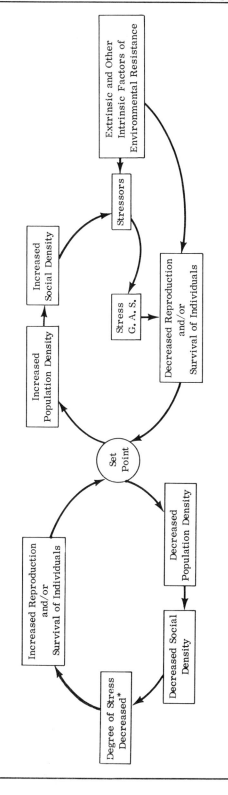

Figure 9.13   A cybernetic system of population regulation (After Sutton, 1953)

*Organism better able to cope with other mortality factors.

Many such interactions have been documented, and there are many others yet to be investigated. (For instance, is a well-fed population better able to withstand severe climatic change than a starved one?) What is important to remember about the model, however, is that regulation is considered to result from the interplay between any of these extrinsic and intrinsic factors and the changing quality of the organisms accompanying changing population size.

SELF-TEST

This Self-Test is designed to show you whether or not you have mastered this chapter's objectives. Answer each question to the best of your ability. Correct answers and review instructions are given at the end of the test.

1. Define environmental resistance. _____

    _____

2. Describe extrinsic environmental resistance. _____

    _____

3. Describe intrinsic environmental resistance. _____

    _____

4. Intraspecific competition is a good example of _____
    environmental resistance.

5. Interspecific competition is a good example of _____
    environmental resistance.

6. Explain the Law of Tolerances. _____

    _____

    _____

7. What are some of the abiotic factors that can limit an organism's growth

    and reproduction? _____

    _____

    _____

8. Define symbiotic relationship. _____

    _____

    _____

9. Match the following terms (more than one may match).

_____ (a) cooperation

_____ (b) mutualism

_____ (c) commensalism

_____ (d) amensalism

_____ (e) competition

_____ (f) parasitism

_____ (g) predation

(1) One population is inhibited; the other is unaffected (–/0)

(2) One population benefits; the other is unaffected (+/0)

(3) Each population benefits. The interaction is optional for both species (+/+)

(4) Each population benefits. The interaction is necessary for the survival and growth of both species (+/+)

(5) One population benefits; the interaction is necessary for the survival of the population that benefits (+/–)

(6) Both populations suffer; finally one eliminates the other (–/–)

10. Identify the type of interaction described in each of the following examples. Refer to the terms from question 9 if you wish.

(a) A man puts out a salt block for deer because he likes seeing them around his house. This is an example of _____.

(b) Starlings thrive in U.S. cities. Assume people don't care if they are there or not. This would be an example of _____.

(c) Man has hunted several species of whales to near–extinction. This is an example of _____.

(d) Most people in the world have some sort of worms living in their intestines. This is an example of _____.

(e) People casually dump wastes into streams thereby killing fish. This is an example of _____.

11. Explain the Competitive Exclusion Principle and the process of niche differentiation. _____

_____

_____

_____

12. Define territory. _____

_____

_____

13. Explain how increasing social density can act as a form of intrinsic environmental resistance. _____

_____

_____

_____

14. Explain why one single factor is hardly ever solely responsible for a
population becoming extinct. _____

_____

_____

_____

ANSWERS TO SELF-TEST

Compare your answers to the questions on the Self-Test with the answers given below. If all of your answers are correct, you are ready to go on to the next chapter. If you missed any questions, review the frames indicated in parentheses following the answer. If you miss several questions, you should probably reread the entire chapter carefully.

1. Environmental resistance refers to environmental factors that operate to decrease the fertility and survival of the individuals comprising a population. (frame 1)

2. Extrinsic environmental resistance refers to factors existing in the environment outside of the population itself. (frames 1 and 14)

3. Intrinsic environmental resistance refers to factors that originate within the population itself. (frames 1 and 14)

4. intrinsic (frames 10, 14, and 15)

5. extrinsic (frame 10)

6. The Law of Tolerances holds that for each abiotic factor, an organism has a range of tolerances within which it can survive. Toward the upper and lower extreme of this tolerance range, that factor exerts a limiting influence on the survival of the organism. (frame 2)

7. Some of the factors you could have mentioned that commonly limit organisms are climate, including temperature and moisture; and nutrients, including macronutrients and micronutrients. (frames 2, 3, and 4)

8. All relationships between organisms are referred to as symbiotic relationships. (frame 5)

9. (a) 3; (b) 4; (c) 2; (d) 1; (e) 6; (f) 5; (g) 5 (frames 5-14)

10. (a) cooperation (frames 5 and 6)
    (b) commensalism (frames 5 and 8)
    (c) predation (frames 5 and 12)
    (d) parasitism (frames 5 and 13)
    (e) amensalism (frames 5 and 9)

11. The Competitive Exclusion Principle states that in the long run, only one species can occupy a single niche. If two species occupy a part of the same niche, competition occurs until one species is eliminated from that part. One way a species can be eliminated from a niche is by niche differentiation, which occurs when a species evolves to switch its resource requirements (and hence its niche). (frame 11)

12. Territory refers to the part of an organism's home range that it defends against intrusion by other members of its own species. (frame 16)

13. Increasing social density refers to an increasing number of social encounters. If these encounters are perceived as stressful, they can produce the G.A.S. If the stress persists or if others are added, the members of the population may become, through the stress syndrome, more
vulnerable to other mortality factors or unable to normally reproduce.
(frames 17 and 18)

14. A single factor is hardly ever responsible for a population becoming extinct because no single factor ever acts on a population independent of
all other factors. Almost any factor that seriously affects a population
will activate the general adaptation syndrome. This, in turn, means
that the organisms will act less efficiently and thereby subject themselves to even more external and internal effects, and so forth. For
example, as a population increases in density not only does predation
tend to increase, but organisms tend to feel crowded and become more
likely to fight among themselves, not breed, etc. Hormone influences
leading to diseases, as well as external epidemics, are likely to occur,
and these in turn lead to more stress. All of these factors interacting
reduce the population's size (either to extinction, or to some lower and
more tolerable level, when all the factors acting to reduce the population tend to reduce themselves by mutual interaction). (frame 18)

CHAPTER TEN
Human Populations

OBJECTIVES

When you complete this chapter, you will be able to

- explain in what way the human population growth pattern is unique among animal populations;

- explain and name the three periods of rapid increase in human population;

- explain what checked human population in previous periods of man's history;

- describe the current world human population trend and discuss possible future results.

If you think that you have already mastered these objectives and might skip all or part of this chapter, turn to page 224 at the end of the chapter and take the Self-Test. The results will allow you to evaluate your current knowledge of this chapter's contents. If you answer all of the questions correctly, you are ready to begin the next chapter. If you miss any questions, you should study the frames indicated after the answers to the Self-Test.

If this material is new to you, or if you choose not to take the Self-Test now, proceed to frame 1.

1.   Unique among animal populations, the number of human beings has been gradually increasing since they first appeared. Because human population is growing exponentially, its <u>doubling time</u> is constantly being reduced. The human population has recently begun the extremely rapid increase characteristic of the late stage of exponential growth.

The previous two chapters were intended as a primer in population ecology, introducing you to some of the basic principles. With this foundation we will consider how these principles can be applied to the populations of man. In this chapter, we will consider the history of human population growth, its current state, and possible future trends.

With respect to population growth, the human species is conspicuously out of line with the rest of the animal kingdom. Man stands alone in showing a long-term upward trend in numbers as shown in figure 10.1.

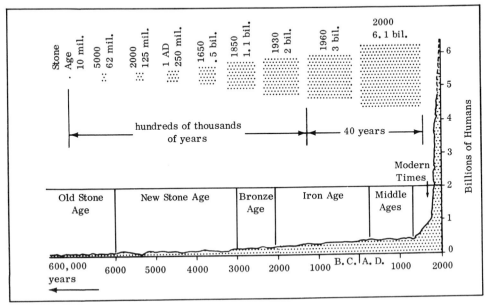

Figure 10.1 The growth of human numbers

Note that this graph includes only a very small percentage of the epoch of man, only the time since the Stone Age. To give you a full perspective, to include the time since the first signs of human activity (between 1 and 2 million years ago), the horizontal axis of the graph would have to be extended about 100 feet to the left. Figure 10.2 provides us with a different overall perspective of this same period.

Date	Estimated World Population	Doubling Time
8000 B.C.	5 million	1,500 years
A.D. 1650	500 million	200 years
A.D. 1850	1,000 million (1 billion)	80 years
A.D. 1930	2,000 million (2 billion)	45 years
A.D. 1975	4,000 million (4 billion)	35 years
A.D. 2010	8 billion?	30 years
A.D. 2040	16 billion?	

Figure 10.2 Doubling times for
human population (After Keyfitz, 1962)

One column is labeled "doubling time." This is a convenient measure used by demographers and refers to the time required for the population to double in size. Note that not only has the world's human population continued to increase over the entire period, but that it has done so at an ever-increasing rate (each doubling has taken less time).

(a) Define doubling time. _____

_____

(b) Approximately how long will it take the human population to double in

size? _____

— — — — — — — — — — — — — — — — — —

(a) the time required for the population to double in size;   (b) approximately 35 years

2.   Only in the very recent past has the human population curve begun its rapid vertical ascent. Population growth was gradual for a very long period because it was subject to the negative feedback controls of environmental resistance. Although not a perfect check, for as we know, the human population has never ceased to increase, there does appear to be a human demostat.

When population growth and the demostatic model were discussed earlier (see page 152), we showed how the biotic potential of a species is held in check by the negative feedback of environmental resistance. This causes the numbers of many populations to fluctuate about a set point (the carrying capacity of the environment). We now should ask: Is there a demostat for the human species? If so, what are the factors that counteract the positive feedback of reproduction? What is the environmental set point or carrying capacity?

A human population demostat can be visualized in figure 10.3 on the next page.[1] The environmental set point is determined by the means of subsistence (food, water, and other necessary resources) available to the population. With "overpopulation" (numbers of people beyond the means of support), disease, starvation, warfare, and crime set in and reduce the population back to within the environment's capacity to support it. A decrease in population size below the means of subsistence creates a surplus—a period of "unusual prosperity," which again stimulates increased reproduction. If rapid, the population quickly returns to its set point.

---

1. As early as 1798, Thomas Robert Malthus, an English clergyman and economist, implied that such a demostat operated in human populations. See his celebrated book, An Essay on the Principle of Populations as It Affects the Future Improvement of Mankind.

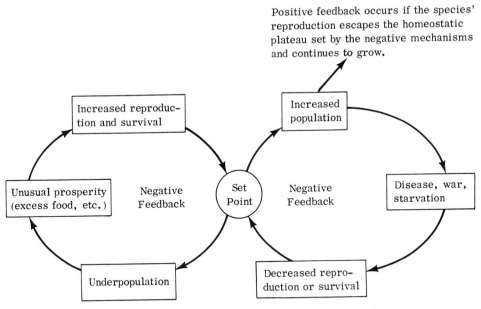

Positive feedback occurs if the species'
reproduction escapes the homeostatic
plateau set by the negative mechanisms
and continues to grow.

Figure 10.3   Human population demostat   (After Hardin, 1966)

The human population throughout most of its history has undergone a <u>slow</u>
gradual increase (rarely realizing its biotic potential) because of

the negative feedback of environmental resistance such as disease,
starvation, and war, which act to reduce reproduction and survival

3.   When the growth of the human population is analyzed with
      special log-log graphs, we see that at certain points growth
      has been very rapid, yet most of the time it has been gradual.
      The rapid increases in human population occurred when man
      made technological breakthroughs that allowed him to sub-
      stantially increase the carrying capacity of the earth. The
      three major "revolutions" or breakthroughs include the tool-
      making revolution, the agricultural and social revolution,
      and the ongoing industrial-scientific revolution which began
      approximately 600,000, 8,000, and 200 years ago respectively.

      Figure 10.4 on the next page depicts the demographic history of man on
a log-log scale. (A log-log scale emphasizes rapid changes in the overall
growth rate.) This figure pictures the growth of the human population as
occurring essentially in three surges, each a result of a technological revo-

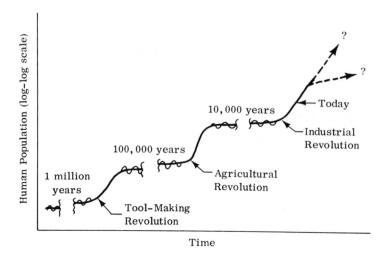

Figure 10.4   Man's major alterations of the demostatic
set point and past homeostatic plateaus

lution. In each case, an elevation of the set point is followed by an extended
period of demostatically controlled growth (a homeostatic plateau). Each
period of controlled growth persisted for many thousands of years until a
major set of technological innovations occurred. With this new means of expanding the "means of subsistence," another set point (or carrying capacity)
was established, which allowed for a marked increase in population growth.
This rapid growth continued until the population reached the new maximum
permitted by the improved technology—the new homeostatic plateau.

From the full historical perspective then, human population growth appears, except for several relatively short periods (one in which we are now
living), to be demostatically controlled. Those periods not conforming to the
demostatic model resulted from a technological revolution that moved the
demostatic set point to a higher level, increasing the means of subsistence.
In each case, however, following the period of unprecedented growth, elements
of environmental resistance imposed their toll to level off growth and establish a new homeostatic plateau. The growth rate of each of these plateaus
was maintained at a very low level by the negative feedback elements of the
demostat.

A population can begin to increase because of the increased availability
of resources needed by that population and/or the decreased severity of environmental resistance. Each of the major technological revolutions in human
history have done both.

The first major increase in the human population occurred with the so-
called tool-making revolution (about 600,000 B.C.). The advent of flint knives
and spearheads made primitive man a more efficient hunter and assured a
better livelihood from the land than was possible before. Learning how to
make tools and more effective weapons increased the food resources available to these early humans and at the same time afforded them a greater degree of security against human and nonhuman enemies.

The second revolution in human technology occurred with the discovery and development of agriculture around 8,000 B.C. Planted crops and domestic animals were a far more assured and potentially larger source of food for human populations than hunting. As long as agricultural practices did not destroy the fertility of the soil or induce widespread deforestation and erosion, people were able to remain in one place and set up permanent dwellings. Moreover, fixed locations were greatly encouraged by the difficulty of moving recently domesticated animals and by the need to stay in one place to care for and harvest crops. The increased ease in obtaining food made it possible for these populations to develop cultures and build cities. In addition, a significant portion of the population was freed from the necessity of working to supply their own food. Thus it became possible for the society to support a number of people not engaged in agricultural pursuits. These people were free to become craftsmen, which had enormous ramifications on the development of the culture's technology. A degree of specialization of function took place and led to a more effective ability to control the environment through the use of increasingly sophisticated tools.

A period of rapid population growth accompanied these developments of the <u>agricultural</u> <u>revolution</u>. This period of growth also originated primarily from decreases in mortality. The supply of food was more dependable and periodic famines became less common. Improved nutrition undoubtedly lessened infant mortality, since a well-fed child is far less likely to fall sick and die. Finally, survival became less risky in general. The dangers and accidents of farming were far less severe than those involved in hunting or moving through a wilderness to gather plants.

The domestication of plants and animals was the process that enabled man to control and increase the supply of biological converters of energy. This made possible larger populations, occasional food surpluses, and even minimal leisure for invention, specialization, art, and speculation. The human population reached a level of roughly 250 million (1/4 billion) at the time of Christ and then began to level off. After reaching this homeostatic plateau, a relatively slow rate of growth was maintained for several thousand years.

(a) Name two revolutions or breakthroughs that allowed the human population to rapidly increase its numbers. _____

_____

(b) How did these revolutions permit an increased population growth rate?

_____

_____

(c) The agricultural-social organization revolution that resulted in tribes, then cities and nations, began about 8,000 B.C. When did the increasing population resulting from this technological breakthrough begin to level

off again? _____

— — — — — — — — — — — — — — — — — — — —

(a) tool-making, agricultural-social organization; (b) They elevated the demostatic set point (increased the means of subsistence) and decreased the death rate. (c) about the time of Christ—A. D. 1

4.   During most of man's recent history, disease has been the chief cause of death. Bubonic plague played a very important role, but effectively disappeared in Europe in the 17th century. This disappearance marked a new increase in the growth of the human population that was soon supplemented by the Industrial Revolution.

During most of the classical and middle ages, mortality remained very high by modern standards. About one-half of all children died before growing old enough to reproduce. Moreover, the death rate for the entire population was usually between 30-40/thousand/year. Combined with the annual birth rate of between 35-50/thousand this would have led to a steady growth rate of between 0.5 percent and 1.0 percent/year. This gradual increase did not occur, however. The usual excess of births above the number of deaths was counterbalanced by recurring, severe peaks in the death rate. Usually due to disease, war, or famine, there were occasional periods when mortality stood as high as 150-500/thousand/year.

During most of man's recent history, there can be little doubt that disease was the chief cause of death. Of course, such things as famine and warfare have been important periodic contributors to high death rates, but even their action is not so much one of direct effect but one that indirectly favors the transmission and onset of disease. (For example, more people died during World War I of typhus and influenza than from gunshot wounds.)

It is quite likely that Stone-Age man was no more affected by disease than were the other animal populations with which he shared the natural Paleolithic environment. It was not until men became "civilized" and developed complex cultures in villages, towns, and cities that disease asserted its dominant role in controlling human populations.

Cities developed as men found that they could clear more, grow more, and build more if they pooled their manpower resources. In addition to bringing large numbers of people in contact with one another, villages and towns brought the human inhabitants in contact with other species capable of transmitting disease. Rivers were used for sewers and, as time passed, large cities developed. With the sewers and cities came the black rat, whose flea harbors the bacteria responsible for bubonic plague. The Black Death, as it was called, along with typhus, smallpox, malaria, sleeping sickness, and yellow fever, has been among the greatest killers of mankind throughout history. Some have gone so far as to propose that the fall of Rome was caused by recurring epidemics throughout the Empire culminating with the Plague of Justinian in A.D. 530. These plagues, it is argued, sapped the intellectual and physical strength of the cities of the ancient world, leaving them empty shells that fell before barbarian hordes. During the Middle Ages, an estimated 25 to 33 percent of the European population was lost to bubonic plague between 1348 and 1350. Many cities lost one-half of their inhabitants; indeed, England's population was reduced by almost 50 percent (from 3.8 million to 2.1 million)!

By A.D. 1400, however, the population had begun to increase again. The rate of growth became more marked by 1650. Explanations of this increase are largely speculative. It began too early for medical advances in public health to have made any inroads on the death rate. So far as is known, there had been no technological changes great enough to make a significant difference in the amount or dependability of food and energy available to man. Too little is known about cultural attitudes of the period, especially outside of Europe, to ascribe the increase to some factor such as average age of marriage or desired number of children.

One possibility that has been advanced is a change in the ecology of these death-dealing diseases. Many disease-causing organisms have very elaborate life-histories. Each step in the life cycle requires a very specific coupling with another organism or its physical environment. The rat-flea-bacteria association accompanying human settlement and causing the plague reflects this interdependency of disease-causing organisms. A major change in any link could drastically alter the possibility of the successful transmission of the disease. During the late Middle Ages many personal habits that were not normally regarded as being related to disease at all became widespread. For example, such things as eating from tables instead of from dirt floors, or using footwear, may have limited disease transmission. The decrease in plague that seems to have occurred during this period might have been a result of just such a change. The final disappearance of the plague in Europe in the late 17th century has been attributed to distinct changes in the ecology of rats. The black rat, which established itself in wooden houses, was displaced by the sewer-loving brown rat. This lessened the rat-to-man contact and its subsequent incidence of the plague. To be sure, the rebuilding of London after the great fire of 1666 with brick and stone in place of wood virtually brought an end to the black rat and contributed to a new and sustained period of population growth.

In any event, the gradual increase in the number of people continued, and by 1825 the population reached the 1 billion mark. Along with those unconscious changes that helped to contain outbreaks of disease were several more direct medical developments. With the realization that diseases were caused by specific organisms, not devils and demons, came the first direct attempts at introducing public health measures. The control and monitoring of the community water supply and other public health measures in cities greatly reduced infectious diseases. The beginnings of widespread inoculation and continually improving nutrition enhanced individual health and also substantially cut death rates. These advances, along with the more modern examples of personal health care, have virtually eliminated the misery of infectious diseases and accounted for the most recent period of rapid population growth.

(a) How did the incidence of disease effect overall human population growth during the ancient and middle ages? _____

_____

_____

(b) How is bubonic plague transmitted? _____

_____

(c) Why has the plague lessened its control over Western man's death rate?

_____

_____

_____

- - - - - - - - - - - - - - - - - -

(a) Disease was the main cause of human death. Through periodic sharp increases in disease-related deaths, human population growth was kept in check.
(b) black rat—flea—bacteria—man
(c) Changes in the ecology of city environments, such as brick houses and improved sewers, probably broke the human-black rat link and contributed to the plague's decline.

5. With the beginning of the Industrial Revolution, the present period of rapid human population growth began. As of yet, no new plateau has been reached.

The Industrial Revolution has, in a comparatively brief period of time, already had more profound and far-reaching implications than the agricultural revolution. If agricultural improvements gave civilization a measure of control over the biological converters of energy, then the Industrial Revolution gave man a parallel control over inanimate sources of energy. Man could not only channel and direct energy flow within ecosystems, he could exploit the energy that had been stored in past ages as fossil fuels. A multitude of technological advances, from the steam engine to mass production methods, combined to increase man's access to energy and the material things that power can produce. The application of machinery and rationalized production methods to agriculture enormously increased farm output, freeing even more rural people to pursue manufacturing occupations in growing urban industrial areas.

It would be false to picture these changes as uniformly pleasant. Working conditions in early factories were awful. Moreover, the movement of workers from the countryside to the city was accompanied by massive social dislocations. The cities, until quite recently, were as much centers of disease as of medicine. Indeed, the growing population density of urban areas and consequent crowding made public health a morbid joke. Still, the changes wrought by industrialization did have a marked influence on death rates. Mortality fell steadily from the 30 to 40 deaths per thousand per year of agricultural societies to a low of 10 to 15 deaths per thousand per year in a very few modern industrial nations. Additionally, the periodic peaks in the death rate no longer occurred. Inoculations, purer water, better sewage systems, and improved transportation made famine and disease far less capable of causing periodic large scale mortality. The Industrial Revolution set off a period of population growth that is still continuing. Mortality rates declined and birth rates remained high.

Birth rates tend to fall as an industrial nation becomes more prosperous. The drop in births seems to be tied to a rise in the standard of living. The falling of birth rates following industrialization is referred to as a demographic transition. Such a transition began in Europe around the turn of the 20th century and has begun more recently in North America, to some extent. It balances the continuing reduction in death rates. Because this phenomenon is a consequence of the late stages of industrialization, it has not occurred in the nations of India, Asia, Africa, and Latin America. These countries have received death control technology from the "developed countries" without having the industrial capacity to become prosperous at the same time. Since the major contribution to world population growth comes from these "under-developed countries," the demographic transition of Europe and North America has had very little effect on the overall growth of the world's population. The net result is that today's world population is growing at an unprecedented rate.

(a) Define demographic transition. _____

_____

(b) How has it affected world population growth? _____

_____

_____

– – – – – – – – – – – – – – – – – –

(a) the drop in birth rates following industrialization;   (b) It has had very little effect on world population growth because it has occurred only in a few industrialized countries which contribute very little to the world's total growth rate.

6.   Today, human population growth, as well as the consumption of natural resources, is advancing at an exponential rate. Projections indicate that if this trend continues, the human population will soon reach another homeostatic plateau where the negative feedback elements of the demostat will again exact their toll. The only reasonable alternative is a decrease in current growth and consumption rates.

As we have seen, past technological revolutions have allowed only an initial period of exponential growth which is then followed by an extended period of slow growth maintained on a homeostatic plateau by either the land's carrying capacity or by various factors of environmental resistance (e.g., disease). What about a new homeostatic plateau?

The amount of arable land imposes a most obvious limit to the world population's means of subsistence. Figure 10.5 shows the amount of land needed to feed the growing world population, assuming that the present world average is sufficient. The lower curve represents the land <u>needed</u>, the upper curve represents the actual amount of arable land <u>available</u>. The land available decreases because it is needed for additional urban-industrial areas as the population grows. The dotted curves show land needed if present productivity is doubled or quadrupled. Even under these most optimistic assumptions, the graph indicates that there will be a serious land shortage before the end of the 21st century if population growth continues at the present rate.

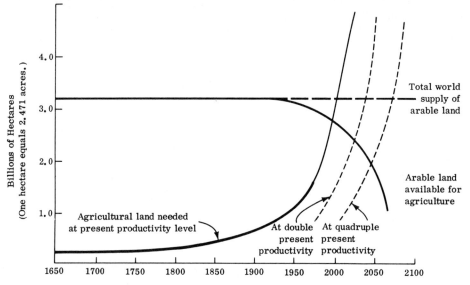

Figure 10.5 Arable land available and required by the growing human population (After Meadows, <u>et al.</u>, 1972)

In the introduction to this book, we discussed a recent study in human ecology made at the Massachusetts Institute of Technology (MIT) and published in a book, <u>The Limits to Growth</u>. That study group found that they could not predict the long-term trend of any major ecosystem component without considering the simultaneous changes in others as well. They studied five major components and their interactions: human population, industrial output, agricultural production, consumption of nonrenewable natural resources, and pollution. Their studies, based on present trends, indicated that there is indeed a limit to human population growth.

In light of this, continued elevation of the demostatic set point is not likely. As a result of the population straining at its means of subsistence, negative feedback controls will sooner or later establish a new homeostatic plateau. The negative natural checks of starvation, disease, and war threaten to provide the necessary controls. Indeed, the greatest famine the world has ever known is happening right now! If starvation is defined as a worldwide problem instead of an isolated event happening in a particular country, the great world famine of 1973-74 will destroy 15 million human beings, over half of whom will be children under the age of five.

Perhaps more serious than starvation are the possible effects of disease. Modern cities, for example, although centers of medical advancement, are becoming sources of new epidemics. Psychological stress and social pathology are on the rise in all of our urban centers. More than any other era in history, people are concentrated in smaller areas, and at the same time are constantly traveling about the world. As a result, the effects of an outbreak of some lethal virus or an "accident" with a chemical or biological warfare agent could be transmitted around the world in hours, affecting millions to billions of people, the majority of whom are malnourished and lacking in adequate medical facilities. The potential for mass fatalities is frightening. Moreover, the prospects of war are equally high and hardly need to be reaffirmed here.

In 1912 the English social theorist Edward Isaacson prefaced his book, The Malthusian Limit, with the assertion that "the most important question for the human race" was how human society could limit its numbers "to figures which can make best use of the world's natural resources." More than a half century later, his words are even more valid. Clearly, a reduction in birth rate is the only alternative. The question is whether or not the world will accept and practice effective birth control measures in time. If not, history forcefully indicates that we will experience the natural population controls of disease, famine, and war.

SELF–TEST

This Self–Test is designed to show you whether or not you have mastered this chapter's objectives. Answer each question to the best of your ability. Correct answers and review instructions are given at the end of the test.

1.   How is the human population's growth pattern unique in the world of animals? _____

_____

_____

2.   At three different periods, the human population has increased very rapidly. When did these increases occur and what are they called?

_____

_____

_____

3.   During most of civilized man's existence, his population has remained on one or another homeostatic plateau. What kept it in check? _____

_____

4.   What is happening to the human population today? _____

_____

_____

ANSWERS TO SELF-TEST

Compare your answers to the questions on the Self-Test with the answers given below. If all of your answers are correct, you are ready to go on to the next chapter. If you missed any questions, review the frames indicated in parentheses following the answer. If you miss several questions, you should probably reread the entire chapter carefully.

1. The human population is unique because the number of humans has been gradually increasing throughout its history. (frame 1)

2. about 600,000 years ago—the tool-making revolution; about 8,000 years ago—the agricultural and social revolution; beginning about 200 years ago—the Industrial-Scientific Revolution (frame 3)

3. Disease was the principal check on the human population. (frame 4)

4. Since the onset of the Industrial-Scientific Revolution, human population has been growing at an exponential rate and that trend is continuing today. (frames 5 and 6)

PART FIVE
Ecosystems

We have seen how organisms respond to the abiotic environment and how they interact with one another. In this part we focus on the product of these interactions—the ecosystem. We analyze the various structures that the ecosystem can assume as it continually cycles its substance between components and draws its power and order from the sun.

Chapter 11 investigates those ecosystems that are relatively free from the influences of man. After briefly classifying communities, we consider species diversity, ecosystem complexity and stability, and the dynamic process of ecological succession, which brings together many concepts from earlier chapters.

Chapter 12 focuses on ecosystems managed by man, which takes us through a wide range of ecosystems, from the intensely managed urban megalopolis and industrialized agricultural lands to the recreation areas of our natural parks and wilderness areas. In each case, we consider some of the possible long- and short-term consequences of man's manipulation.

CHAPTER ELEVEN

The Structure and Function of Ecosystems

OBJECTIVES

When you complete this chapter, you will be able to

- define ecosystem;
- define biotic community and biome;
- explain how biologists classify terrestrial and ocean areas into life zones;
- explain the relationship between species diversity and ecosystem stability;
- discuss spatial (vertical/horizontal) and temporal stratifications;
- explain the importance of stratification;
- explain the process of ecological succession;
- identify various types and stages of ecological succession;
- indicate some of the major characteristics of a mature ecosystem.

If you think that you have already mastered these objectives and might skip all or part of this chapter, turn to page 256 at the end of this chapter and take the Self-Test. The results will allow you to evaluate your current knowledge of this chapter's contents. If you answer all of the questions correctly, you are ready to begin the next chapter. If you miss any questions, you should study the frames indicated after the answers to the Self-Test.

If this material is new to you, or if you choose not to take the Self-Test now, proceed to frame 1.

1. An ecosystem is composed of populations interacting with each other and with the abiotic environment in a given area. Ecosystems have cybernetic mechanisms that maintain certain ecosystem-level characteristics such as stratifications, biomes, and successions.

Just as populations have characteristics not displayed by individual organisms, so ecosystems have characteristics not shown by the individual populations that compose them.

All ecosystems are open systems; they depend upon energy inputs and they produce outputs of heat (energy). Ecosystems also depend upon the biogeochemical, water, and other cycles for inputs of nutrients, water, and so forth; and they make outputs of nutrients and water. Further, most ecosystems have plants, animals, and microorganisms entering and leaving them.

In spite of being open and dynamic, ecosystems display certain characteristic structures and functions that result from the operation of various cybernetic systems operating at the ecosystem level, including stratifications, biotic communities, biomes, and ecological successions. Let's briefly define these terms:

- Biotic Communities: All plant and animal populations interacting in a given area constitute a biotic community. Most community analysis is a detailed description or classification of organisms that exist together at a given point in time. Communities that cover large geographical areas and that exhibit similar plant and animal associations as well as community structure are called biomes.

- Stratification: A layering or series of separations that differentially distributes the organisms occurring within an ecosystem. Stratifications can be described in terms of separations between organisms in space (vertical and horizontal stratifications) or in terms of separations between organisms in time (periodicity).

- Ecological Succession: The dynamic process by which ecosystems change in order to develop greater stability over the course of time.

2.   All living organisms interacting in a given area make up a biotic community. Ecologists have developed elaborate community classification schemes that allow them to predict which organisms will be found together.

The species composition of any community is determined by both the interaction between the species and the environmental conditions present. For example, seeds may be carried by wind and animals to a specific habitat, but only those that are able to dominate or coexist with species present in the community will survive and grow. One species may inhabit an area, become dominant, and prevent other less well-suited species from entering. Likewise, abiotic environmental conditions also limit the membership in a particular ecosystem. A species must be able to tolerate the limits of moisture, light intensity, wind velocity, soil composition, and temperature to remain in a particular area.

Because of the large number of different habitats[1] that may develop

---

1. The place or area that any species occupies is called its habitat. An ecosystem contains many habitats determined in part by the biotic community's structure (i.e., by the other organisms present in the ecosystem).

within very similar ecosystems (e.g., rotting logs, a clump of ferns), species composition from ecosystem to ecosystem varies considerably.

Historically, <u>biotic communities</u> have been very important to biologists. Early naturalists spent considerable time determining just which plants and animals were commonly found together, and they developed many classification systems for identifying the different biotic communities. The biotic community concept is a type of model which helps an ecologist make predictions. For example, if he locates a forest with a large number of beech and maple trees he can reasonably predict that deer and thrush will be in that same area.

A biotic community is an ecosystem minus _____.

_ _ _ _ _ _ _ _ _ _ _ _ _ _ _ _ _ _

    abiotic components

3.   The world is often divided up into large communities called <u>biomes</u>. The largest possible major community, comprised of all living organisms on or about the planet earth, is called the biosphere.

The term <u>biome</u> is used to designate very large terrestrial biotic communities. There are several different biome classifications. One classification developed by 19th century botanists is based on the dominant plant species. This classification is illustrated in figure 11.1 on the facing page.

Another system classifies biomes according to the abiotic factors in the physical habitat (which makes it, for practical purposes, also an ecosystem classification).

Holdridge's system (figure 11.2, page 232) relates the gradients of only a few abiotic factors but it can be used to predict a generalized worldwide vegetarian pattern. We might call this a biogeophysical classification system. (Note that this chart is much less reliable for areas where man has a large agricultural or urbanizing influence.) In figure 11.2 terrestrial biomes are plotted against climate, geographical, and latitudinal factors. Point A on figure 11.2, for example, designates the following conditions: mean temperature: 62°F; annual rainfall: 125 millimeters; humidity: superarid (very dry). This particular interaction of humidity, temperature, and rainfall results in a set of conditions that almost surely dictates a desert environment. Some kind of coniferous (e.g., pine, fir) forest, on the other hand, would be found where humidity is superhumid, rainfall is about 2000 millimeters per year, and mean temperature is around 39°F (point B).

Each of the biomes shown in figure 11.2 occupies a specific range on each of the three environmental gradients. Generally speaking, the tolerance limits of a species peculiar to one of these biomes will be within the area occupied by that biome. Hence, a maple forest (in the deciduous biome) and the species inhabiting it would have little difficulty becoming established in an area with the following ranges:

    temperature: between 40° and 75° Fahrenheit
    rainfall: between 500 and 9000 millimeters
    humidity: humid or perhumid

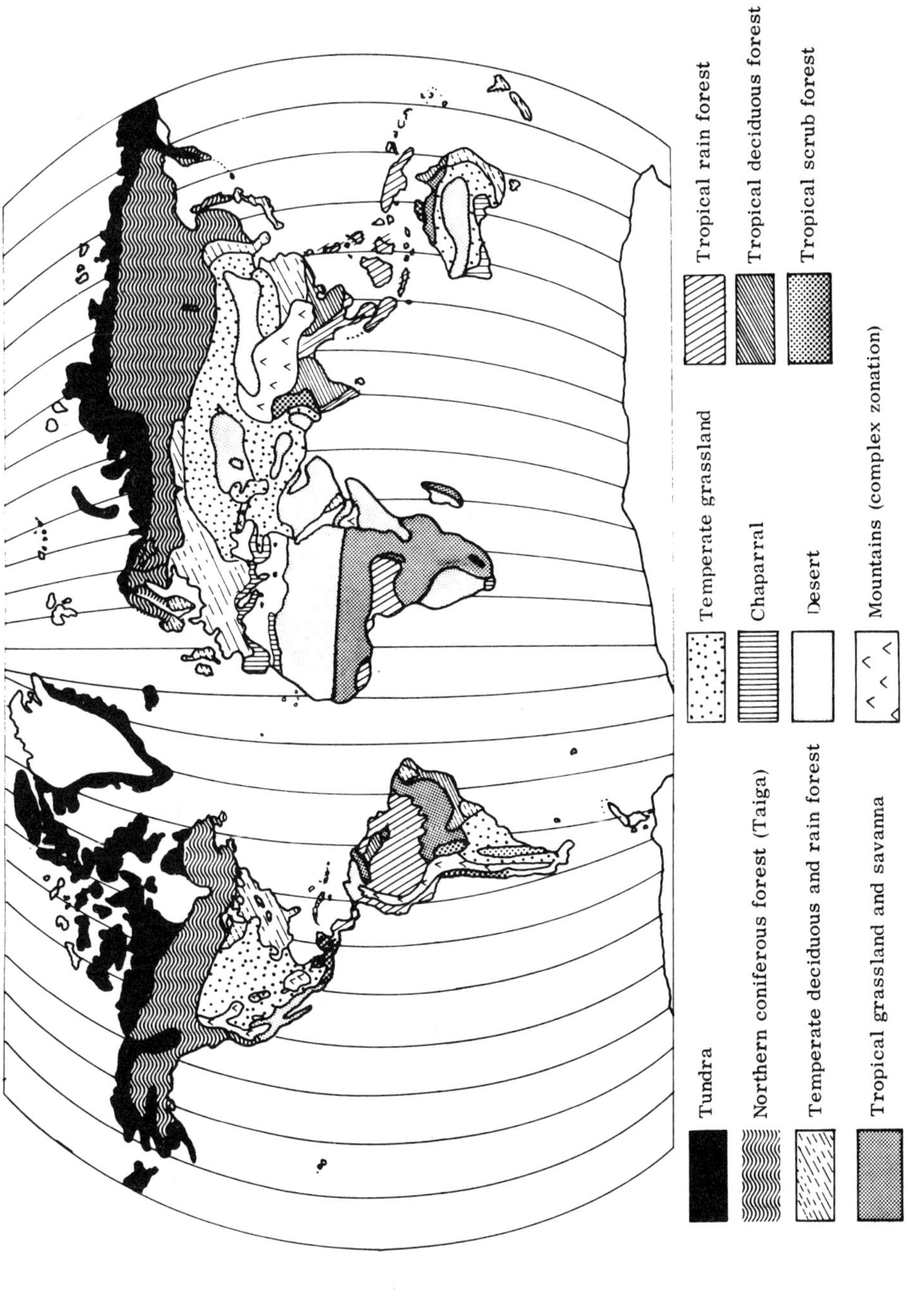

Figure 11.1   The major biome types of the world   (After Odum, 1971)

Tundra

Northern coniferous forest (Taiga)

Temperate deciduous and rain forest

Tropical grassland and savanna

Temperate grassland

Chaparral

Desert

Mountains (complex zonation)

Tropical rain forest

Tropical deciduous forest

Tropical scrub forest

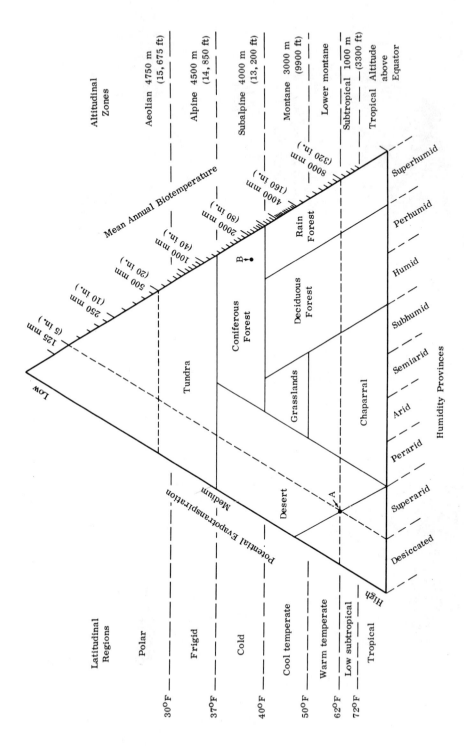

Figure 11.2 A modification of the Holdridge system of classification of the world's terrestrial life zones (After Holdridge, 1947)

Plants and animals inhabiting the deciduous forest biome can exist in an area with as little rainfall as 500 millimeters per year or as much as about 9000 millimeters per year. However, for a deciduous forest itself to exist in these extreme precipitation conditions, special altitude and temperature conditions must be met. That is, for a deciduous forest biome to appear in heavy rainfall, humidity and temperatures must be relatively high. A deciduous forest receiving light rainfall could exist only in relatively cool temperatures where humidity is lower. Although this chart generally relates rainfall, temperature, and humidity (which are shown also to relate to latitude and/or altitude), remember that it does not exhaust all of the abiotic factors.

There are also many possible biomes that are not listed in figure 11.2. For instance, a climate with wet, cool winters and long, dry, hot summers produces a forest and shrub biome that is distinct from any given one on this diagram.

All biomes, taken together, constitute the biosphere, the largest possible community, containing all living organisms on earth.

Examine figure 11.1 to determine what biome you live in. Based on that, use figure 11.2 to determine the area's limits of mean annual precipitation:

_____ and mean annual temperature:

_____. Indicate the humidity province

your biome occupies: _____.

— — — — — — — — — — — — — — — — — — — —

See figures 11.1 and 11.2. (If you live in San Francisco, for example, you would have decided that your biome was chaparral, based on figure 11.1. Then, going to figure 11.2, you would have seen that chaparral's annual precipitation ranged from 10 to 80", that its annual temperature ranged from 48° to 75°F, and that its humidity provinces included arid, semiarid, and subhumid. If you live in Washington, D.C., you would have consulted figure 11.1 and decided you lived in a deciduous forest biome. Based on that knowledge, and consulting figure 11.2, you would have decided that annual precipitation could range from 2 to 160", that annual temperature could range from 40° to 75°F, and that humidity provinces include humid and perhumid conditions.)

4.   Just as the world's land areas can be divided into biomes (sometimes called terrestrial life zones), the oceans are also divisible into life zones. The ocean's zones are classified based on water depth, temperature, water density, available light, and chemical factors such as the salt content, the amount of dissolved oxygen, and the available nitrogen and phosphate.

The most common ocean zone classification system is based on the depth of the ocean—see figure 11.3. Over 77 percent of the ocean is at least 3000 meters deep.

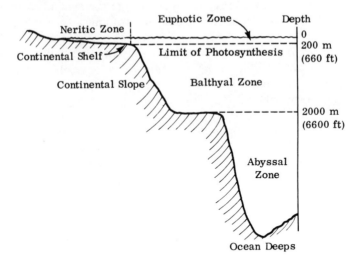

Figure 11.3   Classification of marine environments

The limited transparency of ocean water, the great depths of the oceans, and the water's salt content make ocean organisms quite different from those that inhabit the land. Photosynthesis can occur only near the ocean's surface, since bright sunlight only penetrates a short distance. (Ninety-eight percent of the sunlight entering the ocean's water is absorbed within eight feet of the surface.) Because of this, marine plants of the open ocean cannot touch the bottom of the ocean. Most ocean producers are very small, having a large surface-to-volume ratio, and sink or rise very slowly in the water. They tend to have short lifespans (often measured in hours or days rather than in the seasons or decades that often characterize large terrestrial producers). Because of their small size, their metabolism (and hence the gross production of the ocean) is very high. But also because of their small size, they use most of their energy just staying alive and reproducing, so that the net production (standing crop) of the oceans is very, very low. The total biomass in the oceans, compared to that on land, is very small.

The basic distribution of organisms in the deep oceans displays the following general pattern. Primary production occurs very near the surface and is carried out by phytoplankton (usually single-celled or very simple organisms like algae). The phytoplankton are usually eaten by zooplankton—the single-celled herbivores of the ocean. The zooplankton, in turn, are eaten by primary carnivores such as crustaceans (e.g., crabs and shrimp). Fish usually serve as secondary carnivores. Large fish eat the smaller fish. As each organism eats others, particles of the prey as well as droppings of the predator join a "rain" of organic detritus material that slowly and constantly settles to the ocean floor. Several deep-living ocean organisms live as scavengers on this falling debris. The decomposers of the ocean live in two places: among the living organisms where the detritus originates, and on the bottom, where it eventually settles and is finally digested. Upwellings of water caused by various ocean currents bring some nutrients back to the surface of the ocean to be used by the phytoplankton. Likewise, run-off from the land and detritus from the rich flora of the coastal waters also are washed into the deep oceans where they provide nutrients and foodstuffs for the phytoplankton. Usually, the deep oceans are most productive where either run-off from the land or upwellings from the ocean depths occur. Since the greatest upwellings of deep ocean material occur in the Arctic and Antarctic Oceans (caused by the cooling water temperatures), these oceans sustain the largest and most complex food webs. The center areas of the Atlantic, Pacific, and Indian Oceans have next to zero productivity.

(a) The life zones in the ocean are classified mainly by _____.

(b) The primary producers of the oceans are _____.

(c) The oceans will probably not be a storehouse from which future generations can derive rich food supplies. Why? _____

_____

- - - - - - - - - - - - - - - - - - - -

(a) water depth; (b) phytoplankton (small one-celled plants, usually algae); (c) The oceans have a very low net productivity (nearly zero). They support very little biomass. Phytoplankton are very small and use up most of the energy they fix in metabolism. Oceanic animal life is limited by this small base.

If you are considering taking a break soon, this would be a good point to stop.

5.   A generalization that has grown from the studies of biotic communities is that species diversity enhances stability in ecosystems. As with all generalizations, there are undoubtedly exceptions to this rule; however, there is ample evidence to include it as a valid principle of community ecology.

Ecosystems with many species have more complex food relationships. Individual food chains become part of a multidimensional community food web, in which there are more feeding alternatives for each species. With more species (species diversity), there are more interconnections, which ultimately tie all elements of the system tightly together. In essence a system of multiple feedback loops emerges, so that a disturbance in one part of the system is cushioned by the action of some other part. The concept of diversity should also include diversity in the physical structure of the environment and differences within individual species (e.g., age). Note that these kinds of ecological diversity are mutually reinforcing. For example, increasing the number of plant species results in more habitats, which in turn stimulates more new species to occupy those habitats.

Based on your knowledge of the relationship between species diversity and ecosystem stability, rate the following ecosystems from 1—most stable, to 3—least stable.

_____ (a) a large Iowa farm—miles and miles of one variety of wheat with no other plant allowed

_____ (b) a wild grassland field in Iowa

_____ (c) a small farm in Iowa—small fields of different crops with a small woods interspaced

– – – – – – – – – – – – – – – – – –

(a) 3;   (b) 1;   (c) 2

6. All ecosystems are stratified to some extent. <u>Stratification</u> refers to separations between organisms in space or time. An ecosystem can be stratified in space either vertically (layers) or horizontally (concentric circles). Organisms within ecosystems can also display daily, lunar, seasonal, or irregular patterns that separate them in time. In terrestrial ecosystems spatial stratification is largely determined by the plant forms present. In aquatic ecosystems, spatial stratification is usually determined by the depth, light penetration, and temperature of the water.

Communities (both aquatic and terrestrial) exhibit some form of layering or stratification. This type of environmental diversity increases the number of microhabitats and allows for a greater degree of community diversity and hence community stability. Let us look at the various ways that a community might be structurally or temporally subdivided.

• <u>Vertical Stratification</u>: Two layers of vertical stratification are commonly recognized: an <u>upper stratum</u> of light penetration, and a <u>lower regenerating stratum</u> where organic matter accumulates.

The upper stratum of light penetration is dominated by autotrophic organisms. In a terrestrial ecosystem the upper stratum is often the forest vegetation; in an aquatic ecosystem it consists of the entire upper water layer of the sea, lake, or pond. The lower regenerating stratum where organic matter accumulates is dominated by decomposers. In terrestrial ecosystems this stratum is the soil; in aquatic ecosystems it is the sediment. Both the upper and lower stratum can be divided into substrata.

The <u>upper stratum</u> of a terrestrial ecosystem, such as a forest, can be divided vertically into various layers according to the various heights of its vegetation. The great variety of life forms in a forest indicates that it is usually stratified. A deciduous forest, for example, has four main layers:

1. The tallest trees (<u>overstory</u>) which make up the <u>canopy</u> and receive the full sunlight. The foliage of these trees may absorb and scatter more than half of the available sunlight.

2. The shorter trees (<u>understory</u>) which contain some of the younger individuals of the canopy species as well as other mature species that will not reach canopy height. These trees prefer some shade.
3. The shrubs which receive only about 10 percent of the sunlight after it has filtered down through the overstory and understory.
4. The herbs, ferns, and mosses (<u>ground layer</u>) which need very little light (usually 1 to 5 percent) to exist. In a dense forest, less than 1 percent of the sunlight reaches the woodland floor.

The number of layers of vegetation above the soil and the degree to which each layer has developed varies with the type of forest. The tropical rain forest is the most highly stratified with as many as five or six layers. The well-developed deciduous forest, usually with four layers, is the next most highly stratified, while the coniferous forest, generally composed of three layers, is the least stratified. The profiles of these three forest types are illustrated in figure 11.4.

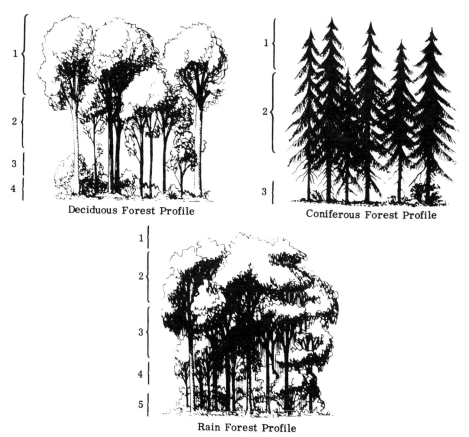

Deciduous Forest Profile

Coniferous Forest Profile

Rain Forest Profile

Figure 11.4   Stratification in main forest types

Along with stratification of the vegetation within a forest, there exists a
stratification of temperature, light, and moisture. The canopy of the forest
plays a major role in the process of this stratification since it receives the
full force of the weather. The canopy serves to modify the light intensity,
temperature, wind velocity, and moisture downward to the lower regenerating
stratum.

The lower regenerating stratum is the soil of the forest floor. Soil is
composed of three basic layers or horizons: topsoil, subsoil, and parent
material.

The soil profile and the relative thickness of the horizons vary a great
deal depending on the climate, topography, vegetation, and original material
of a particular region. An examination of the horizons of a level grassland,
a coniferous forest, and a deciduous forest show markedly different soil profiles because of the great differences in drainage, slope, wind, vegetation,
and so forth (figure 11.5). Various soils play an important role in determining the density and types of plant life that will grow in an area. The plant
life, in turn, influences the existence of soil animals such as bacteria, earthworms, millipedes, mites, and moles.

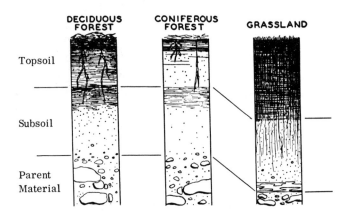

Figure 11.5   Three major soil profiles characteristic
of three major biomes (After Odum, 1971)

- Horizontal Stratification: Studying vegetation in concentric rings from
  the outer boundary of the ecosystem toward the center.

Horizontal stratification is another way of subdividing an ecosystem. Differences in vegetation are caused primarily by the climate and local conditions.
This type of stratification is most noticeable around ponds and bogs.

Horizontal changes in major communities do not begin and end abruptly.
Sometimes communities are separated by rather clear-cut boundaries, for
example, a pond bordering on a woodland. But usually communities blend
into one another so that it is difficult to determine where one starts and the
other ends. Transition areas in which two large biotic communities meet
and blend are called ecotones. A seashore, for example, is the ecotone be-

tween the terrestrial and marine communities. Ecotones usually contain organisms from both communities as well as species specifically adapted to the ecotone. This species diversity in an ecotone is sometimes called the edge effect. For instance, birds are often present in greater variety and density at the edge of a forest than in either the forest or the field proper.

Each of the substrata of an ecosystem has its own type of food, shelter, temperature, light, and humidity conditions. And thus each is suitable for particular organisms. The diversity of animal life depends upon the stratification of the plant life. Although some interchange does take place between the various layers, many of the animals that are quite mobile still spend most of their time in a single layer. For example, figure 11.6 shows the foraging niches of several birds in a spruce-fir forest in Wyoming.

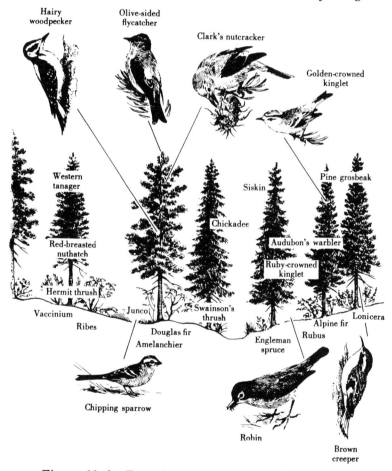

Figure 11.6 Foraging niches of some birds in a
spruce-fir forest in Wyoming (After Smith, 1966)

If we studied the deciduous forest discussed earlier, we would find that the greatest diversity and density of animal life is located on and just below the ground layer where the climate is most constant. Many of the animals such as bacteria, earthworms, moles, insects, and mites live in the lower regenerating layer below the ground layer. Other animals such as mice, ground squirrels, and foxes dig tunnels in the soil for shelter and food but spend a great deal of their time on the ground layer. Larger mammals such as the white-tailed deer, elk, and black bear live on the ground layer and feed on the herbs, shrubs, and understory of the forest. Various species of birds occupy the three higher strata, as well as herbivorous insects, tree frogs, blacksnakes, and other small mammals.

Stratification within a major community can range from one feeding layer above the ground (grassland) to as many as six feeding layers (tropical rain forest). As the degree of stratification increases, the number of available habitats also increases, leading to a greater diversity of species. Thus, greater stratification leads to more complex food webs which in turn lead to a more stable community.

(a)   Use figure 11.7 to fill in the blanks.

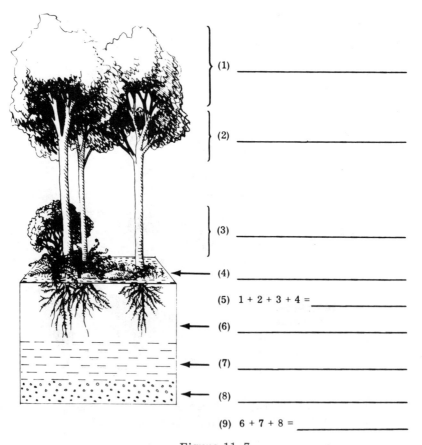

(1) _____

(2) _____

(3) _____

(4) _____

(5) 1 + 2 + 3 + 4 = _____

(6) _____

(7) _____

(8) _____

(9) 6 + 7 + 8 = _____

Figure 11.7

(b) What is the major effect of layering or vertical stratification? _____

_____

_____

(c) Figure 11.8 shows the results of a study of insect species diversity in three adjacent patches of vegetation—a beanfield, a hedge, and a pasture.

What does the figure graphically demonstrate? _____

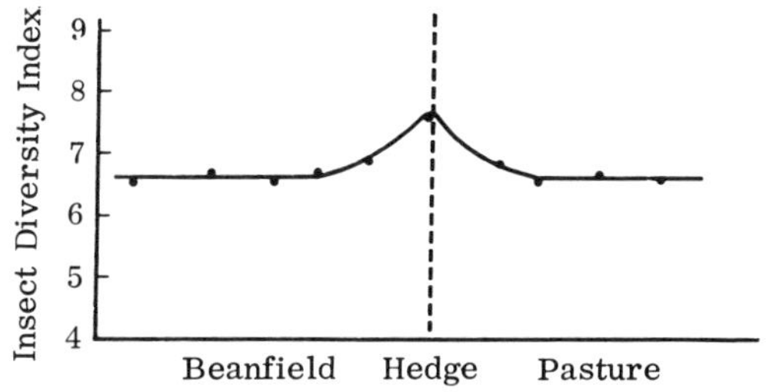

Figure 11.8   Insect species diversity on
three adjacent patches of vegetation

(d) We can say that the hedge is an _____ between

what two communities? _____

_____

(e) We said earlier that as a general rule, species diversity increases the stability of an ecosystem. Rewrite that statement to include what you

now know about stratification. _____

_____

_____

_____

- - - - - - - - - - - - - - - - - - -

(a) (1) overstory,   (2) understory,   (3) shrub,   (4) ground layer,
(5) upper stratum,   (6) topsoil,   (7) subsoil,   (8) parent material,
(9) lower regenerating stratum
(b) It increases the number of subcommunities or microhabitats in the ecosystem and therefore increases species diversity.
(c) the edge effect;
(d) ecotone, the beanfield community and the pasture community;
(e) As the degree of stratification increases, the number of available habitats also increases, leading to greater diversity of species. Thus, greater stratification leads to greater species diversity that in turn increases the stability of the ecosystem.

7.   Vertical and horizontal stratification are spatial concepts. Periodicity is another type of stratification—temporal (time) stratification. Periodicity refers to regular recurring changes that are more or less determined by the rhythmic or cyclic changes in the activities of the organisms within that ecosystem.

Most of the activities of communities are periodic. They are synchronized with physical influences such as length of day and night (photoperiodicity), light intensity, humidity, temperature, and tides. The existence of any community is dependent upon this synchronization of its activities with its environment.

Ecosystem periodicity is a result of changes in plants and animals that result from daily rhythms, lunar rhythms, and seasonal rhythms. Investigators have found that a timing function—some sort of biological clock—is virtually a universal characteristic of plants and animals. This biological function may be chemically controlled at the cellular level. Hormones—chemical substances carried in blood and body fluids—often control periodicity in animals. The immediate internal trigger for the release of the hormones themselves is the result of some action in the brain and central nervous system. Ordinarily, this trigger is set for 24 hours by external cues such as light, humidity, and temperature, which synchronize the activities of the organisms with their physical environment.

- Daily Rhythms: Most plants and animals coordinate their activities with the 24-hour photoperiod of day and night. Photoperiodism is the response of an organism to the duration and timing of light and dark conditions.

Dawn and dusk signal the beginning and end of activity depending on whether the organism is diurnal (light active) or nocturnal (dark active). These daily rhythms are often called circadian rhythms. Although the biological clock is usually set by external time cues, the 24-hour rhythms will continue, for a time at least, even if the external day/night stimuli are absent.

Photosynthesis is a good example of daily periodicity. In order to manufacture carbohydrates, a plant must have light. Therefore, the dawn signals the beginning of the food-producing process. Dusk ends the process of photosynthesis, but during the dark hours the carbohydrates are distributed throughout the plant. Another cycle begins with the new dawn.

The vertical migration of various animal plankton in shallow coastal waters illustrates a daily rhythm and photoperiodism. At night the zooplankton migrate upward to the surface waters, and then migrate downward to the bottom when day arrives. Some of the phytoplankton (diatoms) have a reverse procedure. They migrate to the surface during the day to carry on photosynthesis and move downward during the night. See figure 11.9 on the next page. This migratory activity is brought about by the plankton's response to light intensity as well as the daily currents or waves in the water.

Many mechanisms determine whether a species is diurnal or nocturnal. Each species has different requirements of light, humidity, and temperature.

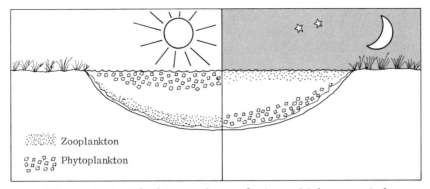

Figure 11.9   Plankton exchange during a 24-hour period

As night approaches, humidity increases and temperature decreases. Organisms such as centipedes and millipedes are not well adapted to the dry daytime air, therefore, they tend to find refuge under logs and stones during the day and come out only at night when the air has a higher relative humidity. Bees are active when flowers are open. Predators must be active when their prey is available. The adjustment of each organism's activity cycle to the light-dark cycle is a complicated process that has evolved over eons of time to accommodate the organism's particular requirements.

Since man has also been subject to these rhythms throughout his evolution, it seems likely that he also possesses daily rhythms and considerable research has shown this to be the case. Man is a diurnal animal with the peak of his activities occurring during the day. Research indicates that a man does not function as efficiently if his activities are switched to the night. This helps explain such problems as jet lag: jet travel can put a traveler out of phase with his intrinsic time schedule and can result in psychological and physical upsets.

- Lunar Rhythms: Rhythms that correspond with lunar or monthly periods.

Most organisms that show lunar periodicity are marine organisms. This is not surprising considering the moon's strong effect on the ocean tides.

- Seasonal Rhythms: Rhythms that correspond to the seasons of the year.

The biological clock is also useful in timing the activities of the community to the seasons of the year. By comparing their internal rhythms to those of their environment, organisms within the community manage to be prepared for forthcoming situations such as spring or winter. Therefore, as a result of generations of evolutionary selection, animals and plants generally reproduce at a time of year when chances for survival are optimum. Seasonal activities include the growing season of plants, mating and migration of animals, flowering and dormancy of plants, and hibernation of animals.

(a) What are the two major clues that trigger most land animals to make seasonal changes?

_____   _____

(b)   Match the following.

_____ (1) daily rhythms

_____ (2) lunar rhythms

_____ (3) seasonal rhythms

A. Organism A comes out only at night and sleeps during the day.

B. Organism B feeds only during the twilight hours.

C. Organism C folds up its leaves at night.

D. Organism D mates on beaches once every 30 days at low tide.

E. Organism E breeds in the spring and has young in midsummer, and leaves the young to fend for themselves in the late fall.

— — — — — — — — — — — — — — — — — —

(a) temperature and photoperiod (or 24-hour or day/night periods);

(b) (1) A, B, C;   (2) D;   (3) E

If you are considering taking a break soon, this would be a good point to stop.

8.   <u>Ecological succession</u> is the process by which ecosystems change over time. A particular succession progresses as a result of complex interactions of biotic and abiotic factors. One dominant species modifies the ecosystem's stratification and soil, making it less favorable for its own offspring and more favorable for the entry of some new species. In time, the new species becomes dominant and modifies its surroundings in ways that suppress the activities of the existing species and prepare for the entry of yet other new species, which in their turn also alter the environment. This gradual and continuous replacement process continues until a relatively complex and stable ecosystem develops. When this steady-state or mature ecosystem is reached, it remains in possession of the area and is self-perpetuating unless some unusual change such as a forest fire, flood, or hurricane reduces the ecosystem to a simpler stage. If a mature ecosystem is reduced to a simpler stage, the dynamic processes begin again and the ecosystem proceeds again to its mature or balanced state.

Until now we have been concerned with static or structural concepts of community stratification. Now we want to consider the dynamic nature of the ecosystem, a concept called ecological succession.

Consider this example: a Michigan farmer cleared an acre of his forested land in order to establish an irrigation pond. At first the pond was surrounded by bare soil and there was no observable plant life (though soil organisms probably remained). After a year or two, the area rimming the pond contained grasses and other small plants. A few years later this same area began to be invaded by brushes—blueberries, blackberries, and pussy willows. Later small pines and aspen trees appeared. After many years passed (assuming that the farmer did not disturb the new vegetation), the pond would be surrounded by a forest of maples, pines, oaks, and other trees. The sequence of changes that reestablished the forest was not accidental. Such a process is predictable, provided that man does not interfere. The process whereby an ecosystem changes from a simple community into a complex and relatively stable one is called ecological succession. The whole progression of communities—from the pioneer or beginning stage to the mature or stable ecosystem —is called a series. Each of the individual stages (or transitory communities) is referred to as seral community, which is temporary and may exist for a short span of time or for a great number of years. Sometimes one or more seral stages may be bypassed. For example, a grassland may grow directly into a forest of trees bypassing the brush or shrub stage. The final stage or community in a succession is called the climax community or mature ecosystem.

Although animals are by no means passive agents in ecosystem succession, the most significant changes are brought about by plants. Thus ecological successions are often called plant successions.

Figure 11.10 on the next page illustrates a generalized terrestrial succession that results in a forest climax. This succession could easily occur on any abandoned farmland in the northeastern United States. This abandoned farmland succession begins with a pioneer stage of grassland. The dominant species—grass—alters the soil and the climate near the surface of the earth, making it less favorable for grass and more favorable for shrubs. Then the shrub species becomes dominant and again alters the environment, making it more desirable for other species such as low trees. Then the low trees are succeeded by high trees. Figure 11.10 also shows the changes in bird and mammal species that occur during this succession. Gradual replacement of one plant and animal by another continues until a relatively stable forest ecosystem is established. As each stage succeeds the former, the ecosystem becomes more complex. More habitats are created and consequently species diversity increases, as the table below indicates.

	Grassland 1-10 years	Shrubs 10-25 years	Low Trees 25-100 years	High Trees 100 or more years
Number of Different Species	2	8	15	18
Density (pairs per 100 acres)	27	123	113	233

Figure 11.10   Changes in the variety of birds and mammals in a northeastern U.S. ecosystem as that system changed into a climax or mature ecosystem   (After Smith, 1966)

(a) Define ecological succession. _____

_____

_____

(b) Briefly explain what is happening in figure 11.11.

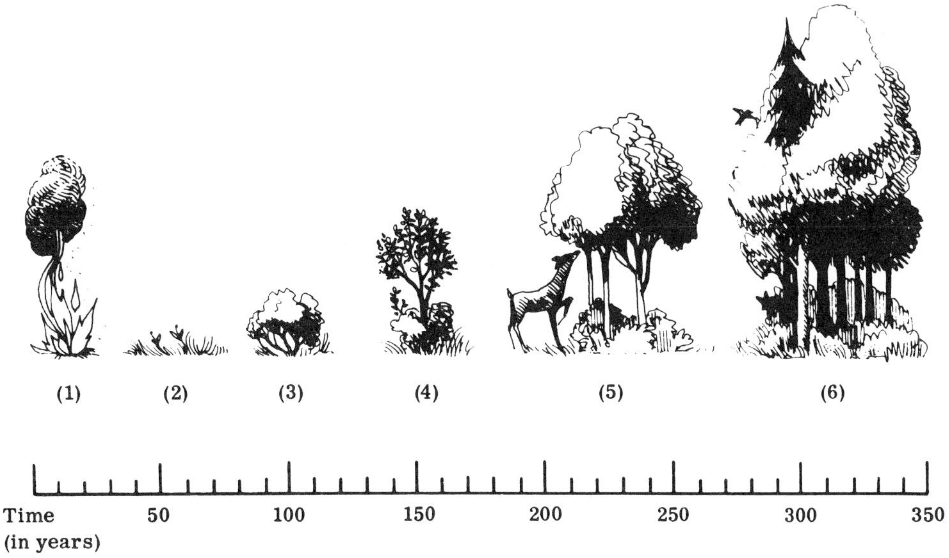

| (1) | (2) | (3) | (4) | (5) | (6) |

Time   50   100   150   200   250   300   350
(in years)

Figure 11.11

(1) Fire destroys a beech-maple climax forest, leaving only burned
     ground. The community begins again with only soil organisms and
     no surface animals (or habitats).

(2) _____

_____

(3) _____

_____

(4) _____

_____

(5) _____

_____

(6) _____

_____

- - - - - - - - - - - - - - - - - - - -

(a) Ecological succession is an orderly process whereby ecosystems
change over the course of time. Succession results from the interaction
of biotic and abiotic factors and finally results in a complex, stable,

mature ecosystem (or climax community).

(b) (2) Grass begins to grow. As it lives and dies, soil slowly accumulates. Insects and new microbes come into the community and it becomes slightly more complex.

(3) Bushes begin to grow in the field. Rabbits and mice and perhaps a fox arrive. Birds that nest and live in fields establish residence. The soil becomes rich. The ground is more protected by the shrubs from sunlight by day and cold winds at night.

(4) Trees spring up and the animal life multiplies. The numbers of trees and shrubs increase yearly.

(5) A forest is established. Some trees become taller and other, smaller trees and shrubs grow beneath them, so that there are many layers of foliage and, consequently, more animals. Forest birds move in and field birds move elsewhere.

(6) Finally, an established or climax beech-maple forest ecosystem results again. Huge trees grow up and shade the ground. The ground cover consists of ferns and other shade-loving plants. Animals that live in the deep beech-maple forest become established again.

9.   Successions in water environments are called <u>aquatic successions</u>.

If the man-made pond we discussed in frame 8 were left unattended, an aquatic succession would take place. The first form of life that would inhabit the man-made pond would be floating organisms (plankton) consisting of algae (phytoplankton) and microscopic animal life (zooplankton). As the pond became older, it would become more and more populated with vegetation. Its size would decrease as it filled with organic sediment created by the accumulation of dead plant tissue. As this sediment continued to accumulate, the vegetation at the edge of the pond would change from floating plants to aquatic rooted vegetation, and then to terrestrial vegetation. The pond would gradually become a swamp. This aquatic succession would continue until the former pond became dry land. Once the former pond became dry land, the aquatic succession would be ended and a terrestrial succession would begin. Figure 11.12 on the facing page shows three stages in this aquatic succession.

Not all aquatic successions result in dry land. If a particular body of water is very large and deep, or if a powerful physical condition such as strong wave action is present, a stable aquatic ecosystem will result.

Man has often tried to maintain "desirable" communities without realizing that succession is inevitable in most aquatic and terrestrial communities. For example, in Lake Tahoe, California, unwanted plant species, such as algae, arrowhead plants, or cattails, which detract from the lake's appearance and recreational usefulness, are constantly being removed, yet continually reappear. This effort is costly and will continue to be necessary as long as men want Lake Tahoe to remain at an immature aquatic successional stage.

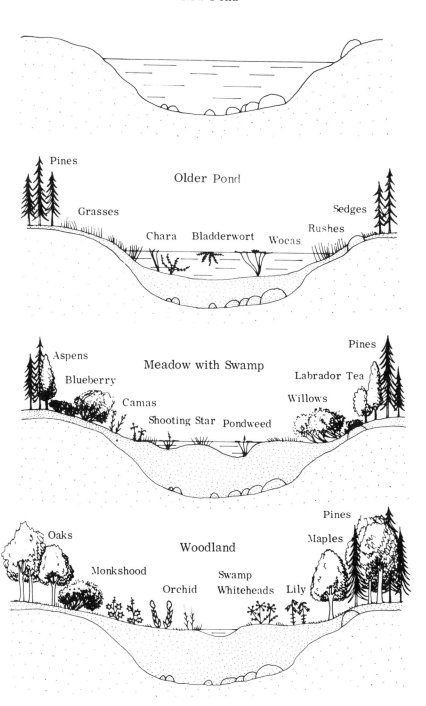

Figure 11.12   Stages in a typical aquatic succession

The evolution of a bend in a slow moving river into an isolated pond (as the river shifts its channel) and then into a swamp and finally into a rich valley bottom is an example of _____.

_ _ _ _ _ _ _ _ _ _ _ _ _ _ _ _ _ _

    an aquatic succession

10.   After a succession has passed through its many seral stages, it eventually reaches a somewhat steady state or equilibrium with its environment. This final stage in the successional process is commonly referred to as a mature ecosystem or climax community. This stage contains a relatively stable and diverse set of species interacting through complex food web patterns. The overall ecosystem production and respiration tend to be balanced.

Mature ecosystems are not static. Instead, they are slowly changing as self-destructive biological changes continually occur. Major shifts in the biotic or abiotic environment can cause rapid change. For the most part, climax communities are those ecosystems that have adapted to gross climatic and topographical patterns and reflect stability only insofar as they are capable of responding favorably to various short-term environmental disturbances (such as the change of seasons or a frost). Only time and the specific conditions that arise in the environment can determine future stability of these systems.

What is a mature ecosystem like? Will it last forever? _____

_____

_____

_____

_ _ _ _ _ _ _ _ _ _ _ _ _ _ _ _ _ _

    A mature ecosystem is the end product of a succession. It is a balanced ecosystem that shows little tendency to change further. Mature ecosystems are often destroyed by natural disasters (fire, flood) and by man.

11.   While climate and other physical factors influence the composition of the ecosystem, it is essentially the ecosystem itself which brings about succession.

No one can completely explain the process of ecological succession. We know that it is influenced by climate since climax communities vary with the type of climate (such as the desert or the Arctic). But it is not caused by climate because even in an area with a stable climate the ecological succession activity continues. Succession appears to be caused by the ecosystem itself. As each early successional species modifies its environment, it makes it less favorable for itself and more favorable for a new species. This process continues until the equilibrium or steady state is finally reached. The final outcome is determined, therefore, by the total environment and not by only one factor such as climate.

What causes ecological succession? _____

_____

_____

_____

– – – – – – – – – – – – – – – – – – –

You should have said something like: There is no one complete answer. Climate and other physical factors influence the composition of the ecosystem, but basically it is the community itself, interacting dynamically, that brings about succession.

12. Succession can be related to energy flow within the ecosystem. Productivity—the rate at which organisms fix biomass—varies with ecological succession. Immature or early successional communities have high net productivity, whereas mature or climax ecosystems tend toward zero net productivity. This process dictates that climax communities be made up of large, long-lived organisms, many niches, and complex food webs. All tissue growth is consumed, thus maintaining a balance.

We said earlier that productivity refers to the rate at which an ecosystem fixes or accumulates biomass. Gross productivity includes the production of tissue that organisms will later break down in photosynthesis or respiration. Net productivity refers to the biomass accumulated in excess of that used for respiration. Using these concepts, as well as what we know about energy flow in general, we can consider how energy helps to determine the organization and succession of particular ecosystems. Ecosystems tend toward a state in which the energy entering the ecosystem is balanced by the energy consumed by the ecosystem. Simple ecosystems are prone to many fluctuations, hence ecosystems tend to become more complex so that energy inputs and outputs will become balanced. An ecosystem keeps changing toward a combination of plants and animals that can use all of the energy the system can fix. This is what we meant in Chapter 1 when we said that energy acts to organize a system.

By examining the amount of energy that is exported from an ecosystem, we can gain some insight into the "maturity" of the ecosystem.

In an oak-pine forest at the Brookhaven National Laboratory, Dr. George M. Woodwell determined that 80 percent of the production was expended in respiration. Thus, about 20 percent was stored for the future. Significantly, a forester would say that this forest was in a "late successional" stage, meaning that it had been developing for a good while but was not yet fully mature since the trees had not yet reached their full or maximum growth. Applying what we know about an ecosystem tending toward zero net productivity, we can predict that the producers of this community (the oak and pine trees) will get larger and therefore more efficient and that larger herbivores and carnivores will settle there until the ecosystem's total ability to utilize the energy that it fixes is equal to its gross production.

Climax communities, as transient as they sometimes turn out to be, seem to be ecological approximations of the most efficient way that the resources of a particular area can be used to support life without adversely affecting neighboring ecosystems or causing them to adversely affect that particular site.

The process of ecological succession, viewed as a tendency toward the efficient use of all available energy, is diagrammed in figure 11.14, on the facing page.

Label each of the diagrams in figure 11.13 below, describing what succession stage it is probably in.

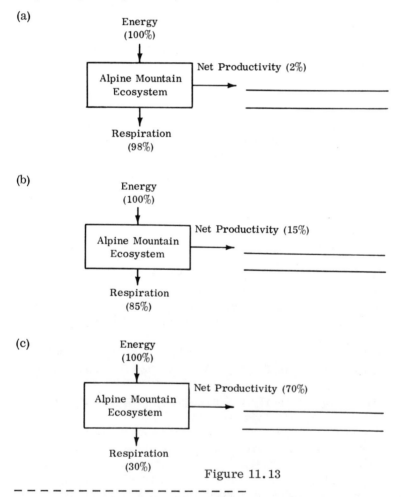

Figure 11.13

- - - - - - - - - - - - - - - - - -

(a) very late successional or mature community; (b) developing or late successional community; (c) early or new successional community

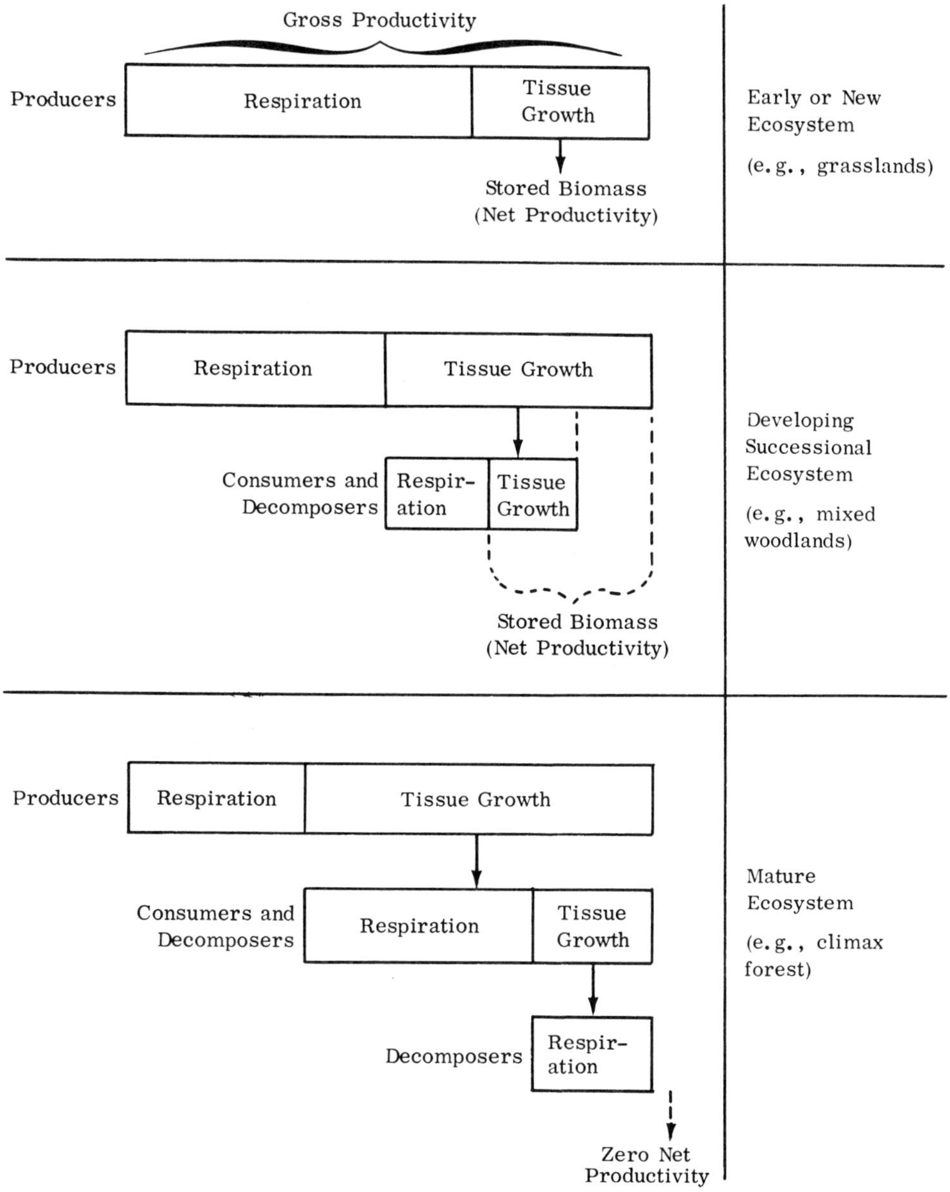

Gross Productivity

Producers	Respiration	Tissue Growth

Early or New
Ecosystem

(e.g., grasslands)

Stored Biomass
(Net Productivity)

Producers	Respiration	Tissue Growth

Consumers and Decomposers	Respiration	Tissue Growth

Developing
Successional
Ecosystem

(e.g., mixed
woodlands)

Stored Biomass
(Net Productivity)

Producers	Respiration	Tissue Growth

Consumers and Decomposers	Respiration	Tissue Growth

Decomposers	Respiration

Mature
Ecosystem

(e.g., climax
forest)

Zero Net
Productivity

Figure 11.14   Ecological succession as a process
of maximizing use of available energy

13.   Summary of ecological succession tendencies:

Figure 11.15 Ecosystem Successional Tendencies (Modified after Odum, 1969)		
Viewpoint and Attribute	Early Stages	Mature Ecosystem
• <u>Energy</u>		
1. Gross production/community respiration (P/R ratio)	Greater or less than 1	Approaches 1
2. Biomass supported/unit energy flow (B/E ratio)	Low	High
3. Net community production (e.g., agricultural yield)	High	Low
4. Food relationships	Simple, linear, predominantly grazing	Complex, weblike, predominantly detritus
5. Loss of energy	High	Low
• <u>Cycles</u>		
6. Total biomass	Small	Large
7. Inorganic nutrients	Mostly from outside	Mostly from within
8. Biochemical diversity	Low	High
9. Mineral cycles	Open	Closed
10. Nutrient exchange rate (between organisms and environment)	Rapid	Slow
11. Role of detritus in nutrient regeneration	Unimportant	Important
12. Nutrient conservation	Poor	Good
• <u>Populations</u>		
13. Niche specialization	Broad (few niches)	Narrow (many niches)
14. Size of dominant organisms	Small	Large
15. Organisms' life cycles	Short, simple	Long, complex
16. Symbiotic relationships	Undeveloped	Developed
17. Natural selection pressures on member organisms	Selected for rapid growth	Selected for ability to adjust to minor changes

Viewpoint and Attribute	Early Stages	Mature Ecosystem
• Ecosystems		
18. Species diversity	Low	High
19. Objective of biomass production	Quantity	Quality
20. Stratification	Simple	Complex
21. Resistance to external disturbances	Poor	Good

Figure 11.15 is a modified form of a model developed by E. P. Odum that summarizes trends to be expected as ecosystems change from immature to mature systems. This model is interesting because it illustrates how many of the viewpoints and concepts we have studied separately can be integrated by a single dynamic model like ecological succession.

We can summarize the ecological succession process itself as follows:

- Ecosystems change in an orderly, directed fashion and in a predictable way.
- The change results from modifications of the abiotic environment by the biotic community.
- This change continues, increasing in complexity, until it results in a stabilized ecosystem in which the maximum biomass and largest number of organism interrelations (symbiotic functions) are maintained relative to the total energy available to the ecosystem.
- If a climax community is simplified by some outside force, it redevelops until it again attains stability.

Match the following columns. In a <u>mature</u> ecosystem, we can assume the following:

_____ (a) high or large or complex

_____ (b) low or small or simple

(1) species diversity
(2) loss of energy
(3) nutrient conservation
(4) net productivity
(5) food relationships
(6) size of organisms
(7) stratification
(8) biochemical diversity
(9) total biomass
(10) size of typical niche
(11) stability

- - - - - - - - - - - - - - - - -

(a) 1, 3, 5, 6, 7, 8, 9, 11; (b) 2, 4, 10

SELF-TEST

This Self-Test is designed to show you whether or not you have mastered this chapter's objectives. Answer each question to the best of your ability. Correct answers and review instructions are given at the end of the test.

1. Define ecosystem. Explain how it can be both an open and a closed system. Give examples. _____

   _____

   _____

   _____

   _____

2. Explain the relationship between species diversity and ecosytem stability.

   _____

   _____

3. Define biotic community. _____

   _____

   _____

4. Explain what happens where two biotic communities blend together.

   _____

   _____

   _____

5. Define biome. Explain two systems for classifying them. _____

   _____

   _____

   _____

   _____

   _____

6. Is the ocean one large life zone? Explain your answer. _____

   _____

   _____

   _____

   _____

7. Explain vertical, horizontal, and temporal stratification. Give examples.

_____

_____

_____

8. Explain the importance of stratification. _____

_____

_____

_____

9. Examine figure 11.16. Explain what is happening. Go into some detail.

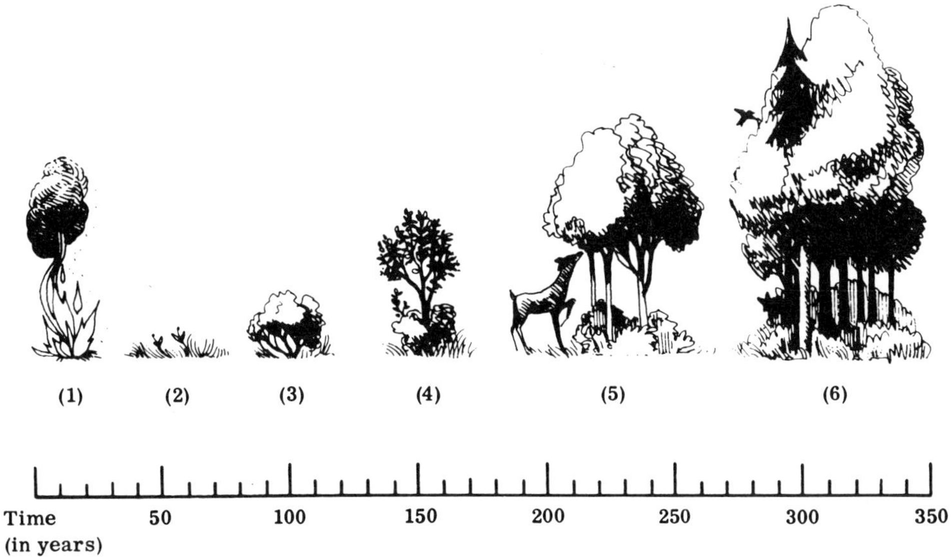

(1)   (2)   (3)   (4)   (5)   (6)

Time   50   100   150   200   250   300   350
(in years)

Figure 11.16

_____

_____

_____

_____

_____

_____

_____

_____

_____

_____

10. If the same sort of thing that is pictured in figure 11.16 happened in a lake ecosystem, what would it be called? _____

11. Assume you are examining an <u>immature</u> ecosystem. Label each item <u>H</u> if you expect it to be high, or large, or complex; and <u>L</u> if it is low, or small, or simple.

_____ (a) species diversity

_____ (b) loss of energy

_____ (c) nutrient conservation

_____ (d) net productivity

_____ (e) food relationships

_____ (f) size of organisms

_____ (g) stratification

_____ (h) biochemical diversity

_____ (i) total biomass

_____ (j) size of typical niche

_____ (k) stability

ANSWERS TO SELF-TEST

Compare your answers to the questions on the Self-Test with the answers given below. If all of your answers are correct, you are ready to go on to the next chapter. If you missed any questions, review the frames indicated in parentheses following the answer. If you miss several questions, you should probably reread the entire chapter carefully.

1. An ecosystem is composed of all the populations living in a given area interacting with each other and with the abiotic environment. All ecosystems are open systems: they need energy, nutrients, and occasional organisms from outside themselves to continue to function. They are also closed systems since they have certain cybernetic mechanisms that give them certain characteristic structures and functions including communities, stratifications, and ecological successions. (frame 1)

2. The greater the species diversity, the greater the stability of the ecosystem. (frames 5, 6, and 13)

3. all of the living organisms in an ecosystem (or given area) interacting together (minus the abiotic components of the ecosystem) (frame 2)

4. The area where two biotic communities blend together is called an ecotone. Plant and animal life is especially varied, complex, and dense there—an effect referred to as the edge effect. (frame 6)

5. A biome is a large terrestrial community. One common biome classification is based on the dominant plant species and uses such designations as tundra, northern coniferous forest, grassland, desert. Another system—the Holdridge—plots climate, geographical, and latitudinal factors against each other to arrive at biogeophysical descriptions of biomes. (frame 3)

6. No, like the land the ocean can be divided into many life zones depending upon such variables as light, depth of water, salinity of water, nutrients present, and temperature. (frame 4)

7. All ecosystems exhibit some form of stratification. Stratification refers to consistent general patterns of organism distribution, occurrence and abundance, or activity level, within the area of the ecosystem. In terms of space, a community can be stratified either vertically or horizontally. In terms of time, organisms within an ecosystem can display daily, lunar, or seasonal stratification (or periodicity, or rhythms). In terrestrial ecosystems, the spatial stratification is largely determined by the plant forms present. In aquatic ecosystems, spatial stratification is usually determined by the depth of the water. (frames 6 and 7)

8. As the degree of ecosystem stratification increases, the number of available habitats also increases, leading to a greater diversity of species. Thus, greater stratification leads to greater species diversity, which in turn increases the stability of the ecosystem. (frames 5, 6, and 13)

9. Figure 11.16 depicts an ecological succession. Ecological succession is a process by which ecosystems change over the course of time. It is an orderly process resulting from the interaction of biotic and abiotic factors and finally results in a complex, stable, mature ecosystem (or climax community). In this particular diagram, by numbered stages:
    (1) Fire burns the ground, leaving only soil microbes—an ecosystem without any complexity or stability.
    (2) Grass begins to grow. As it lives and dies, soil slowly, slowly accumulates. Insects and new microbes come into the community and it becomes slightly more complex—an early or immature successional stage.
    (3) Bushes begin to grow in the field. Rabbits and mice and perhaps a fox arrive. Birds that nest and live in fields establish residence. The soil becomes rich. The ground is more protected by the shrubs from sunlight by day and cold winds at night.
    (4) Trees spring up and the animal life multiplies. The number of trees and shrubs increases yearly.
    (5) A forest is established. Some trees become taller and other smaller trees and shrubs grow beneath them, so that there are many layers of foliage and, consequently, more animals. Forest birds move in and field birds move elsewhere.
    (6) Finally, an established, mature or climax (beech-maple) forest ecosystem results again. Huge trees grow up and shade the ground. The ground cover consists of ferns and other shade-loving plants. Animals that live in the deep beech-maple forest become established again. This climax community will continue to exist in a steady state unless a major natural disaster (fire, earthquake) or man interferes.
    (frame 8)

10. aquatic succession (frame 9)

11. (a) L; (b) H; (c) L; (d) H; (e) L; (f) L; (g) L; (h) L;
    (i) L; (j) H; (k) L (frame 13)

CHAPTER TWELVE

Human Ecosystems

OBJECTIVES

When you complete this chapter, you will be able to

- give examples of "human ecosystems";
- explain some of the basic kinds of environments required by man;
- explain some of the purposes and dangers of agricultural ecosystems;
- explain the basic ecological nature of urban ecosystems.

If you think that you have already mastered these objectives and might skip all or part of this chapter, turn to page 271 at the end of the chapter and take the Self-Test. The results will allow you to evaluate your current knowledge of this chapter's contents. If you answer all of the questions correctly, you can skip this chapter. If you miss any questions, you should study the frames indicated after the answers to the Self-Test.

If this material is new to you, or if you choose not to take the Self-Test now, proceed to frame 1.

1.   The needs and desires of an expanding world population have required intensive environmental management. Indeed, man's interventions have created entirely new environments which we shall call <u>human</u> <u>ecosystems</u>.

These intensely managed areas, especially cities, have succeeded in shielding their human inhabitants from the rigors of the external world to such a degree that some people may have forgotten that these areas depend upon the life-sustaining properties of the earth's natural ecosystems. In attempts to maximize yields in agricultural systems, for example, we often lose other beneficial qualities of less productive but more diverse communities. We will consider human environments from the ecosystem perspective developed in the last chapter. You will quickly learn that they do not exist in isolation, but depend, like any other ecosystem, on an external source of energy, on various cycles, and on intricate interrelationships with natural ecosystems.

2.   Since the Industrial Revolution, man has sharply increased
        his control over the land surface of the world ecosystem.

For at least 10,000 years, ever since man assumed a dominant role in the world, he has exercised some degree of control over it. The intensity and prevalence of such management, however, has seen its most dramatic increase in the last two hundred years since the beginning of the Industrial Revolution. Today it is estimated that approximately 11 percent of the earth's land surface is intensely managed; 30 percent moderately managed; and 59 percent only slightly utilized by human societies.

Match the following:

_____ (a) 11 percent intensely managed

_____ (b) 30 percent moderately managed

_____ (c) 50 percent slightly utilized

(1) New York City
(2) African hunting preserve
(3) large automated farm
(4) the Antarctic region
(5) farmland in India
(6) rice paddies in China
(7) grazing land in the outback of Australia
(8) high mountain regions

- - - - - - - - - - - - - - - - - -

(a) 1, 3, 6;   (b) 2, 5, 7;   (c) 4, 8

3.   Man manages ecosystems to obtain high agricultural yields.
        High yields (high net productivity) necessitate holding the eco-
        system at an early successional stage, and hence increasing
        its instability.

The activities of man have been involved in maximizing the productivity of ecosystems, usually by increasing the numbers of one or two species of organisms. Here we find a dangerous conflict between the goals of man and the strategy of ecosystem development. Recall from the last chapter that the successional process is directed toward the maximization of a complex community structure, in which the amount of diversity and biomass is increased, and the yield or community production decreases until virtually all energy fixed goes into the maintenance of the community structure (community respiration). We have also seen that accompanying the many tendencies of ecosystem development is an increase in the system's ability to resist external disturbances (an increase in stability). Yet man actively arrests this process by developing and maintaining early successional types of ecosystems as he strives for the highest possible yields.

We can divide ecosystems, from a human point of view, into four general classes.

1. Mature Natural Ecosystems: ecosystems that are more or less in their natural states. These are generally unused and uninhabited by man (e. g. , wilderness areas, mountains, deserts).

2. Managed Natural Ecosystems: ecosystems that are managed by man for recreational use or for the production of natural products (e. g. , parks, managed forests, hunting areas, some areas of the oceans).

3. Productive Ecosystems: ecosystems used by man for the intensive production of foodstuffs or natural resources (e. g. , farms, cattle ranches, stripmined areas).

4. Urban Ecosystems: ecosystems in which man lives and works (e. g. , industrial areas, cities, and towns).

As human population has grown, ecosystems in classes 2, 3, and 4 have increased sharply, ultimately at the expense of class 1. In fact, given population growth there is no alternative to this pattern.

Ecologists, however, have always argued for some balance between all of the classes since each of these types is required by man. His need for urban and productive ecosystems is obvious. The necessity for parks and other semi-wild areas is also usually conceded. It is man's requirement for wilderness that is less generally understood, for traditionally he has considered open land nonproductive, and hence of little value. Yet mature natural ecosystems must not be measured in strictly economic terms. Their cleansing effect on the atmosphere and their value for the study of undisturbed natural areas are only two examples of their benefit to man. Mature natural ecosystems not only maintain themselves, but they function as a filter for more intensively used ecosystems. The forests and mountains help purify an area just as the ocean dilutes the pollutants that wash into it. If a balance is maintained, natural ecosystems can absorb and neutralize man's pollution as they have in the past. If wilderness regions are reduced sharply at the same time that pollution is increased, however, environmental problems will worsen considerably.

(a) When man creates an ecosystem, what is his usual aim?

_____

(b) In what way is his aim efficient; in what way inefficient?

_____

_____

_____

_____

(a) maximizing productivity; (b) It is usually efficient in producing the maximum biomass the area can produce. It is usually inefficient in that he uses the maximum amount of energy to produce this biomass and the maximum productivity requires simplification of the ecosystem, which increases its instability.

4. Mechanized agriculture areas are some of man's most intensively manipulated productive ecosystems. Tremendous amounts of energy are necessary to obtain great harvests from these systems, and the larger harvests needed in the near future will require even more energy inputs. Because agricultural ecosystems tend to have only one crop, they are called monocultures. Although this practice makes planting, care, and harvesting of crops more efficient, it also creates simplified and therefore very unstable ecosystems that are especially subject to diseases and insect epidemics.

Productive ecosystems include all ecosystems that man intensively manages for the harvest of food or resources. Agricultural ecosystems are typical productive ecosystems; they are simplified systems that depend upon repeated additional inputs. Accompanying the impressive yields of the "green revolution," for instance, is an equally impressive roster of inputs needed to sustain that yield. The new crop varieties produce high yields only when cared for properly. Technology, in the form of fertilizer, pest and weed control, irrigation or proper water management, and the machinery required to harvest and transport the crops, is indispensable.

Indeed, it is estimated that the energy requirements necessary for the production and transport of these subsidies is increasing faster than the yield itself. Although productivity is constantly pushed higher and higher, it has been calculated that to double present world food resources it will take 6.5 times as much fertilizer, 6 times as much pesticides, and 2.8 times more power than required today. This is because more and more marginal land must be forced to grow the crops needed by man. At such an energy deficit, it is hard to conceive of this type of system resulting in a dependable sustained yield over the long run.

Some people think of wheat growing in the desert as a "miracle" because man could not get food there before. Yet if the wheat were measured as calories of energy, from which were subtracted the calories consumed in irrigation, mechanical plowing and harvesting, fertilizing, and fighting insect pests, we would find that deserts produce only the same net calorie energy as they did before man intervened. In the short run, of course, a gain appears evident, since hungry people can eat wheat but not cactus or the fuel oil and fertilizers required in production of the crop. But what happens when the earth's limited supply of oil, gas, and fertilizers runs out?

Let's examine some of the simplifying features of modern agricultural practices. Almost every aspect of ecological diversity described in the last chapter is reduced in an agricultural community. Probably the most obvious consequence is the enormous decrease in species diversity. Most mechanized agricultural ecosystems are designed to use a single crop species while at the same time removing all competing and interfering species. Obviously these monocultures lack the inherent system of checks and balances present in diversified natural communities. We know that a highly stratified (both vertically and horizontally) community is likely to harbor a greater number of species and has a potentially greater capacity to resist disruption. Simplifying the physical structure in agricultural systems may do several things. It can eliminate barriers to the crop-wide spread of pest infestation as well as eliminate the habitats that would otherwise support a variety of the pest's natural enemies. The quaint acreage of hedgerows and assorted patches of crops in England, for example, have elements of native wisdom as well as landscape aesthetics. We have seen how hedges, with their consequent increase in edge effect, enriches the insect species diversity and hence the checks and balances available in that ecosystem. In England, however, the hedges are now giving way to the mechanized plow as the British seek more short-term efficiency.

A large expanse of one crop may be harvested more efficiently by man, but it also represents a paradise for organisms that compete with man for a share of it. These "pests" can multiply into huge numbers in environments that lack diverse varieties of predators and competitors which act to limit the success of one another. Large monocultures, with their constant threat of pest epidemics, have thus created an ever increasing demand for chemical means of control.

Another biological pitfall of the "green revolution" and its high yield grains involves the reduction in genetic diversity in the crops themselves. The new plants, called hybrids, are developed from stock taken from around the world, and are bred for high yield, responsiveness to fertilizer, and adaptability to various climatic conditions. Many times, however, the move to higher yields has sacrificed other beneficial plant characteristics, such as protein content, palatability, and, most important, resistance to disease and pest epidemics. New crops usually have been developed upon a very narrow genetic base and contain a minimum of genetic variability. Because of the high degree of biological uniformity and the fact that large tracts of adjoining land are planted in the same variety, the crops are much more susceptible to new disease outbreaks or pest infestations. With little genetic variability, there is little chance that these plants will be naturally resistant to these new threats and thus be able to survive.

This is not just wild conjecture, but a biological reality that has shown its gruesome face more than once. The story of "Victory" oats and "Hope" wheat bears out this tragic scenario. Two decades ago, U.S. oat breeders developed a strain called Victory oats, with a gene for crown rust resistance.[1] Just as Victory oats became widely accepted, however, another fungus

---

1. Rusts are types of fungus that commonly attack grain plants.

specific to them appeared. Within two years, this new rust became so wide-spread in the U.S. that Victory oats no longer could be safely grown. It was a short-term "Victory" at best. Wheat farmers hoped for the end of their wheat rust problems with the development of a "Hope" gene in the 1930s. Because the new gene showed great promise of rendering the wheat resistant to the stem rust, it was not long before the entire wheat-growing region of the U.S. from Texas to North Dakota displayed monocultures of Hope wheat. By the late 1940s, however, yet another new stem rust fungus appeared and spread across the western U.S., nearly bringing a halt to wheat production in the northern Great Plains.

Presently there are 18 million acres of a new high yield dwarf wheat (developed by Dr. Norman Borlaug, for which he was awarded the 1970 Nobel Prize) planted around the world. It is widely grown throughout Mexico, the western U.S., and the wheat-growing areas of South America. At the moment man is enjoying greatly increased yields from this new strain. In the future, however, we should not be surprised if the chemical control methods constantly used to maintain this production suddenly prove inadequate to curtail some newly evolved disease or pest species.

Of course, advanced agricultural practices have made a tremendous contribution to the immediate welfare of mankind, and it is not our intention to belittle this contribution. It is our concern, however, that short-term boosts in the immediate yield lead to many biological oversights which jeopardize future prospects of the system to sustain itself. The ability to modify and manage ecosystems is undoubtedly one of man's most powerful traits. It is crucial, however, that he recognize the probable consequences of his actions. Men must consider the risks of modern agricultural techniques in light of current ecological knowledge about the structure and function of ecosystems. Ultimately the goal must be the reduction of these risks. It is important that this reduction be started at once.

(a) Define monoculture. _____

_____

(b) Is a monoculture an early or mature stage of succession? Why?

_____

_____

_____

(c) What are some of the ecological problems inherent in monocultures?

_____

_____

_____

- - - - - - - - - - - - - - - - - -

(a) an agricultural ecosystem with a single crop (e.g., a huge area of one species of wheat or corn); (b) It is a very early stage of a succession. Mature ecosystem successions are characterized by complexity, species diversity, energy conservation, many niches, and checks and balances. A monoculture lacks all of these characteristics—it is as simple as man can make it. (c) Because of its ecological simplicity, a monoculture lacks the ability to exist without constant care and protection by man. This care includes tractor planting, fertilization, irrigation, and a constant fight against insects and plant diseases. At the same time, insects and disease are constantly evolving new resistances to man's sprays and threatening to become epidemic on the large areas covered by a single crop.

5. An urban ecosystem is man's most intensively managed environment. It requires constant inputs, makes constant outputs, and has many internal feedback cycles. Men in cities have both biological and cultural requirements.

Men began to create the special ecosystems we call cities about 8 to 10 thousand years ago when his discovery of agriculture led him to establish permanent living areas, storage areas, and irrigation systems. Today, the majority of the people living in industrialized countries live in urban regions. Even in underdeveloped countries people are rapidly moving into large cities. About 20 percent of the world's population lives in urban concentrations of more than 100,000 people. As cities have grown in size they have also grown in complexity and man has developed very elaborate systems to control the land, air, water, and energy flow through them. Yet for all man's influence and intensive control, cities are still ecosystems.

Like all ecosystems, the city is an open system. It must receive inputs of both matter and energy from ecosystems outside itself and it must make outputs of products, wastes, and heat to continue to exist. Within a city there are numerous feedback loops or cycles that keep various city subsystems in balance. See figure 12.1 on the following page. A city's populations interact with the external environment to draw in continuous inputs of food, fuel, materials, air, and water. These inputs are then concentrated, transformed, stored, and ultimately expelled as a stream of outputs including waste products, foul air and water, and the useful products of technology, education, and culture. The modern city must import a tremendous quantity of materials to maintain itself. The American urban dweller, for example, uses (directly or indirectly) about 3,500 gallons of water, 4 pounds of food, and 19 pounds of fossil fuels each day. His daily output includes about 120 gallons of sewage, 4 pounds of refuse, and 1.9 pounds of air pollutants.

In analyzing urban ecosystems, we consider two broad types of requirements: (1) biological requirements and (2) cultural requirements.

Biological Requirements: Urban man has the same biological requirements as man in other ecosystems. He needs, for example, air, water, space,

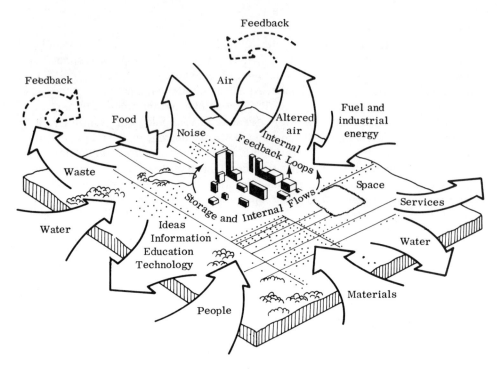

Figure 12.1   Diagram of some of the inputs and outputs
of a typical urban ecosystem (After Detwyler, et al., 1972)

energy (food and heat), shelter, and areas to dispose of wastes. Because of
the high population densities of urban areas, many of these resources are
not available within the ecosystem and must be drawn from outside. Systems
for supplying urban air and water needs are under particular stress because
of the large amounts of pollution produced in cities. At the same time the
cultural and technological creations of modern urban societies allow man to
operate more effectively outside the city and hence make it possible for cities
to obtain the large inputs that their dense populations require.

Cultural Requirements: By culture, we mean all of the ways of living that
human beings have developed and passed on to each new generation. Man is
a social animal and has cultural requirements just as he has biological requirements. Urban ecosystems exist because they help man obtain his cultural requirements. At the same time, more and more sophisticated cultural developments in the form of technology, transportation, and communication have made larger and larger cities possible. Some of modern man's
cultural requirements include political organizations, an economic-exchange
system, technology, transportation and communication, educational systems,
social and intellectual activities, and safety and security systems.

We might diagram a city ecosystem like this:

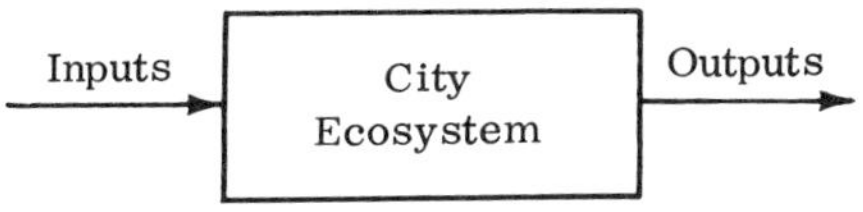

Inputs → City Ecosystem → Outputs

Figure 12.2

(a) List some inputs: _____

(b) List some outputs: _____

(c) Name the two general types of requirements of men living in cities.

_____

- - - - - - - - - - - - - - - -

(a) air, water, energy (food, fuel), natural resources, people;
(b) products, wastes, garbage, heat, people, ideas, education, technology; (c) biological requirements, cultural requirements

6. The ability to modify and manage ecosystems undoubtedly is one of man's most powerful and unique traits. Whether or not modern civilization succeeds in finding a better way of life for the world's inhabitants depends on the wise use of these talents for ecological modification. The maintenance of the vital balance between human and natural ecosystems must be a part of man's future land use planning.

Ecology is concerned with the integrity of the whole living world. The success of man's attempts to manage the world's ecosystems will depend on how well he has first studied them. Obtaining optimum sustained yields and efficiency from the earth's resources can only come from the knowledge of how natural ecosystems develop and maintain themselves. We must always be careful in what we consider the most "efficient" use of the earth's ecosystems. As E. P. Odum has put it, "man does not live by food and fiber alone; he also needs . . . the buffers provided by oceans and masses of vegetation, and clean (that is, unproductive) water for cultural and industrial uses" (Odum, 1969). Furthermore, Odum has maintained, many "essential life-cycle resources, not to mention recreational and esthetic needs, are best provided man by the less 'productive' landscapes."

As Odum has recognized, the earth is our home, not merely a "supply depot." Yet in his quest for short-term efficiency, man has sacrificed long-term stability for the immediate gains of high productivity. Gas exchanges in the atmosphere, natural water purification, nutrient cycles, and "other protective functions of self-maintaining ecosystems" have been taken for granted. "Now," writes Odum, "it is painfully evident that such balances are being affected, often detrimentally." Unless man considers himself "a part of, not apart from the environment," Odum claims, natural ecological defenses and stability will be adversely affected.

Yet man has not considered these external environmental costs. In maximizing yields, damming rivers, laying roads, and building cities, he has given up much of the earth's diversity and inherent stability. In 1864 George Perkins Marsh, a New England popular scientist, argued that the destruction of natural diversity would irreparably damage the functions of the natural world. He argued for fixed ratios between agricultural and forested lands, in other words, between specialization and diversity in the environment. Since his time, however, more extensive forests have been toppled, rivers impounded, and monoculture communities established. More than a century after Marsh and his warnings, man has still failed to recognize the wisdom of this New England scholar. In large part, Odum's plea is a redefinition of Marsh's earlier call for the protection of diversity in the natural world.

We have seen how the world's ecosystems can be divided into four general classes (see frame 3). The problem now facing us is one of balance. What limits must be eventually imposed on the size and capacity of each general class to maintain the vital balance between human and natural communities? Of course, the welfare of modern man depends on urban and productive ecosystems, yet these environments do not exist in isolation, but depend on the more "protective" environments (i.e., climax communities, national parks, open spaces) to absorb their impact on regional and global balances. Such natural areas not only maintain themselves but have a buffering effect on surrounding areas—regulating run-off and erosion, ameliorating local climatic conditions, and absorbing pollutants. We do not know how long we can continue expanding intensive agriculture and urban sprawl at the expense of the protective landscape. But we should be at least asking the question. The point is that at some point natural diversity should be consciously protected. The health and survival of our urban and agricultural ecosystems are directly related to the continued presence of natural ecosystems.

SELF-TEST

This Self-Test is designed to show you whether or not you have mastered this chapter's objectives. Answer each question to the best of your ability. Correct answers and review instructions are given at the end of the test.

1. Define human ecosystems. Give some specific examples.

_____

_____

_____

_____

2. Explain how man's productive (agricultural) ecosystems are different from natural ecosystems. Why does man maintain the unique characteristics of the productive ecosystem?

_____

_____

_____

_____

3. What are some of the potential dangers inherent in man's current agricultural practice?

_____

_____

_____

_____

4. Briefly describe an urban ecosystem.

_____

_____

_____

_____

5. List the four general types or classes of ecosystems that the world can be divided into.

_____

_____

_____

ANSWERS TO SELF-TEST

Compare your answers to the questions on the Self-Test with the answers given below. If you missed any questions, review the frames indicated in parentheses following the answer. If you miss several questions, you should probably reread the entire chapter carefully.

1. Human ecosystems refer to ecosystems that man manages. They include urban ecosystems, productive ecosystems, and managed natural ecosystems. (frames 1, 2, and 3)

2. Productive (agricultural) ecosystems are monocultures (single crop) that require constant pest control programs and constant fertilization. They are very immature ecosystems that have a very high net productivity (they produce lots of biomass for a <u>very</u> high input of energy). They are often monocultures of hybrid genetic species (and have replaced natural species). (frame 4)

3. The dangers in agricultural ecosystems include instability; possibility of disease and pest epidemics; depletion of fertilizers (nutrients) and energy (fossil fuels) that are in limited supply; elimination of other crop species (loss of genetic information) and other ecosystems. (frames 3 and 4)

4. Urban ecosystems include man's towns and cities. They are essentially open systems requiring constant inputs of matter and energy, while eliminating a stream of outputs including wastes, fouled air and water, and the useful products of technology. (frame 5)

5. mature natural ecosystems, managed natural ecosystems, productive ecosystems, and urban ecosystems (frame 3)

Bibliography

INTRODUCTION
PART I: THE NATURE OF ECOSYSTEMS

Bates, M. 1964. Man in nature. Englewood Cliffs, N. J.: Prentice-Hall.

Bertalanffy, Ludwig von. 1968. General system theory. New York: George Braziller.

Cole, L. C. 1958. The ecosphere. Scientific American 198(4):83-92.

Dasmann, R. F. 1972. Environmental conservation. New York: John Wiley & Sons.

Ehrlich, P. R.; Ehrlich, A. H.; and Holdren, J. P. 1973. Human ecology: problems and solutions. San Francisco: W. H. Freeman.

Greenwood, N. H.; and Edwards, J. M. B. 1973. Human environments and natural systems: a conflict of dominion. North Scituate, Mass.: Duxbury Press.

Hardin, G. 1959. Nature and man's fate. New York: Rinehart.

Leopold, Aldo. 1949. A Sand County Almanac. New York: Oxford University Press.

Meadows, D. H.; Meadows, D. L.; Randers, J.; and Behrens, W. 1972. The limits to growth: a global challenge. New York: Universe Books.

Miller, G. Tyler. 1972. Replenish the earth: a primer in human ecology. Belmont, Cal.: Wadsworth.

Nagel, Ernst. 1961. The structure of science. New York: Harcourt, Brace & World.

Popper, Karl R. 1968. The logic of scientific discovery. New York: Harper & Row.

Shepard, P.; and McKinley, D. (eds). 1969. The subversive science: essays toward an ecology of man. New York: Houghton Mifflin.

Smith, R. L. 1972. The ecology of man: an ecosystem approach. New York: Harper & Row.

Toffler, Alvin. 1970. Future shock. New York: Random House.

PART II: ENERGY IN ECOSYSTEMS

Cook, Earl. 1971. The flow of energy in an industrial society. Scientific American 224(3): 135–144.

Baker, J. J.; and Allen, G. E. 1970. Matter, energy and life. Reading, Mass.: Addison-Wesley.

Cowan, R. L. 1962. Physiology of nutrition as related to deer. Proceedings of First National White-Tailed Deer Disease Symposium, pp. 1–8.

Energy and Power. 1971. A Scientific American Book. San Francisco: W. H. Freeman.

Holdren, J.; and Herrera, P. 1971. Energy: a crisis in power. San Francisco: Sierra Club.

Hubbert, M. K. 1969. Energy resources. In Resources and man (Preston Cloud, ed.). San Francisco: W. H. Freeman.

Landsberg, H. H. 1964. National resources for U.S. growth: a look ahead to the year 2000. Washington, D.C.: Resources for the Future, Inc.

Lehninger, A. L. 1971. Bioenergetics. Menlo Park, Cal.: W. A. Benjamin, Inc.

Lindeman, R. L. 1942. The trophic-dynamic aspect of ecology. Ecology 23:399–418.

Miller, G. Tyler. 1972. Replenish the earth: a primer in human ecology. Belmont, Cal.: Wadsworth.

Odum, H. T. 1957. Trophic structure and productivity of Silver Springs, Florida. Ecological Monographs 27:55–112.

Ophel, Ivan L. 1963. The fate of radiostrontium in a freshwater community. In Radioecology (U. Schultz and W. Klement, eds.). New York: Reinhold.

Phillipson, J. 1966. Ecological energetics. London: Edward Arnold Publishers.

Swan, Lawrence W. 1961. The ecology of the high Himalayas. Scientific American 205:68–78.

Woodwell, G. M. 1967. Toxic substances and ecological cycles. Scientific American 216(3):2–91.

PART III: ECOLOGICAL CYCLES

Borgstrom, Georg A. 1970. Too many: a study of earth's biological limitations. New York: Macmillan.

Bormann, F. H.; Likens, G. E.; and Eaton, J. J. 1969. Biotic regulation of particulate and solution losses from forest ecosystem. Bioscience 19(7):600-610.

Clark, J. R. 1969. Thermal pollution and aquatic life. Scientific American 220(3):13-27.

Day, J. A. 1966. The science of weather. Reading, Mass.: Addison-Wesley.

Deevey, E. S. 1970. Mineral cycles. Scientific American 223)3): 148-159.

Delwiche, C. D. 1970. The nitrogen cycle. Scientific American 223(3): 136-147.

Haagen-Smit, A. J. 1968. Reactions in the atmosphere. In Air Pollution (A. C. Stern, ed.). New York: Academic Press.

Penman, H. L. 1970. The water cycle. Scientific American 223(3):98-109.

Skinner, B. J. 1969. Earth resources. Englewood Cliffs, N. J.: Prentice-Hall.

Tarling, D.; and Tarling, M. 1971. Continental drift: a study of the earth's moving surface. New York: Anchor Books.

Thornthwaite, C. W. 1955. Discussions on the relationships between meteorology and oceanography. Journal of Marine Research 14:510-515.

Wilson, T. J. (ed.). 1972. Continents adrift. San Francisco: W. H. Freeman

Witherspoon, J. P. 1964. Cycling of cesium-134 in white oak trees. Ecological Monographs 34:403-420.

PART IV: ECOLOGY OF POPULATIONS

Bell, R. H. V. 1971. A grazing ecosystem in the Serengeti. Scientific American 224(1):86-93.

Birdsell, J. B. 1953. Some environmental and cultural factors influencing the structuring of Australian aboriginal populations. American Naturalist. 87:179.

Boughey, A. S. 1973. Ecology of populations, 2nd ed. New York: Macmillan.

Cheng, T. C. 1970. Symbiosis: organisms living together. New York: Pegasus.

Christian, J. J.; and Davis, D. E. 1964. Endocrines, behavior and populations. Science 146:1550-1560.

Connell, J. 1961. The influence of interspecific competition and other factors on the distribution of the barnacle Chtamalus stellatus. Ecology 42:710-723.

Davidson, J. 1938. The Proceedings of the Royal Academy of South Africa.

Deevey, Edward S. 1960. The human population. Scientific American 203(3):194-204.

Ehrlich, P. R.; and Holdren, J. P. 1971. Impact of population growth. Science 171:1212-1217.

Esser, A. H. (ed.). 1971. Behavior and environment: the use of space by animals and man. New York: Plenum Press.

Gause, G. F. 1969. The struggle for existence. New York: Hafner Publishing Co.

Hardin, G. 1966. Biology: its principles and implications. 2nd ed. San Francisco: W. H. Freeman.

Hardin, G. (ed.). 1969. Population, evolution and birth control: a collage of controversial ideas. San Francisco: W. H. Freeman.

Keeton, W. T. 1967. Biological Sciences. New York: Norton.

Keyfitz, Nathan. 1966. How many people have ever lived on earth? Demography 3:581-582.

Klein, D. R. 1968. The introduction, increase, and crash of reindeer on St. Matthew Island. Journal of Wildlife Management 32:350-367.

Langer, William L. 1964. The black death. Scientific American 210(2): 114-121.

MacArthur, R. H.; and Connell, J. H. 1966. The biology of populations. New York: John Wiley & Sons.

MacLulich, D. A. 1937. Fluctuations in the numbers of the varying hare (Lepus americanus). University of Toronto Studies, Biology Series, No. 43.

Malthus, T. R. 1798. An essay on the principle of populations as it affects the future improvement of mankind. Reprinted for the Royal Economic Society, 1926. London: Macmillan.

Meadows, D. H.; Meadows, D. L.; Randers, J.; and Behrens, W. 1972. The limits to growth: a global challenge. New York: Universe Books.

Population Bulletin. Published six times yearly by the Population Reference Bureau, Inc., 1755 Massachusetts Ave., N.W., Washington, D.C. 20036.

Population Reference Bureau, Washington, D.C. Population Data Sheet. Published annually.

President's Commission on Population Growth and the American Future. Population growth and the American future. Interim Report, March 1971. Washington, D.C.: U.S. Government Printing Office.

Stankovic, S. 1960. Monographiae Biologicae 9:1–357.

Terao, Arata; and Tanaka, T. 1928. Population growth of the water-flea, Moina macrocopa strauss. Proceedings of the Imperial Academy (Japan) 4:550–552.

Thompson, W. S.; and Lewis, D. J. 1965. Population problems, 5th ed. New York: McGraw-Hill.

PART V: ECOSYSTEMS

Biosphere. 1971. A Scientific American Book. San Francisco: W. H. Freeman.

Detwyler, T. R.; and Marcus, M. G. 1972. Urbanization and environment: the physical geography of the city. North Scituate, Mass: Duxbury Press.

Evans, F. C. 1956. Ecosystem as the basic unit in ecology. Science 123: 1127–1128.

Geiger, R. 1965. The climate near the ground, 4th ed. Cambridge: Harvard University Press.

Holdridge, L. R. 1947. Determination of world plant formations from simple climatic data. Science 105:367–368.

Iltis, H. H.; Loucks, O. L.; and Andrews, P. 1970. Criteria for an optimum human environment. Bulletin of the Atomic Scientists, January 1970.

Odum, Eugene P. 1969. Strategy of ecosystem development. Science 164: 262–270.

Paddock, W. C. 1970. How green is the green revolution? Bioscience 20(16):897–902.

Rudd, R. L. 1964. Pesticides and the living landscape. Madison: University of Wisconsin Press.

Salt, G. W. 1957. An analysis of avifaunas in the Teton mountains and Jackson Hole, Wyoming. Condor 59:373–393.

Smith, Robert. 1966. Ecology and Field Biology. New York: Harper & Row.

Whittaker, R. H. 1970. Communities and ecosystems. New York: Macmillan.

Woodwell, G. M. 1970. Effects of pollution on the structure and physiology of ecosystems. Science 178:429–433.

Woodwell, G. M. 1970. The energy cycle of the biosphere. Scientific American 223(3):64–74.

Glossary

Abiotic: nonliving.

Aeolian zone: a zone occurring on mountains above the alpine zone supported by windblown matter.

Amensalism: a type of interaction between two species populations where one population is inhibited; the other is unaffected.

Aquatic successions: ecological succession in water environments.

Atmosphere: the gaseous envelope that surrounds the surface of the earth.

Atmospheric cycle (circulation): the movement of warm or cold air over the earth's surface.

A.T.P. (adenosine triphosphate): a chemical compound that acts as a carrier of chemical energy in biological systems.

Autotrophs: "self-feeding" organisms that can build large compounds from simple nutrient molecules.

Biogeochemical cycle: the cycling of elements between biological organisms and their environment.

Biomass: the total amount of living matter in an area.

Biomes: large biotic communities that exhibit similar plant and animal associations as well as community structure.

Biosphere: that portion of the earth occupied by living forms.

Biotic: living.

Biotic community: all of the populations of organisms that exist and interact in a given area.

Biotic potential: ability of organisms to reproduce themselves under optimal conditions.

Bonds (chemical): chemical forces holding atoms together to form molecules.

Carbon dioxide: CO_2, a colorless gas in the atmosphere, formed by the burning of carbon-containing (organic) compounds utilized by plants.

Carnivore: a flesh-eating animal that obtains its energy indirectly from primary producers by eating other animals.

Carrying capacity: the capability of a particular environment to support life.

Cell: basic structural component of all living things.

Climax community (mature ecosystem): the final stage in the successional process.

Commensalism: a type of interaction between two species populations where one population benefits and the other is unaffected.

Competition: a type of interaction between two populations in which they vie for the same limited resource.

Competitive exclusion principle: the principle that if two populations compete for some resource that is necessary for the survival of each and is in short supply, one of the populations will be eliminated.

Coniferous (forest biome): trees having needles.

Consumers: organisms that derive their nutrition directly from plants (herbivores) or indirectly from the producer by way of the herbivore (carnivores).

Continental drift: the concept that the earth's continental land masses were once one large land mass which has since broken into pieces that have drifted apart.

Convection current: a circulation process or pattern that is created and maintained by differences in the distribution of temperature and density.

Cooperation: a type of interaction between two species populations where each population benefits; the interaction is optional for both species.

Crude birth rate: number of births in one year for each 1000 persons in a population.

Crude death rate: number of deaths in one year for each 1000 persons in a population.

Cultural eutrophication: the eutrophication process greatly accelerated by man's nutrient inputs.

Cultural sedimentation: dumping of solid wastes in water beyond natural inputs of solid material.

Cybernetic system: a system that exhibits some degree of self-control through the use of negative feedback mechanisms.

Cycle: a sequence of events that recur regularly.

DDT: a persistent, water insoluble insecticide.

Deciduous (forest biome): trees having broad leaves that are commonly shed in the fall.

Decomposers: organisms (i.e., bacteria and fungi) that break down dead plant and animal material to obtain their energy requirements.

Demographic transition: the falling of birth rates following a period of industrialization.

Detritus: dead organic material.

Differential reproduction: the difference in success in leaving offspring by individuals possessing different inheritable characteristics.

Doubling time: the time required for a population to double in size.

Ecological succession: the dynamic process by which ecosystems change over time.

Ecology: the science that deals with the interactions between living organisms and their environment; the study of ecosystems.

Ecosystem: system of living organisms and the media through which they exchange matter and energy.

Ecotone (edge effect): transition area between two biotic communities.

Element (chemical): a substance that is composed entirely of one type of atom.

Energy: the ability to do work.

Energy consumption (external): energy that man uses to power his machines and maintain his culture.

Energy consumption (internal): energy that man uses to maintain his bodily processes.

Environmental resistance: all the biotic and abiotic factors that tend to decrease the fertility and survival of the individuals in a population.

Environmental resistance (extrinsic factors): those factors that affect a population from outside itself (i.e., weather, food supply, predation).

Environmental resistance (intrinsic factors): those factors that are generated within the population itself (i.e., territoriality, social stress).

Eutrophication: a naturally occurring "aging" process in aquatic communities where productivity increases with a gradual increase in nutrient input.

Erosion: the wearing away of the earth's surface by wind and water action.

Evaporation: the process by which liquid water changes into water vapor.

Evapotranspiration: evaporation and transpiration taken together.

Evolution: process by which species populations change their characteristics in the course of time.

Exponential growth: any growth pattern that increases at a constant rate (a common example is the progression 1, 2, 4, 8, 16, . . .).

Feedback (negative): feedback that slows down and eventually halts or reverses a tendency or movement away from the set point.

Feedback (positive): an increasing accentuation of a tendency away from the system's set point.

Fertility rate: births per 1000 female members (ages 15-45) of a population.

Food chain: a series of feeding relationships between organisms that shows who eats whom.

Food chain concentration: the concentration of certain substances as they pass along the food chain.

Food web: a relatively complex series of interconnected food chains.

Fossil fuels: coal, oil, gas; organic matter of former plants and animals transformed through geologic time by temperature and pressure.

Gaseous nutrient cycle: a biogeochemical cycle with the atmosphere as the main reservoir of the nutrient.

Gene pool: the collective genetic material within a population.

Geologic cycle: refers to the creation, movement, and destruction of the material comprising the surface of the earth.

Glucose: $C_6H_{12}O_6$, complex carbon-based molecule storing energy (i.e., sugar).

Gross primary productivity: the total rate of photosynthesis, including energy that is fixed and then used in respiration as well as energy used to create new tissue in excess of the plant's respiration.

Ground water: water in the saturated zone under the ground.

Habitat: the place or area that a species occupies.

Herbivores: animals that feed on plants.

Heterotroph: "other-feeding," organisms whose nutritional needs are met by feeding on other organisms.

Human ecology: the study of ecosystems as they affect and are affected by human beings.

Human ecosystems: environments created and maintained by the intervention of mankind.

Hydrosphere: the water on or surrounding the solid surface of the earth.

Interspecific competition: competition between individuals of two different species.

Intraspecific competition: competition between members of the same species.

Law of Tolerances: the principle that an organism has a range of tolerances for each abiotic factor, within which it can survive.

Life zones: regions displaying common assemblages of plants and animals.

Lithosphere: the solid part of the earth.

Metabolism: all of the chemical reactions taking place within an organism.

Minerals: generally, all nonliving, naturally occurring substances that are useful to man.

Molecule: the smallest particle of an element or compound that retains the chemical properties of that substance.

Monocultures: greatly simplified agricultural ecosystems having only one crop.

Mutations: changes in genetic material.

Mutualism: a type of interaction between two species populations where each population benefits and is dependent on the relationship.

Natural selection: the process tending to cause the survival of those forms of plants and animals best suited to the conditions under which they live.

Net primary productivity: rate that plants store energy as organic matter in excess of that used in respiration.

Niche: a set of characteristics that describe the precise requirements an organism needs to survive.

Niche differentiation: a shift in a population's requirement to minimize its interaction with a competing species.

Nutrient: a substance necessary for the normal growth and development of an organism.

Nutrient budget (external): nutrient inputs and outputs of an entire ecosystem.

Nutrient budget (internal): nutrient exchanges between the subsystems or components of a particular ecosystem.

Omnivore: an organism that eats both plants and animals.

Open system: a system that depends upon the outside environment to provide inputs and accept outputs.

Parasitism: a type of interaction between two species populations where one nourishes itself at the expense of the other (called the host).

Photosynthesis: the process by which carbon dioxide, water, sunlight, and chlorophyll are utilized to produce glucose in plant cells.

Plate tectonics: study of lateral surface movements of the earth's crustal plates.

Pollution: sediments, foodstuffs, poisons, and heat that are entering an ecosystem at a rate exceeding the normal ability of the ecosystem to process and distribute them.

Population: a group of organisms, all of one kind, living within a given area.

Population density: number of organisms per unit area.

Population growth: increase or decrease in the total number of organisms in a population due to the interplay between their biotic potential and environmental resistance.

Population growth rate: rate of population change, calculated by subtracting the death rate from the birth rate.

Precipitation: water falling to the earth, including snow, sleet, and rain.

Predation: a type of interaction between two species in which one species (the predator) attacks and kills another species (the prey).

Primary productivity (or primary production): the rate at which energy is bound or organic material is created by photosynthesis.

Producers: organisms that can convert the radiant energy from the sun into chemical energy by producing energy-rich carbon compounds.

Respiration: chemical process which occurs within cells releasing chemical energy to carry out metabolic processes.

Science: the activity that is basically concerned with making predictions about the future.

Seral community: a transitory community in the process of ecological succession.

Sedimentary nutrient cycle: a biogeochemical cycle with sedimentary rock as the main reservoir of the nutrient.

Social density: number of social interactions between individuals in a given area.

Species diversity: refers to the number of different species occupying the same area.

Standing crop: amount of biomass present at a particular time.

Stratification: a layering or series of separations that divide up an ecosystem.

Stress: specific series of bodily reactions that an organism undergoes in response to many different stimuli.

Survivorship curve: a curve showing the numbers of organisms in a population that survive to any particular age (survivors per 1000).

Symbiosis: "living together," refers to all relationships between organisms.

System: a collection of parts or events (called components, elements, or subsystems) that can be seen as a single whole thing because of the consistent interdependence and interaction of those parts or events.

Systems approach: a way of thinking about problem solving and model development which involves thinking about a complex series of events or things as a single whole.

Ten Percent Law (or Rule of Ecological Tithe): states that only about 10 percent of the energy from one level can be captured by organisms on the next higher trophic level.

Territory: refers to an area that an organism will defend against intruders.

Thermal pollution: an abnormal increase in heat in some part of the environment, usually in aquatic systems.

Thermodynamics, First Law of: the principle that energy can be transformed from one form to another, but can never be created or destroyed.

Thermodynamics, Second Law of: the principle that each time energy is transformed, it tends to go from a more organized and concentrated form to a less organized and more dispersed form.

Topography: the land's surface features.

Transpiration: the process by which water vapor escapes from a living plant (principally from the leaves) and enters the atmosphere.

Trophic level: position along food chain, or feeding level, measured as the number of steps from primary production.

Watershed: the whole region or drainage area that contributes to a water supply point.

Index

Abiotic, 11
Adaptive traits, 148, 149
Aeolian zone, 54, 232
Age pyramids, 163-166
Agricultural (productive) ecosystems, 134, 261-267
Agricultural revolution, 215-217
Altitudinal zones, 232
Amensalism, 184, 188
Aquatic successions, 248-250
Astronomical cycles, 91, 92
Atmosphere, 93, 99
Atmospheric cycle (circulation), 93, 94, 95
Atmospheric pollution, 95, 96, 97
A.T.P. (adenosine triphosphate), 38
Autotrophs, 37

Biogeochemical cycle, 125, 128, 135, 254. See also Gaseous nutrient cycle; Sedimentary nutrient cycle
Biological clock, 242-243
Biomass, 134, 254
Biomes, 229, 230-233
Biosphere, 12, 230, 233
Biotic, 11
Biotic community, 12, 229, 230, 236, 254-255
Biotic potential, 152-154, 157
Bonds (chemical), 37, 38
Borgstom, Georg, 116, 117
Bubonic plague, 218-220

Carbon cycle, 127
Carbon dioxide, 35, 37, 38
Carnivore, 51
Carrying capacity, 73, 155, 216
Climax community, 245, 250, 254, 255, 263

Commensalism, 184, 187, 188
Community. See Biotic community
Competition, 184, 189-191. See also Interspecific competition; Intraspecific competition
Competitive exclusion principle, 189-192
Coniferous, 237, 239
Connell, J. H., 189, 191
Consumers, 47
Continental drift, 101, 102, 104
Convection current, 94, 104
Cooperation, 184, 186
Crude birth rate, 158-160, 163, 164
Crude death rate, 158-160, 161
Cultural eutrophication, 119
Cultural sedimentation, 118
Cybernetic system, 17, 23, 152, 153, 215, 228, 229
Cycle, 13

DDT, 64, 65, 96
Deciduous, 233, 236, 239
Decomposers, 47, 52, 62
Demographic transition, 221
Demostat model, 152, 153, 214, 215
Detritus, 53, 254
Differential reproduction, 148-151
Doubling time, 212-214

Ecological diversity, 235
Ecological succession, 229, 244-246, 250, 251-253, 254-255, 262, 263
Ecology, 9
Ecosystem, 9, 12, 14, 24, 137-139, 228, 229, 254, 255, 262, 263, 269, 270
Ecosystem stability, 235, 244, 245, 254, 255, 262, 263
Ecotone (edge effect), 238-239